GOMERSAL
A WINDOW ON THE PAST

Seventeenth century mullions at Spen Hall

Cover illustration: Seventeenth Century window at Oakwell Hall

GOMERSAL

A WINDOW ON THE PAST

by

GILLIAN COOKSON and NEIL A. COOKSON

Published by Kirklees Cultural Services, Red Doles Lane, Huddersfield, HD2 1YF

Technical and Commercial Unit

ISBN 0 900746 53 X

© Gillian Cookson and Neil A. Cookson 1992

Typesetting by The Mouse House, Harrogate 0423 879393.   Printed by Thornton & Pearson, Bradford BD8 9AS

CONTENTS

ILLUSTRATIONS

ABBREVIATIONS

Abbreviations used in the chapter notes:

Archives and Record Offices:

BL	British Library.
Borthwick	University of York, Borthwick Institute of Historical Research.
Bretton	Bretton Hall College of Higher Education, West Bretton.
NYCRO	North Yorkshire County Record Office, Northallerton.
Thoresby	Thoresby Society, Claremont, Leeds.
WYAS B	West Yorkshire Archive Service, Bradford.
WYAS C	West Yorkshire Archive Service, Calderdale.
WYAS HQ	West Yorkshire Archive Service, Wakefield.
WYAS L	West Yorkshire Archive Service, Leeds.
WYAS K	West Yorkshire Archive Service, Kirklees.
WYAS SMR	West Yorkshire Archaeology Service: Sites and Monuments Record, Wakefield.
YAS	Yorkshire Archaeological Society, Claremont, Leeds.

Other abbreviations used:

BL Add Ch	*British Library* Additional Charters - Unpublished.
BPR	Birstall Parish Registers; see Nussey (ed.) 1983 and 1987.
Census	Gomersal Census Enumerators' Returns for 1841, 1851 and 1861. Copy at Cleckheaton Library, etc.
DoE	Department of the Environment list of Buildings of Special Architectural or Historic Interest – Borough of Kirklees.
KCS	Kirklees Cultural Services
RCHME	Royal Commission on Historical Monuments (England).
YAJ	*Yorkshire Archaeological Journal.*
YASRS	*Yorkshire Archaeological Society Record Series.*

ACKNOWLEDGEMENTS

We are fortunate to have been helped by many people in the preparation of this book. To all those inhabitants of Gomersal who have generously allowed access to buildings, documents and photographs, and trusted various items to us, we are very grateful. In particular we would like to acknowledge the help of Mrs Hazel Burns, verger of Birstall Church, Mr and Mrs G.Calvert, Mr Gordon Cooper, Mr Michael Dobson (formerly of the Black Bull), Mr Harold Hepworth, Mr John Holroyd, the Rev. Bob Hopwood of Gomersal Moravian Church, Mrs Joan King, Mr and Mrs Micklethwaite, Mr Joe Richardson, and Mr John G.Walker. We owe special thanks to Mrs Mabel Hellewell. We would also like to record our appreciation of the work of the late Mr Frank Hellewell who ensured that antiquarian material on Gomersal would be available for research in public archives.

The assistance of Dr Stephen Caunce, Mr Steve McGlynn and Mr Barry O'Neill, who have shared with us their ideas and knowledge about the buildings and landscape of Gomersal, is gratefully acknowledged. Mr Andrew Nicholson has given us technical help, and Mr John H. Fenton made our work easier by lending a number of scarce local books over a long period.

Staff in the headquarters and district offices of the West Yorkshire Archive Service have given prompt and courteous attention to our requests for information, as have Dr Bob Yarwood and Mrs Helen Gomersall of West Yorkshire Archaeology Service. We have also been assisted by archivists and librarians at the Yorkshire Archaeological Society, the Thoresby Society, Bretton Hall College of Higher Education, the Brotherton Library at Leeds University, and Kirklees Cultural Services. In particular we would like to mention the help given by Mr Robert Frost, head of West Yorkshire Archive Service; and also the contribution of Miss Margaret Roberts of Cleckheaton Library, whose efficient collection and organization of local material has made our task much less onerous than it might otherwise have been.

For permission to reproduce material we are grateful to Lord Allendale; the Bretton Estate Archive; the Yorkshire Archaeological Society; Dibb Lupton Broomhead and Prior, Solicitors; the West Yorkshire Archive Service; and Kirklees Cultural Services. Staff of the latter organization have also assisted with the retrieval and loan of many photographs and helped us to bring this volume to publication.

We would like to thank the Yorkshire Archaeological Society for a generous grant which enabled us to reproduce the 1714 map of Ibbetson's estate and the 1770 map of the church glebelands.

Finally we should record the contribution made by our family and friends, in various ways, to help us complete this book. The encouragement we have received has helped a great deal. In particular, our parents have assisted in many ways. Our greatest debt however is to our sons, Joseph, who accompanied us on much of the fieldwork, and Francis, who arrived after the fieldwork was complete. We dedicate this volume to them in the hope that this will compensate for a certain amount of parental neglect during the writing.

INTRODUCTION

There is still something special about Gomersal, even after a century and a half of continuous growth. It was in an attempt to capture something of this unique atmosphere and to explain how Gomersal has become what it is, that we set about this work.

We have concentrated upon what interested us, that is, the buildings and landscapes, particularly in the period 1600 to 1850 which was the formative age of modern Gomersal. Perhaps this book will help to develop an awareness of what is unique and irreplaceable in the village. It would be satisfying to see other historians and archaeologists build upon our work and investigate further the sites of importance we believe our survey has identified. But above all we hope to be read by non-specialists, people interested in an up-to-date collection of historical observations.

It is now over sixty years since the publication of H. Ashwell Cadman's *Gomersal Past and Present*. That work leaves much unsaid on important topics such as the role in Gomersal life of Birstall Church and Oakwell, while following a detailed vein of reminiscence which is perhaps of less interest than it once was. Cadman presents what is essentially a folk history. He did not consider the change from medieval to modern society in Gomersal, the pattern of landholding and economic development between 1600 and 1850, or the particular evidence of archaeology and architecture – all of which are major concerns of our work. Of course, fresh information has surfaced and new methods of investigation

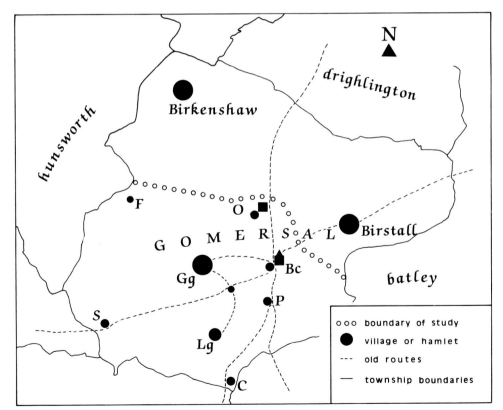

Map A.
Gomersal township, showing boundary of study area

Key:
Bc	*Birstall Church*
C	*Castle Hill*
F	*Fieldhead*
Gg	*Great Gomersal*
Lg	*Little Gomersal*
O	*Oakwell*
P	*Popeley*
S	*Spen*

Map A: *Gomersal township, showing boundary of study area*

have been adopted since the 1920s, when Cadman was writing. We feel sure too that organization of the main material, with proper references and an index, is an improvement on what existed previously; anyone who has tried to read Cadman will instantly recognize the value of this exercise.

This volume is arranged on an 'area basis', using together historical, archaeological and architectural evidence wherever possible. We have also adopted a narrow topographical definition of Gomersal. Both approaches require a few words of explanation.

Taking the latter point first: historically, the name Gomersal referred to the entire township of Gomersal, including Great and Little Gomersal as far west as Cleckheaton, but also encompassing the villages of

Birstall and Birkenshaw in the east. Birstall and Birkenshaw, however, are not readily recognisable as part of Gomersal in landscape terms, and it is doubtful whether the several villages in the township ever functioned as a unit. Consequently, what follows is restricted to the area still known as Great and Little Gomersal, together with important sites at its periphery. Anyone looking for a history of the whole township of Gomersal will be disappointed. Our main purpose is to trace the origins and growth of the most distinctive parts of the township and so come a little closer to an appreciation of its historic culture.

The 'area basis' simply refers to the method of looking at particular parts of the study area in turn. The overall picture is made up of several elements, each represented by a single chapter. In this way we hope to convey something of the spirit of each small settlement. An important advantage of this approach is that the subject matter is more accessible to readers familiar with a locality than it would be if arranged by theme or chronology. The exceptions are Chapter 7, an examination of Gomersal's most important industry, textiles, and, by way of refreshment, a short final chapter on the village's public houses.

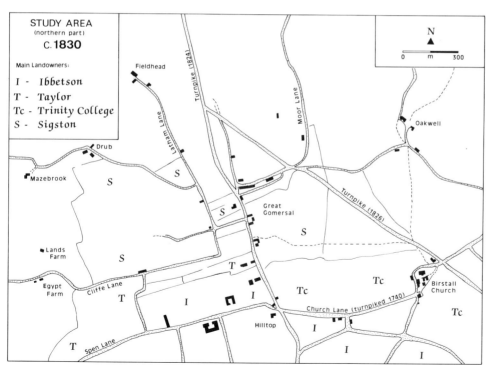

Map B: *Study Area: northern part*

Gomersal is not a place which can claim significant pre-historic or Roman remains. A neolithic stone axe was found at Birkenshaw in 1963 and Roman tesserae are said to have been unearthed on the site of the recreation ground at Birstall.[1] But the former had probably been lost in

x

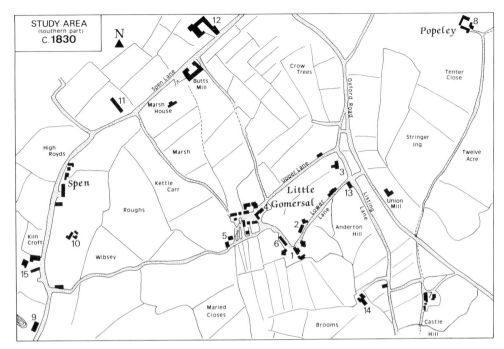

Map C.
Study Area: southern part

Key:
1. Low Fold
   (Gomersal House)
2. Sisters' Houses
3. Moravian settlement
4. Little Court or Upper
   House
5. Royds Farm and barn
6. Dryhouse
7. Castle Hill House
8. Popeley
9. Spen Mill
10. Spen House
11. Cloth Hall dryhouse
12. Cloth Hall
    (Gomersal Mills)
13. The Bull's Head
14. Castle Hill Mill
15. Spen Hall

Map C: *Study Area: southern part*

modern times, while the latter are reported only by way of hearsay. Aerial photography, over several years, has also failed to reveal any significant early features. A Roman road is said to follow what is now Whitehall Road; likewise Castle Hill, Little Gomersal, is reputed by some to have prehistoric antecedents (see chapter 4). Like almost all talk of such settlement in the township, these assertions, however plausible, have yet to be supported by firm evidence.

The earliest convincing evidence of human occupation in Gomersal, as defined above, is of the late Saxon period. This takes the form of a carved stone of tenth or eleventh century date at Birstall Church (see chapter 1) and the names themselves of 'Gomersal' and 'Birstall', both of which are of pre-conquest origin. No church was mentioned at Birstall in the Domesday survey of 1086, though there was probably some religious activity in the

locality of the church in that period; in any event the survey was never intended to record all churches in a locality. Domesday also provides the clearest early record of agriculture in Gomersal when it says: 'Dunstan and Gamel had 14 carucates [2] of land to be taxed where seven ploughs may be. Ilbert [de Lacy] has [it] and it is waste'.

From the eleventh century until the end of the fourteenth century information is more plentiful, though mostly concerning the descent of the manor or the tenure of the manor at a particular time. Evidence of local economic and social matters is very limited. Documentary and archaeological evidence begins to fill this gap only in the fifteenth century. It is primarily for the years after 1400 that what we have called 'historic culture' begins to be accessible, by the physical survival of remains and especially by written records which are now readily available in public archives.

Some new or previously little used evidence is presented in this book. Of special note is the long medieval lineage of the Popeley family and the more recent history of Popeley fields, including a formerly unpublished map of 1714. Also noteworthy are lists of early seventeenth century pew holders in Birstall church, and a schedule of Gomersal tax payers for the mid.seventeenth century. Much greater use is made of the early Birstall parish registers than was possible in days before their indexing and publication.[3] Maps of the church glebelands have also been examined, and one of these is reproduced here for the first time. Some of the evidence used has been known to exist for many years but has previously been recorded very cursorily in print, for example the archaeological evidence for medieval settlement at Oakwell Hall, or the Batt family's seventeenth century rent books. Two prominent seventeenth century families, the Gomersalls of Little Gomersal and the Norcliffes of Great Gomersal, are discussed at length. The former is especially interesting as a settlement of their property in the early seventeenth century resulted in a survey of the estate at the hand of Robert Saxton. The Norcliffe estate of the mid seventeenth century was later recorded in a sketch plan of 1732 and eventually came to form the bulk of the Sigston family's holding in the village. Of other Gomersal families, there are insights into the textile manufacturing of the Burnleys and the involved dynastic history of the Knowles family. Two outlying sites are also considered in more detail than hitherto, namely Castle Hill and Spen Mill. Indeed the latter has never been properly studied in spite of its importance to both the manor and the local economy.

A book which covers a variety of particular sites and historical details should also attempt to draw out the common threads of each and provide a general summary of developments. In the medieval period it seems that Little and Great Gomersal were the largest of a group of hamlets which included Oakwell, Popeley, and Castle Hill. There was no true settlement centre to Gomersal township; instead the church and manorial seat were simply located centrally for ease of access to and from all surrounding areas. This is a pattern strongly influenced by a 'highland' type of settlement, in which settlements can be said to be serving the land rather than vice-versa.

By the mid sixteenth century however such manorial cohesion as existed began to be weakened by the emergence of a number of sizable freeholdings. When the Batt family acquired Oakwell manor in the 1560s this process was already under way. That is not to say that the manor was poorer than before; on the contrary, all the evidence indicates increasing prosperity in the seventeenth century, from which the Batts fared as well as most. Generally, houses became larger and more luxurious. Areas which previously had seen at most only basic timber buildings acquired substantial houses of stone. It is perhaps more accurate to describe the Batts as part, rather than victims, of such changes.

There was no dramatic industrialization in Gomersal to match that of many towns in the West Riding. Gomersal had developed a well-organized and extensive domestic system of cloth production by the seventeenth century, with local clothiers buying in pieces for finishing and transporting to the markets at Leeds and, to a lesser extent, Halifax. Development of this domestic system culminated in the late eighteenth century with the building of Gomersal's own cloth hall. But the village, on the ridge of a hill, lacked an essential resource for further industrial development at that time, that is, water power. Moreover, as the industrial age dawned, Gomersal was well to do when compared with most of her neighbours, including Birstall, Cleckheaton and Heckmondwike; there may consequently have been fewer incentives to change.

Finally, a close connection can be seen between the ownership of property and the pace of change in the village. In the seventeenth century most of the large estates in Gomersal were at least partly occupied by their owners, but by the eighteenth century these properties had come into the possession of absentee landlords. Some estates, notably those of the Beaumonts and Ibbetsons, were broken up and sold to local people in the first half of the nineteenth century. The main periods of growth in Gomersal were the second half of the seventeenth century and the middle years of the nineteenth – in other words, when most property was owned by local people. But even these changes appear to have been at a relatively steady pace and in areas of activity which were thoroughly understood; Gomersal seems always to have been rooted in West Riding tradition, and this is certainly part of its appeal.

NOTES

1. *WYAS SMR.*
2. Carucate: a unit of land measurement used in assessing tax liability, in theory the area which an eight-ox plough team could plough in a single year; though see Faull and Moorhouse 1981, 240-241.
3. Nussey (ed.) 1983 and 1987.

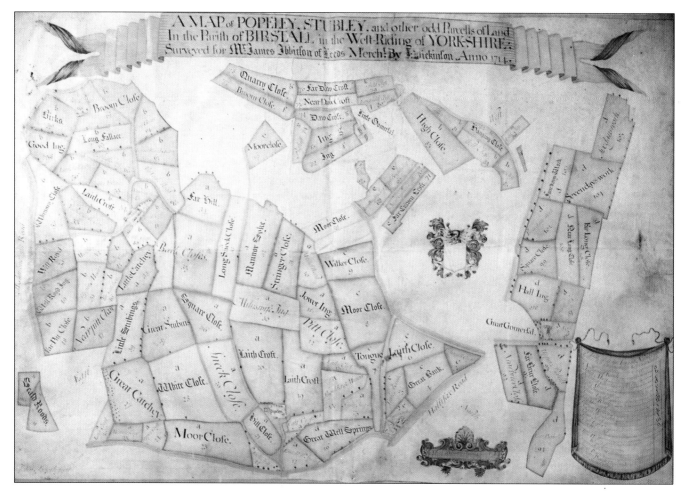

Figure 1: *Ibbetson's estate in 1714*

The road running along the bottom of the plan is Muffit Lane. Outlying parts have been inserted where they will fit on the paper, regardless of their actual relationship to the main estate. The section on the right of this plan includes Pollard Hall and the White Horse, with Spen Lane forming part of the boundary. The fields at the top of the map are those around the abrupt bend in Lower Lane, Little Gomersal. (Reproduced with the kind permission of its private owner, and with the help of a grant from the Yorkshire Archaeological Society).

Chapter 1

BIRSTALL CHURCH

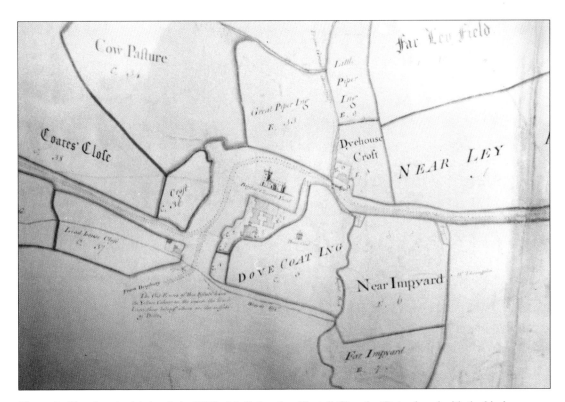

Figure 2: *The church glebelands in 1770: detail showing Birstall Church. (Reproduced with the kind permission of its private owner and with the help of a grant from the Yorkshire Archaeological Society)*

Gomersal did not have its own church until 1851, when St. Mary's, Spen Lane, was consecrated. Consequently, for the whole of the period from the twelfth century to 1850, inhabitants of Gomersal looked instead to the church of St. Peter, Birstall. St. Peter's was easily accessible from both Little and Great Gomersal; it was also the most important church for several miles around.

The parish of Birstall was very large by modern standards, including, amongst others, the townships of Tong, Wyke, Liversedge and Cleckheaton. Both church services and administration for all of these places were originally centred on Birstall. Some outlying areas, most notably Tong and Cleckheaton, acquired their own chapel-of-ease in the medieval period (and later the right to baptise and bury), but for villages such as Gomersal, which were nearer to the parish church, St. Peter's was always the local place of worship.

The impact of the church before the nineteenth century was not, of course, limited to what today would be called religious activities. Whether a person attended with zeal, irregularly or not at all, the church required many obligations to be fulfilled. In particular, at a time when many of the tasks now undertaken by central and local government were shouldered by the local parish, tithes had to be paid to finance good works and services.[1] Church 'briefs' were sometimes levied to relieve disasters or emergencies in other parts of the country. The church was also one of the largest landowners in Gomersal, having the benefit of several tracts of glebeland, the largest of which was on the northern side of Church Lane.

Historically, Birstall Church was also the name given to the settlement around the church, including the mill and millpool, rectory house, rectory farm, an early vicarage, a number of lesser houses, two inns and a grammar school. This name survived into the nineteenth century when various awards and censuses still referred to people as 'of Birstall Church'. St. Peter's therefore appeared less of an outlier to Birstall and Gomersal and more of a distinct community than it seems today. It was well served by a network of local 'kirkgates', some of which are now discernible only as bridleways, which ran from Birstall, Drighlington and Oakwell, Liversedge and Castle Hill, as well as from Great Gomersal.

From Saxon Times to the Reformation

The Domesday Survey of 1086 does not mention a church at Birstall. It is debatable therefore whether one existed in the Anglo-Saxon period. The area occupied by the church seems to have been a religious site, however, since before the conquest. A raised piece of ground adjacent to water and a bridge (or ford) would have been a suitable site; more conclusively, remains of a pre-conquest stone have been found in the churchyard.

Figure 3: *Birstall Church: the Saxon Stone. This face has a tree of life with volutes enclosing ivy leaves; on the other side is a loosely drawn interlace. The stone tapers slightly, from 50 cm at its base to 46 cm at the top*

Until 1865 this Saxon stone was fixed beneath a seat in the porch of the old church. It now lies in the northern aisle of the new. Collingwood judged it to be 'perhaps part of a cross base, though the hollow inside seems too great for the tenon of a shaft'.[2] In an earlier article George Auden arrived at a similar conclusion.[3] The hollow of the stone is indeed very large and its walls correspondingly thin. Because of this any role as the lower portion of a substantial stone structure seems unlikely. As there is also no sign of a tenon or other connection at its base, it is equally difficult to see the stone as the middle section of a cross. It may be that the Birstall stone served an itinerant preacher in some other way, perhaps as a receptacle, or as a more simple form of marker. It is even feasible that the stone merely indicated the extent of a church estate.

There is less doubt surrounding the date of the stone. Dating such artefacts is, even today, not an exact science, but most authorities place the Birstall example towards the end of the Saxon period, usually in the late tenth or early eleventh centuries. Auden, because of a lack of 'Scandinavian influence', placed it in the ninth century, but this is probably too early. Scandinavian styles were never predominant in the Gomersal or Spen Valley areas, and the loose carving of decoration at Birstall has a lot in common with later designs on a stone of similar size at Rastrick. The Birstall stone is also very different in style from the acknowledged ninth or early tenth century stone at Hartshead.

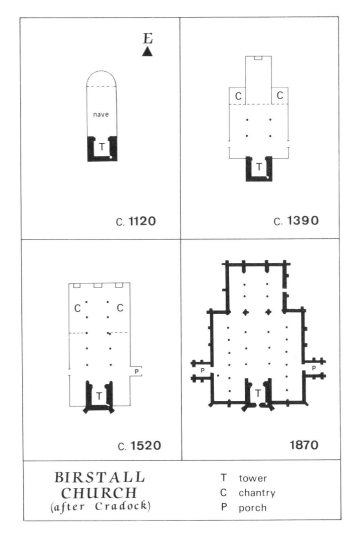

Figure 4: *Evolution of Birstall Church*

most authors agree with a date in the first half of the twelfth century.

The bulk of the building completed at this time did not survive the successive remodellings of the medieval and early modern periods. However, the first and second stages of the tower are a noteworthy exception and now provide the most convincing evidence of the church's early importance in Gomersal.

The tower still possesses two narrow windows in the Norman style, a style which is repeated in the door surrounds and arches of the internal stair at its south-west corner. The stair is especially significant, not only for its good state of preservation but also for its similarity to other narrow service stairs which are undoubtedly of Norman origin.

Figure 5: *Birstall Church: from the south west*

Although no church is recorded there by Domesday, Birstall certainly had one soon afterwards. This was a small affair, probably built of local sandstone, and consisting of a square tower, a nave of equal width and, at the eastern end, a chancel with an apse.[4] The date of this early structure is a matter for conjecture, though

Stephen Glynne, the nineteenth century antiquarian, also recorded some decorated stonework of the Norman period which has since disappeared.[5] This appears to have included elements of a doorway, including columns and the remains of an arch, which had been re-used in the main body of the sixteenth century building. No

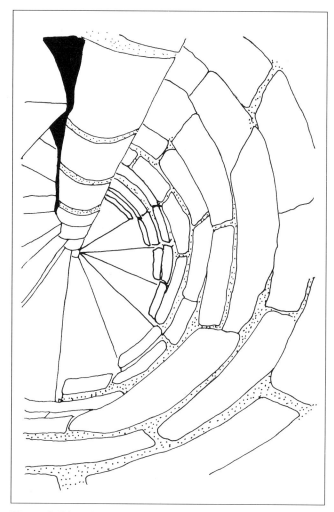

Figure 6: *Birstall Church: the stair of the Norman Tower*

Both Cradock and Lancaster considered the Tilly family to have been responsible for the building of the first church. This was because both believed the Tillys to have been the lords of the manor in the twelfth century. As suggested elsewhere in this book (chapter 2) however, the Tillys may not have been in outright possession of the manor at this time. The question should really remain open, with a strong presumption in favour of whichever family held the manor in the middle years of the twelfth century. It is likely to have been during this latter period that lands were first given by the manor to the church, for in 1204, when a fine was levied for the Manor of Gomersal, two carucates of land were already said to be vested in the first rector of Birstall, Brother Dolfin.[6] Perhaps the most important – as well as the most obvious – point to make is that the church was not built in the village of Birstall, probably because even at this early date Birstall was a separate manor, distinct from the manor of Gomersal.

The Tilly family certainly held Gomersal in the thirteenth century and were by then involved in most major transactions of the local church. In 1229 'Richard de Birstal, clerk' was presented for office by John Tilly;[7] and in 1281 Robert de Tilly was recorded in the Archbishop of York's register as patron of the rectory lands at Birstall.[8] Robert was mentioned again in 1281, when he required the Archbishop's consent to appoint rectory lands to the support of a new vicarage, in other words to divert funds from the support of the church itself and into the local curing of souls. Soon after this consent was granted, in 1286, the Tillys obtained a royal licence to donate their rights of patronage in the rectory to the Prior and Convent of Nostell Priory.[9] This was quickly followed, in 1300, by the Tillys granting to Nostell all rights in the church and rectory on a permanent basis. The Archbishop appropriated the right to appoint the vicar (a right retained by York until 1836) but the monks retained all rights over the rectory, including the glebelands, until the dissolution of the monasteries in the sixteenth century.

other Norman architectural features survive. A grave slab of twelfth century date, decorated with a chevron pattern, and a font with tegulated decoration around its base are the only other monuments of this period now visible in the church. By far the most important of these is the font, testifying to Birstall as a centre of baptism, possibly before the first church was completed.

After 1300 the Tilly family continued to give land to Nostell, most significantly the mill and millpool next to the church. For the next two hundred years the Priory's influence in Gomersal affairs must have been considerable; the name Monk Ings, to describe an area of land just to the north of the church, probably gained currency in this period. Cradock records an agreement of 1342 whereby stones were set up to define the boundary between manorial and monastic holdings in Gomersal.[10] The fourteenth and fifteenth centuries also saw a multiplication of chantries and private chapels at Birstall, all of which added to the growing need to expand and remodel the church. According to Cradock, by 1300 the original Norman structure had already lost its apse, and an aisle had probably been built on the south side of the nave. A northern aisle was added probably in the fourteenth century. This process of rebuilding culminated in the late fifteenth century with the addition of the present third stage of the tower and its embattled top.

Medieval parish churches fulfilled many of the functions which today would attach to town halls, parish halls or even chambers of commerce. Church courts would also sit in order to enforce church law, by which most of the laity were bound. Plays and festivals were performed and contracts were often made within church grounds. Linstrum even believes that the Birstall tower originally had a defensive function.[11]

The clergy frequently had many secular responsibilities and powers. At the turn of the fourteenth century the then vicar, Richard de Liversedge, was a trustee and guardian of Richard Popeley of Gomersal during the latter's minority.[12] This vicar was, and probably needed to be, a shrewd businessman. He also obtained many lands for the benefit of the de Liversedge family. The scale of the church's undertaking at this time is well illustrated by the will of Richard de Liversedge's predecessor, Robert Davy. When Davy died in 1394 he had five chaplains working in the parish, all of whom were probably priests. He gave twenty-six gallons of honey from the church's apiary to the monks at Nostell.

The annual production of beeswax was to go to the maintenance of altar lights in the church. Davy had even obtained licence from the papal authorities for a portable altar, by which he was able to spread the word in remoter parts of the parish.[13]

The general picture is of a practical Christianity. Whether this was a product of a mainly commercial perspective or of a true religious devotion is impossible to say. But it seems clear enough that the arid speculation of medieval scholasticism found little course in the early vicars of Birstall. No doubt they would have readily agreed with the words of the fourteenth century mystic Richard Rolle [14] who wrote:

> Nowadays too many are consumed with a desire for knowledge rather than for love ... shame on them ... an old woman can be more expert in the love of God – and less worldly too – than your theologian with his useless studying. He does it for vanity, to get a reputation, to obtain stipends and official positions. Such a fellow ought to be entitled not 'Doctor' but 'Fool'.[15]

At least one Birstall vicar felt some sympathy with such a view. This was Richard Messing, a Carmelite friar, who held the vicarage from 1460-1462. He is famous for translations of the works of Rolle, and may have been instrumental in establishing at Birstall devotions in keeping with Rolle's teaching.[16]

Medieval Buildings at Birstall Church

There were other important buildings near to the church in the pre-Reformation period. First is the mill. Its existence in the early thirteenth century is suggested by an entry in the Yorkshire Assize rolls *c.*1218-9, where reference was made to the murder of the rector's miller.[17] We can be certain that there was a mill by the early fourteenth century, as a millpool at Birstall church was then given to Nostell. Nothing is known however of the structure of the medieval mill, nor its exact location, though it must have stood close to the dam, just to the north of the present bridge. The dam itself, as depicted on the map of 1770, was of a much narrower construction than the dam visible today.

Second is an inn, supposed to have occupied a site close to that of the Black Bull, Kirkgate (see chapter 8). There are oblique references from various sources suggesting the brewing of ale in the locality of the church, but it is not possible to relate these definitely to any predecessor of the Black Bull. The present building does not appear to have any architectural features of pre-seventeenth century date. The suggestion of a medieval ale house close to the church remains very plausible however, especially when one considers the distances which many parishioners must have travelled to attend church. The rectory and the area around the church would have been self-sufficient in most food produce and it would be surprising if ale had not been easily available.

Thirdly, the rectory buildings were at the heart of the settlement around the church, and as early as the fourteenth century probably consisted of a house for the rector and some farm buildings. One of the earliest references to a house is in 1218, in the assize roll entry mentioned above. Gradually, other houses were built in close proximity to the rectory, at first for chaplains and servants but by the turn of the fourteenth century

Figure 7: *Birstall Church from the south east before the rebuilding of 1865 (KCS)*

including a house for the newly created office of vicar. A charter dated 1293 records the lease to one Randulf, clerk, 'of a toft and croft with the house built on it' in the vicinity of the church in Birstall.[18] As a vicar is not mentioned by name in the deed the reference is probably to a chaplain or lesser officer; though according to Cradock, the first vicar, in 1280-81, did occupy the house of a chaplain.[19]

Nothing now remains of any of the rectory buildings, at least not above ground. The rectory house is shown on the map of 1770 in a position immediately south of the churchyard. A painting reproduced by Cradock shows how parts of the late medieval building may have appeared.[20] Cradock believed that the rectory house experienced two major rebuilds, each involving near total demolition. One is said to have been in about 1550 at the time of Henry Batt's probable residence at Birstall Church, the other in the eighteenth century. However, this is not supported by the style of the buildings shown in the picture which Cradock reproduced. The buildings closest to the churchyard (the rectory house) appear to be largely of the sixteenth century, with some earlier and some later elements. The 'L'-shaped building (the rectory farmhouse) further to the south and nearer to Church Lane, seems to be of the seventeenth or eighteenth century. This is confirmed by one of the few

Figure 8: *The Rectory Farmhouse*

Figure 9: *Birstall Church: bench ends*

surviving photographs of the building, now displayed in the Black Bull Inn. The photograph shows a two storey structure, largely of stone rubble, with large, three-light windows in one elevation and four-light mullions in another. In fact the building had every appearance of an eighteenth century wing added to an earlier housebody (Fig. 8).

As the rectory house survived until 1865, further light is shed on the age of the building by the diary of William Carr of Little Gomersal, a Victorian who took a considerable interest in the history of Gomersal. After visiting the church in September 1865 he observed:

> The old rectory house adjoining Birstall churchyard was pulled down at this time. It was a timber and plaster irregular erection with additions of various periods. The main building was probably of the early part of the reign of Henry VIII. Many massive oak beams were removed from this building and I purchased one oak floor main-beam joists and boards etc with a view to re-erect it in one of the rooms of Gomersal House.[21]

Stephen Glynne had also noticed the rectory, describing it in 1858 as 'a very picturesque house of wood and plaster in good preservation'.[22]

Medieval Monuments in Birstall Church

Several medieval gravestones and other monuments now displayed in the church should also be mentioned. A Norman font and gravestone have already been referred to, and the font's importance noted. Both are early Norman. The gravestone, with its crude chevron design, is an amateurish attempt at a traditional Norman ornament. The font has tegulated decoration at its foot, also in an early style. There are four other gravestones in the church which are clearly of medieval origin. Three are of thick sandstone and have a double cross motif on a stepped base. Cradock and others had no doubts that these are Knights Hospitallers' crosses of about the thirteenth century, although the use of the double cross motif was never restricted to the Hospitallers of that period. In fact these slabs, with their heavy cutting and untapered, rectangular plan could easily be as late at the fifteenth century. The fourth slab survives only as a fragment, but is probably the earliest of the four. It does seem to have been tapered; it is also more delicate and the base of the cross is more finely cut.[]

Other notable objects include a collection of carved, darkly stained, wooden bench ends. Some of these are

Figure 10: *Birstall Church: bench ends with trademarks*

shown in plate 14 of Cradock's book, in the positions which they occupied when last in use in the nineteenth century. But they were pulled out during the rebuilding of 1865 and now exist only as individual museum pieces, propped against walls in the north and south aisles. Several have tracery decoration and may be of late medieval origin (Fig. 9). Some have rosette and peltae designs and are of indeterminate date. Another is clearly inscribed with the date 1616. Perhaps the most interesting of all however are those which have trade motifs such as mason's square and compasses, or wool cropper's teasel and shears (Fig. 10). From their style of representation these latter carvings may also be of medieval date, and indicate a long pedigree for Gomersal's established trades of stone dressing and wool cropping.

The Post-Reformation Church and People

It is this period of the church's history which provides the bulk of evidence of its relationship with the community at large. A surprising quantity of information has survived from the medieval period but, because of the illiteracy and limited participation in church affairs of nearly everybody outside of the church, such information does little to clarify the church's role in local society.

All this changed after the Reformation. Most parishes acceded to royal dictate and began keeping comprehensive registers of births, marriages and deaths from 1558. In about 1550 Birstall church also changed its name. Previously dedicated to St.Peter and St. Paul, it became known simply as St. Peter's. This development can be observed in wills of the period. One of the latest to refer to the church by its original name was that of John Gomersall in 1544 (see chapter 4).

In the sixteenth century the ownership of the rectory also changed hands. In 1538 it was still vested in the monks of Nostell Priory, but the following year it was appropriated by the Crown, and in 1546 was given by Henry VIII to Trinity College, Cambridge. Consequently

the glebelands were no longer under monastic control; instead the rectory and the right to collect tithes were leased out to wealthy laymen. The political spirit of the Reformation therefore had an almost immediate impact on Gomersal. The first lessee was Henry Batt, who according to Cradock took a short lease initially, followed by a term of sixty years in 1555.[23] After Batt's tenure, probably with one eye on his misanthropy (see chapter 2), the College began leasing to two tenants jointly. Cradock assumes this joint ownership to have begun in 1615, though at least one document recites that the rectory was divided into two halves as early as 1609.[24]

The church also began to keep better records of pews and their occupants. In the archives of the Yorkshire Archaeological Society survive lists of the owners of pews in 1606 and 1634.[25] The pews are described by reference to their position in the church.

The earlier list begins:

The stalls or seates in the church of Birstall to whom they belong as followeth:
first in ye bodie of ye church on ye same side beneath ye pulpitt

first stall	John Gomersall
	Robert Liversedge
	John Nettilton
	John Egremond
	Thomas Clayton

In front of the pulpit seven rows are listed – no doubt many of those pews once terminating in the bench ends discussed above. Other areas of the church are also mentioned, for example 'under the roode loft', 'the stall next the queerer [choir]' (paid for by John Nettilton of Oakwell), 'stalls in the bellhouse' (four pews) and the stalls in the 'bodie of the church' (17 pews, including one for Oakwell Hall and one for Edward Popeley).

The second list is essentially an amendment to the first, and indicates that many of the names recorded in the first list relate to persons who had dedicated the pews, and not necessarily to those who occupied them when the inventories were taken.

In the seventeenth century the established church suffered greatly from internal division. By the end of that century an unsteady equilibrium had been achieved, but at the cost of some loss of spiritual vigour by the early eighteenth century. One notable development in these years was the growth of non-conformity, and locally particularly the appearance of congregations of Independents and Quakers. It was partly as a result of concern over church attendance and the growth of non-conformist groups in his province that Archbishop Herring of York organized a very thorough 'Visitation', or report by the vicar of each parish in the diocese. Of note is Birstall's return made in 1743 by Thomas Coleby.[26] At this time there were already estimated to be 300 dissenting families in the parish out of a total of 1,500. John and Charles 'Westley' were said to be active in the parish, and John Nelson was said to be teaching in Birstall (later Vicar Coleby successfully conspired to have Nelson conscripted into the army). Coleby said that five non-conformist meeting houses were licensed at this time but another dozen or so were operating illegally.

In the seventeenth and eighteenth centuries the church in Birstall also became more involved with education. From the early years of Elizabeth I's reign all those who practised as schoolmasters had had to provide evidence of orthodoxy in religious matters, and from 1604 had to be licensed by the appropriate bishop. It appears that all Birstall schoolmasters were in holy orders until 1819.[27]

A grammar school was founded in Birstall in about 1560, by Sir John Neville of Liversedge and Henry Batt. No building was erected, presumably due to Batt's appropriation of part of the endowment. By 1604 however a commission of enquiry had settled the matter and Henry Batt's son, John, was ordered to convey suitable premises to the vicar, Richard Dickinson.[28] The school was never a large one. It had six free places paid for by endowments and out of the fees of other, paying, scholars. The ratio of free to fee payers was probably about 1:4. Education was in reading, writing, the teachings of the Church of England, and some Latin poetry. Pupils had to attend church regularly, particularly if they lived within easy walking distance, as did those from Gomersal. This education probably altered very little until, in 1818, the school was replaced by a new one run by the Anglican National Society.

The church was less directly responsible for relief of the poor. It did make a contribution in this area, but from as early as the sixteenth century a system of poor law administration, established on a secular basis, was in place in most parishes. Poor Law Acts of 1597-1601 required the appointment of two local Overseers of the Poor who, along with churchwardens, were responsible for distributing goods and payments to the infirm, aged and impoverished. Overseers were also empowered to bind the young poor of the parish as apprentices. Justices of the Peace were required to consent to this, just as they had to agree to withdrawal of relief and arbitrate in disagreements about poor law administration.

Relief was financed from a local rate. Most assistance in the seventeenth and eighteenth centuries was in the form of 'out-relief', that is gifts of bread, blankets or money to families in their homes. Some workhouses did exist even at this time, where the number of poor was thought to present too great a burden on the parish; in 1722 an Act of Parliament made it possible to refuse relief to those who would not enter the workhouse. It was not until the nineteenth century however that workhouses proliferated and assumed their Dickensian character.

Several documents survive to illustrate the operation of the Poor Law system in the Gomersal area. There are indentures whereby sons of paupers were apprenticed.

The indenture of John Moore of Gomersal, in 1674, records that:

John Rooke and William Taylor, overseers of the poore in the Township of Gomersall and John Newby churchwarden of the saide Towne ... have put placed and bound John Moore of Gomersall a poore child about the age of 7 yeares with Thomas Taylor of the saide Towne ... to dwell with Thomas Taylor until he John Moore shall attain the age of four and twenty yeares ... dureing which time the saide John Moore his saide master shall obediently and faithfully serve.[29]

The system was enforced by punishment of any recalcitrant parents, a position poignantly chronicled by an entry in the records of the West Riding Quarter Sessions for 14 January 1640:

Forasmuch as this Courte is informed that one Robert Savile of the par. of Birstall, butcher, beinge one of the poore of that parishe and haveinge a boy aged tenn yeares or thereabouts refuseth to allowe the churchwardens and overseeres of the poore to putt his saide sonne apprentice as the lawe in that case hath appointed, ordered that the said Robert Savile shall be committed to the house of Correccon at Wakefeild for his misdeamenner.[30]

For most of the seventeenth and eighteenth centuries this system of out-relief and apprenticeship was the main

way of tackling poverty in Gomersal. There does not appear to have been a workhouse until about 1762 when, as Cadman notes, the overseers decided to build one.[31] Their rationale for doing so was that to reduce the number of people claiming out-relief the threat of a workhouse was necessary. Action soon followed idea, as Fairfax Fearnley of Oakwell conveyed a piece of ground to the overseers for a nominal sum. The land in question was at the junction of Muffit Lane and Church Lane. A large building of four bays and two storeys was constructed upon it (Fig. 11). At third floor level it had a through attic which, in the nineteenth century, was used as extra working space.

The building is of brick. Its form is unusual in Gomersal – a hybrid of domestic and industrial construction set beneath a steeply pitched, stone slate roof. In the gable nearest Church Lane the remains of a taking-in door are still visible. The extension to the right of the main building originally housed a kitchen and the master's quarters.

At first the workhouse must have taken both men and women. But by the time of the 1841 census it was clearly accommodating only women and young children: under the Union system, the poor of one parish could be sent to workhouses in other parishes. and by 1840 the men of Gomersal were sent to Staincliffe in Dewsbury. The census recorded sixty-four women and children in the Gomersal workhouse.

Even though male paupers were no longer available, owners of local coal mines continued to use the Gomersal workhouse as a source of cheap labour. Conditions shocked even those hardened to the standards of the times, for example Thomas Rayner, a surgeon and one of the Guardians of the workhouse:

In some cases boys have been selected at 7 and 8 years of age because they were strong and healthy ... and if in a few months the man found the boy was not strong enough ... he brought him back.[32]

Figure 11: *Gomersal Workhouse*

Consigned to this pitiable fate was Joseph Booth, an eight year old of Gomersal Workhouse, who bravely reported to the commissioners:

> I remember being in the pit; I used to hurry [pull loads of coal] with another; I used to like being in the pit. Please they gave me plenty to eat. We used to go in at five in the morning and they came out at five.... The work did not tire me much.[33]

The Church in the Seventeenth and Eighteenth Centuries

In the seventeenth and eighteenth centuries the church itself did not see any radical alterations. There had been a rebuilding in the early sixteenth century and nothing of this scale was attempted again until 1865. The most notable development was probably several new windows, including triple deckers of seventeenth century style in the north and south aisles. Photographs taken before 1865 also show that in the seventeenth century a new gable had been built on the northern side, at right angles to the nave. No doubt one victim of these improvements was the medieval stained glass recorded by Dodsworth in 1619.

Inside the church, pews started to occupy every available space, until by the eighteenth century they covered the floor of the chancel. Even the roof over the nave had to be heightened to accommodate a second tier of pews on the north and south sides. Perhaps the greatest single development during this period however was the introduction of an organ in 1756. This was placed in a gallery which stood over the tower arch in the western wall. Before 1756 the Birstall congregation had, like most, relied for its musical accompaniment on an ensemble of wind and string instruments, playing from the gallery. But by an agreement of 10 May 1754 the opposition to a new organ by several influential landowners was overcome – they had thought that they would have to foot the bill – and the decision taken:

> to convert 18 feet in length and 9 feet in breadth ... at present made use of as a singing loft ... into an organ loft ... that the sum [150 pounds] which has lately been collected by subscription be used for the purchase of an organ ... and that a sufficient sum of money should be taken up at interest in order to finish a new loft or gallery on the south side.[34]

From about 1650 onwards gravestones and monuments both inside and outside the church also became more numerous. Of special note are the Popeley brass (Fig. 26) and the stone commemorating John Greene of Liversedge. Both were originally outside but are now under cover to aid their preservation. Although Victorian and more modern work was responsible for clearing many tens, perhaps hundreds, of gravestones from the churchyard (apparent from the large, open spaces to the east and west) seventeenth century stones remain a feature. Their lettering is usually well-cut and their messages plain and to the point. To the west of the tower is a broken slab to Francis Popeley of Little Gomersal (died 1643) (Fig. 27); there are also various slabs to the Rayner family of Liversedge. The eighteenth century is represented by a stone to the Birstall religious teacher John Nelson, and the nineteenth century by a memorial to Ellen Nussey, the friend of Charlotte Brontë.

In the eighteenth century additional space for burial also had to be found. First, land lying between the eastern end of the church and the stream was consecrated. This had previously been part of the rectory grounds and was crossed by a road to the rectory house. The parishioners of Tong contributed to this undertaking, in 1764 paying for sixty-three yards of a new boundary wall. An inscribed stone in the eastern portion of the south wall still records their dedication. Even this expansion proved insufficient however, and in 1825 land on the other side of Kirkgate was acquired from Trinity College. This area is still populated with monuments of every description.

In the early nineteenth century church alteration and restoration went at a slow pace, amending what had been handed down by previous generations but at a speed which allowed the work of various periods to subsist as a whole. When Sir Stephen Glynne visited the church in 1858, Norman, Early English and Perpendicular styles were still a significant feature of the nave, while seven centuries of building and interment remained intact beneath the chancel floor. Unfortunately for posterity, all of this was to change. Restoration of churches was a favourite Victorian pastime and Birstall church had the dubious honour of receiving more attention than most. Parts of the building fabric on the south side were in need of replacement and, in spite of new galleries, seating was still in short supply. Indeed, it was said that the whole church was unsafe, having been undermined by the collapse of old coal workings and the sinking of burial vaults. The weight of the galleries added to structural problems, and the old church had no proper foundations.[35] But the true motive for what followed was a desire to put into practice the new architectural canons of the day. Consequently, in 1865, the existing church was almost completely demolished. The new building was wider and seventeen feet longer than its predecessor. Even Hartshead Church, another church heavily restored in this period, escaped lightly by comparison. At Birstall only the tower has survived in its original form.

NOTES

1. Tithes were abolished by the 1836 Tithe Commutation Act and replaced by a monetary tax. The Gomersal revaluation was carried out in 1848.
2. Collingwood 1915, 144.
3. Auden 1909, 20.
4. Cradock 1933, plate 4.
5. Glynne 1918, 187.
6. *YAS* DD 70/15/5.
7. Raine 1872, 27-8.
8. Brown (ed.) 1907, 34.
9. Lancaster 1924, 18.
10. Cradock 1933, 136.
11. Linstrum 1978, 158.
12. *YAS* DD 70/15/5.
13. Cradock 1933, 216.
14. Rolle, born *c.*1300 at Thornton-le-Dale, died in 1349. He is sometimes known as Richard Rolle of Hampole (near Doncaster).
15. Richard Rolle *Incendium Amoris* Ch. 5.
16. For example, the keeping of a feast to the name of Jesus (Cradock 1933, 220).
17. Cradock 1933, 207.
18. *BL* Add Ch 12633.
19. Cradock 1933, 127.
20. Cradock 1933, frontispiece.
21. *WYAS K* DD/CA/6.
22. Glynne 1918, 187.
23. Cradock 1933, 138-9.
24. *YAS* DD 70/9/4.
25. *YAS* DD 70/1.
26. Ollard and Walker (eds.) 1928, 60-2.
27. Cradock 1933, 144.
28. Cradock 1933, 142.
29. *WYAS K* KC/52/19; the William Taylor referred to was probably the same who built Red House, Gomersal. Thomas Taylor may have lived at Fieldhead, Latham Lane.
30. Lister (ed.) 1915, 259.
31. Cadman 1930, 129-130.
32. Parliamentary Papers (House of Commons) 1842 (381) XVI no. 180.
33. Parliamentary Papers (House of Commons) 1842 (381) XVI no. 182.
34. *YAS* DD 70/1. A group of parishioners had agreed to indemnify the landowners against extra burdens on the parish rates. Amongst the voluntary contributors were Vicar Coleby, Joseph Nussey, a Birstall dyer, and Benjamin Crowther, a clothdresser of Great Gomersal. Objectors included Sir George Savile and Sir William Wentworth, of Bretton. The new loft on the south side was needed as space for the congregation would otherwise be lost to the organ.
35. Cradock 1933, 93.

Chapter 2

OAKWELL

On 29 September 1927 *The Times* was able to report that 'There is now every prospect that Oakwell Hall, Birstall, in the West Riding of Yorkshire, will be saved from demolition and removal across the Atlantic ... This well-preserved Elizabethan manor house is not only a good example of the late Tudor period, but it is the scene of incidents in Charlotte Brontë's novel *Shirley*, in which it is pictured under the name of Fieldhead'. In two sentences is expressed perhaps the most important reason for studying Oakwell, namely the historic value of the hall itself. The sixty years following this newspaper article have done nothing to change that. If anything Oakwell's evocative architecture has now even greater appeal. The hall is certainly a vital reference point for an appreciation of early housing in the Gomersal area.

But there are at least two other reasons for treating Oakwell as an integral part of Gomersal's history. Oakwell was the seat of the Lord of the Manor of Gomersal. A study of Oakwell's tenurial descent therefore is the easiest way in which to give an outline history of the township as a whole. In addition, for over six hundred years, Oakwell was the administrative centre of Gomersal township, where the manorial court was held; most inhabitants were either bound to the Lord by suit and service or had dealings with him on a commercial basis. The Lord was invariably one of the largest landowners and the most influential person in the locality.

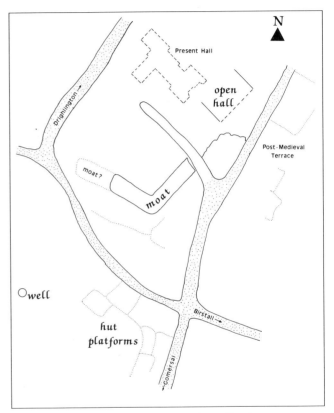

Figure 12: *Oakwell: location of probable medieval structures*

The Hall and Earlier Archaeological Remains

Oakwell hamlet was an area in the ecclesiastical parish of Birstall, including the site of the present hall but centred just to the south. Archaeological investigation has now demonstrated what informed antiquaries and historians had always suspected, that it was the site of agricultural settlement from at least as early as the thirteenth century. Remains of any pre-medieval settlement are still elusive, but excavation and other fieldwork have revealed clear antecedents to the present hall (Fig. 12).

Two sets of excavations are of note: the first undertaken by the University of Bradford in 1977-1978, and the second by John Gilks of Kirklees Metropolitan Borough

Council in 1985. With minor exceptions both concentrated on the area immediately to the east of the hall. The Bradford team claims to have found the remains of seven separate buildings, ranging from sheds and workshops to substantial houses.[1] One building in particular is worthy of comment. This had walls of coursed sandstone rubble. Its internal features included a central hearth, a floor of thin sandstone flags and a baking oven at the northern end. Pottery dated the building to a period from the thirteenth to the early fifteenth century, 150 years before the present hall. Most significantly, the building is said to have been of the open hall type, a basic medieval plan traditionally associated with a large household (perhaps an extended family) where servants and masters occupied different areas of the same room. It was situated immediately to the east of the present hall, and may have been either its forerunner or an ancillary part of such a building.

Although excavation provided no evidence of pre-thirteenth century occupation, the form of the hall and the close proximity of the settlement to a church with Norman architectural features make this a little surprising. Only further archaeological work will illuminate the site's origins. For the moment we can be confident that settlement dating to the time of the Tillys has been discovered and that the present hall had a precursor worthy of the name.

A Break in Occupation?

The 'open hall' was served by at least one barn/cowshed and one workshop. According to the excavators all had been demolished by the fifteenth century (perhaps when the property left the Leedes family). There is thus a gap between the demise of these structures and the building of the present hall, usually dated to 1583, during which there is no clear evidence of normal residential occupation.

Ancillary buildings still existed. The Bradford excavation discovered the sandstone walls of a small building of the fifteenth and early sixteenth century within the then disused open hall; and Gilks recently revealed the complete plan of a rectangular building, with walls of wattle and stake-post construction, whose dates span the fourteenth, fifteenth and sixteenth centuries.[2] But the site of the main residential building, if one existed, between c.1400 and 1550 is unclear. Gilks found evidence of human occupation in the ancillary building mentioned above, but for a number of reasons this was unlikely to have been functioning as the main residential area. It was a low quality building, originally probably used for stalling cattle. Nor was the building intensively occupied, though it appears to have been in use at the time when the Leedes family was strengthening its hand in Gomersal and becoming very active in the township.

There may have been a break in occupation by gentry families between the medieval and modern periods. If this was not so then a hall, probably built at the turn of the fifteenth century, must have existed, either on the site of the present hall or at some as yet undiscovered location. The possibility of a third hall is difficult to accept given the relatively short time span (just over 100 years) in question. It is usual to find a medieval hall replaced by an early modern example but it would be exceptional to find three successive structures. A complete break in occupation by gentry, or by their representative in the form of a bailiff, seems equally unlikely given that Oakwell continued to be the administrative centre of the township.

A more accurate explanation probably lies between these extremes. There may have been an earlier residential building on the site of the present hall. This would certainly help to explain the considerable amounts of structural timber found there, including two re-used timbers tentatively dated to 1199 by recent tree-ring analysis (commissioned by Kirklees Cultural Services). Alternatively, it is also quite possible that excavations did not detect the uppermost occupation layers of the open hall, and that that building had remained in use well into the fifteenth century.

The Present Hall

The hall as it now exists is a large building in stone, an imposing feature in Gomersal since at least the close of the sixteenth century. It is of two storeys, with 11 rooms on the lower floor and 11 or 12 rooms upstairs. These are arranged on either side of a through passage which lies approximately on a north-south axis. To the immediate west of this passage is the central hall, easily the largest room in the house; its width alone at this point links all other rooms lying to the east and west. In plan therefore the building is usually described as a hall with cross-wings.

The rooms had varying functions but in many instances they were used much as they would be today – for sleeping, study and as private apartments upstairs, and for dining, reception of guests and recreation downstairs. An exception to this is the possible use of the better upstairs rooms for public dining and reception of important guests. The main distinction however is with the central hall itself. Used as a manorial courtroom, a place for the formal reception of visitors and, when occasion demanded, as a place for feasts, the hall represents the greatest departure from a modern house of whatever scale.

It has become a habit among historians to describe the house as a timber framed building subsequently encased in stone. Undoubtedly this was a frequent occurrence in the early modern period, and Gomersal has an example with Peel House (see chapter 5). A relatively recent and authoritative survey has however failed to find evidence to support this notion at Oakwell.[3] In fact all the signs are that most, if not all, of the house was from the outset built of stone. There is an absence of main timbers such as posts and beams which could have carried the roof, and even where a number of trusses are found buried in the wall these are not closed or end trusses such as would indicate an initial timber framed building.

If the greater part of the house was originally built of stone it is a very early example of its kind. Nevertheless the dating evidence available confirms this to be the case. At first sight, the date of 1583 cut above the front porch appears unreliable. But this early nineteenth century lettering can be seen to replace a much older, authentic inscription just below it, probably of the late sixteenth or seventeenth century. A date of 1583 can be accepted therefore for at least some of the building. In fact most of the structure may be of 1583 or earlier – not so surprising given the abundance of local stone and the considerable amounts of stone which had been used in the construction of the open hall. The tree-ring analysis, already referred to, has suggested that most of the present roof timbers were felled in 1582/1583.

Figure 13: *Oakwell Hall from the south*

The Hall 1583-1611

The datestone over the porch of the house when taken in conjunction with an inventory of 1611,[4] which refers to the 'new parlour' in the east wing, indicates a remodelling of the east wing in the late sixteenth century rather than a new build of the whole. A remodelling is suggested by the continuous drip course and the use of larger and more regularly cut stone blocks than are used in the west wing.

The inventory shows what would otherwise be revealed only by the most painstaking architectural investigation, namely that at the time that the inventory was taken there was a bedroom ('chamber') over the main hall. In turn, such a two storey arrangement means that the large mullioned window in the south wall was inserted after 1611 and that in 1611 this wall probably had two smaller mullion sets, matching those in the wings. There is no scope for supposing the large window to have been in any way contemporary with the two storey arrangement.

The inventory records the contents of the chamber over:

> In the Hall Chambor. Item, 2 stand bedsteades with teasters and Cordes, 1 other stand bedstead with Cord, 1 truckle bed [low bed on castors] and cord Mr. Waterhouses, 1 long Chest, 1 counter.

The chamber does not appear to have been a small room or loft, but an important private apartment. Indeed some of the timbers of the roof, now in the roof space, are well finished and seem originally to have been visible from the room. The hall below had a ceiling only about 3 metres high, and at this time was heated by a hearth with a firehood placed against the hall's east wall.[5]

It is worth spending a little more time with the inventory, for the light which it sheds on the use of rooms and the lifestyle of the people who occupied them. The early seventeenth century captures the mood of the hall as well as any particular period can. The hall itself (still with a room above) contained two tables, two

Figure 14: *Oakwell Hall: south elevation as it may have appeared in the sixteenth century*

forms and a sideboard. It was the place where touch powder and flax for firing a matchlock were kept. In the 'Great Parlore', downstairs in the west wing, amongst furniture and other effects were found 'mappes ... of the world, Palestine, Ffrance, Spaine, low countries, Greece, Italie, Africa, Asia and England and Tables [i.e. pictures] of both the Universities'. These must at one time have belonged to John Batt [I], the man responsible for the late sixteenth century building, and are an indication of the relative sophistication of the Oakwell household.

In the chambers of the first floor the inventory records: 'Hanginges of Dornicke [a Flemish woollen-silk] with borders' in the Little Parlour Chamber; '1 great stand bedstead that came from Hagg Hall' (the house where Henry Batt died) in the Porch Chamber; and 'in the studdeye over the Taverne' a room in the east wing not the present little cell at the top of the stair – 'all Mr Robert Batte his books to the number of 62 ... 6 pewter dishes ... and 7 porcelain dishes'. There is much else besides recorded in this latter room, which in reality appears to have been more of a lumber room than a study.

The Hall after 1611

The date of the great window in the south wall is not known exactly but it is likely to have been of the period 1630-1660. The loss of the 'hall chamber', above the hall, has already been referred to, but of course the rebuilding had other effects which are still visible.

Externally, a drip course surmounts the window but comes to an abrupt end at the eastern wall of the west wing. A small window in this wall also fits awkwardly, as if at the time when the great window was added the southern wall of the hall was extended a little further to the south. A lower drip course, over the porch, then ends at the angle of the south wall, without any indication that it once continued across that wall towards the great window.

Internally, the main hall achieved the height which it has today. This means that for the first time the hall was visible from the gallery at the top of the stairs (previously this had been a corridor running along the northern wall). This type of open hall was not a particularly seventeenth century feature. In fact Oakwell seems to have been remodelled in this fashion at a time when most houses of similar status were doing away with the open arrangement. There is no real explanation for this other than the personal taste of the owner at this time (probably John Batt [II], owner 1631-1652). Other alterations during the middle years of the seventeenth century included the replacement of a hearth and firehood in the hall with a lateral chimney stack. The grandeur of the house by this date seems to have demanded an impressive entrance from the passage,

and this was impossible whilst the hall was dominated by a firehood at its eastern end. The firehood stood approximately where the entrance to the hall from the through passage is now situated. It rose through the hall chamber and entered the roof at a point now represented by a break in the original ridge.[6] The lateral stack which replaced it is that which still stands against the north wall.

Other rooms benefited from refurbishment at this time. These included the Great Parlour (lower storey of the west wing). Like the hall it received a new plaster ceiling, based on a design of repeating octagons. Unfortunately, neither has survived intact, though an illustration of the Great Parlour ceiling has been preserved.[7]

Some consolation for the loss of such fine workmanship comes from the recent discovery, again in the Great Parlour, of painted panelling. Beneath the overburden of paint, picture panels in a seventeenth century Italian style were found. There were landscapes and garden scenes over the fireplace and geometric designs elsewhere.[8] The house of course has an abundance of oak panelling, but painted panels such as these are much more rare. As well as providing a graphic reminder of the luxury of the 'Stuart' building, their style is further evidence that major embellishment of the house can be dated to the middle years of the seventeenth century. They are also a reminder that the complete story of Oakwell is still to be told.

It is usual in histories of Oakwell to trace the use and development of the hall through the eighteenth and nineteenth centuries, pausing for a while to emphasize its relevance for Brontë literature as the model for Charlotte Brontë's 'Fieldhead'. Such architectural alterations as took place, however, were of a minor nature; for example, two eighteenth century windows over the rear doorway and an early eighteenth century mullioned window over the front doorway. And the Brontë story, though intriguing in its own right, does

Figure 15: *Oakwell Hall: the Great Parlour*

Figure 16: *Oakwell Hall: the seventeenth century window*

little to add to the real value of Oakwell. In some cases the Brontë connection has obscured the significance of the hall, a significance which is first and foremost rooted in the sixteenth and seventeenth centuries. It would be foolish to deny Oakwell's place in Gomersal life after this period. The point is rather that in the early modern period, as in the medieval age, the Manor of Oakwell was central to Gomersal life whereas the same cannot be said of the period which followed.

The Descent and Administration of Oakwell Manor

That Oakwell is the locality's strongest link between the late medieval period and the more familiar surroundings of the eighteenth century is clear in the wealth of documentary evidence which has survived. The papers of the Batt family, now in the custody of the Thoresby Society of Leeds, are an especially valuable collection. They cover in detail the period during which the present hall was built and remodelled, and include several important medieval sources. Other collections, for example the Horton manuscripts,[9] provide significant additional information.

In general, the work of interpreting Oakwell has been much easier since Lancaster first established a virtually complete descent of the manor.[10] He asserted that the two berewics mentioned along with Gomersal in the Domesday survey are likely to be Heckmondwike and Birstall, and not Liversedge.[11] From the pre-conquest period onwards, Liversedge appears to have followed a completely different line of descent from that of Gomersal.

There is no evidence yet to suggest that Oakwell existed at the time of Domesday. After 1086 Lancaster's first reference to Gomersal is of the mid twelfth century when, he believes, following a grant by the Lacys to Hugh de Tilly, Gomersal came to Hugh's son Roger. Lancaster gives no firm evidence in support of the latter statement, and the picture is blurred further by a seventeenth century document which refers to one Eschoche Bulffe as holder of Gomersal and Birstall in 1204.[12] The temptation would be to dismiss the appearance of such an unusually named and otherwise undocumented individual were it not for the accurate circumstantial evidence which accompanies it. The document correctly identifies the descent of the manor after 1204 (from Tilly to Leedes, then to Hussey and Batt) and recognizes it to be held for one knight's fee.[13] The problem arises of course with the date of 1204, because, according to Lancaster, Gomersal had been in the Tilly family's hands since *c.*1150. Nevertheless, the document is quite explicit:

> Eschoche Bulffe levyed a fyne in the county courte at Yorke before Glanville then Sheriffe and Plumpton and others coroners to one Tilly of a whole knights fee in Gomersal ... except for two carucates of land in Birstall held by Brother Dolfin and 80 acres at Popeley held by Popeley.[14]

'Levying a fine' was a method of conveying land, by court judgement rather than private deed. Usually the hearing was an artificial affair, arranged between parties who were already agreed on the outcome. Its special appeal was its simplicity in cases where entitlement had become extremely difficult to establish. It might also be used in cases where settlements of land were proving difficult to administer. There is no reason to believe that a conveyance was not taking place in 1204 between the parties indicated. The manor may have been the subject of a genuinely contested suit against the Tillys, but it is more likely that the fine was either the means by which the Tillys first came by the estate or by which one of the Tillys received the land from a trustee.

The Tilly family certainly held Gomersal in the thirteenth century. First this was in the name of the John who was a co-witness with members of the Popeley family to some early Calverley charters (see chapter 3); afterwards it was in the name of John's son, Ralph. Ralph is mentioned in a deed of *c.*1270-1280, notable for its reserving of a yearly rent of a pair of gilded spurs.[15] Ralph's son was Robert. It was with Robert that the close association of the Tilly family with Birstall church first came to prominence.[16]

In 1281 he was patron of the church, a patron whose consent was required by the Archbishop of York before a vicar could be appointed to the church. Most significantly, it was Robert who in 1286 successfully petitioned Edward I for permission to give the advowson of the church to the Prior and Convent of Augustinian monks at Nostell.[17] The church itself was granted to the Priory in 1300 and from this period onwards the close control which the holders of Gomersal manor must have exercised over the church and its surroundings would have been greatly reduced. There followed further grants to Nostell, notably that by John [II], Robert's son. In the early fourteenth century he gave the millpool at Birstall to the Priory.[18] This was an act which had direct repercussions over four hundred years later when Birstall tenants of the Batts were bound to grind their corn at the manorial mill at Spen and not at the much nearer Birstall mill.

Doubtless these grants to Nostell were motivated by some spiritual conviction. They also coincide with the period when the Lords of the Manor were first associated with a place called 'Okewell'. In 1311 one John de Tilly was described as 'Lord of Okewell'. This is a date which correlates closely with that of the earliest archaeological remains found at the hall.

The description 'Lord of Okewell' was repeated in 1321[19] and appears therefore to be an adopted title. There is no record of the Tillys having used it previously.

From the early fourteenth century the administration of Gomersal was clearly centred on Oakwell. In the year before his death John made a grant of land to one John de Metham and his wife. This was given at 'Gomersale', most likely at Oakwell. Witnesses included many of the major landowners of the locality, including John de Elland, Robert de Nevile, John de Bollyng, Adam de Batelay and (notably) William de Popelay. From the content of the grant it is clear that under this John the Tillys had substantially increased their property in Gomersal.[20]

John [II] died in 1343, the last male of the Tilly family to hold Gomersal. The estate which he had enlarged and organized from Oakwell descended to his daughter, Joan, wife to Roger de Northall of Leeds ('Roger de Leedes'). Not until 1372 however did the de Leedes family finally realise their claim to John's inheritance, but when they did the estate centred on Oakwell was still intact. In the following year, Roger de Leedes, 'Lord of Hokwell', granted a lease of 'a messuage called Spen within the bounds of Gomersal'.[21] Then in 1377 he exchanged some of his lands in Bilham for land in Gomersal, apparently to further consolidate his holding there.

It is worth mentioning that even at this early date Gomersal, and especially Oakwell and Birstall, were coal mining and iron working areas. Numerous fourteenth century leases refer to 'iron pieces', as a form of rent. In 1359, in the period before Roger de Leedes became entitled, a lease of Oakwell was given including 'all mines of ore and coal' and reserving 'twenty shillings and a dozen pieces of iron yearly'.[22] These leases were followed by references to the building of 'smithies' by 'Leedes Lord of Gomersal' in the late fourteenth and early fifteenth centuries. The smithies are said to have been on the commons of Birstall.[23]

Roger de Leedes is best described as an aggressive rather than a merely enthusiastic landowner. In addition to cultivating and building on the Birstall commons, he was central to two incidents unique in the history of Oakwell. In the first, Roger was admittedly an unwilling participant: at a date just before 1384 he was forced to take refuge 'in his house at Okwell' when one Adam de Mirfield and others tried to prevent him from executing a writ.[24] This incident is perhaps most illuminating because it refers to Roger having a house at Oakwell – a very early reference for the Gomersal area – which probably relates to the open hall revealed by archaeology (above). The second incident however, in 1398, shows Roger to have been implicated in the murder of one John Paslew of Leeds. Roger does not appear to have been punished himself, but it certainly seems, following what was initially a very productive period in the 1370s, that by his death in 1400 the security and reputation of the family had been seriously threatened. Only by a Royal Pardon of 21 July 1400 was Roger's son, William, cleared of his part in the murder; and only then did Roger's trustees consider it safe enough to convey the Gomersal inheritance to the heir.

Whether William de Leedes and his wife Joan occupied Oakwell is unknown. Like his father and the Tillys before him he held one knight's fee in an area which, in 1425, included Birstall, Gomersal, Popeley, Heckmondwike, and Birkenshaw. The area undoubtedly also included Oakwell for after William's death in 1440 his wife granted a lease of the 'manor of Oakwell' to one William Nettilton, for a term of twenty years. Lancaster believes that the Gomersal lands may have formed part of Joan's dower. Certainly, lands acquired through marriage, as the Leedes family had acquired Gomersal, were more likely to be treated in this way.

Following William's death in 1433 the Leedes house at Oakwell may have become increasingly peripheral to the rest of the de Leedes estate. Archaeological evidence which suggests less intensive occupation from c.1425 onwards is in keeping with this idea. William had

died childless[25] and, after his wife's death, all the de Leedes estates passed under a settlement to his nephew, Ranulf Pigot.

The Pigot family held Gomersal from 1441 until 1512. Gomersal became a small part of an even larger estate under the Pigots, and the years of this family's tenure appear to have been uneventful. Occupation of the hall may have ceased completely, though the lease granted to Henry Nettilton by Joan, wife to William de Leedes, will have subsisted until 1460. Indeed the lease may have been renewed, for when Henry Batt bought the Oakwell estate in 1565 the Nettilton family was still in occupation of a large part of the Pigot holding in Gomersal. By 1512 the male Pigot line had died out and the inheritance came initially to Elizabeth Pigot (one of whose husbands was Sir Charles Brandon) and, eventually, to Joan Pigot. Joan had two husbands. The first was Giles Hussey of Lincolnshire, by whom she bore a son, Thomas. Thomas therefore became heir to the Gomersal estate. Her second husband was Thomas Falkingham who, along with Joan, conveyed Gomersal, Oakwell and Heckmondwike to Thomas Hussey in 1565. With Thomas Hussey ended the last, tenuous, blood connection with the estate holders of the middle ages. Until 1565 Oakwell had been inherited according to family relationships. All this changed with Thomas Hussey. After owning Oakwell for only about six months he sold it to Henry Batt. The purchase price was £399 plus an annuity for the lives of Thomas's mother and her second husband, Falkingham. Lancaster postulates that the annuity represented a sum which Hussey was already bound to pay his mother. This idea is supported by other conveyances and leases of Gomersal land by Hussey which made a similar arrangement.

Henry Batt already had considerable estates in Halifax. In 1565 however he was living in Gomersal, probably at the rectory house, Birstall (now demolished, see chapter 1), which he held as lessee of the rectory lands from Trinity College, Cambridge. Batt seems to have been resident in Gomersal from as early as 1540.[26] The conveyance from Hussey to Batt is significant for the record which it gives of the manorial property in Gomersal:

> Okewell Hall with appurtenances in Okewell Gomersal Birstall and Heckmondwike now in the occupation of James Nettilton Christopher Nettilton Robert Popelay and William Taylor, also a messuage in Birkenshaye with appurtenances in Birkenshaye and Gomersall in the occupation of Thomas Birtbie, two messuages called Spennes with appurtenances in Spenne and Gomersall in the occupation of Edward Broke and Margaret widow of John Wibsaye, a close of land and pasture called Marshe in Liversedge in the occupation of James Wodde James Ferneley and John Ferneley, a watermill called Spenne Milne and a windmill called Gomersall wynd milne, with the dams watercourses and suits of tenants in Spenne Gomersall and Heton Clak [Cleckheaton] ... [27]

A number of points are of interest. First, the Nettiltons still appear to have been tenants of Oakwell; indeed the conveyance refers to a hall at a time eighteen years before 1583, the year in which the present hall is usually assumed to have been built. Secondly, the manorial property clearly extended across the whole township of Gomersal, from its borders with Liversedge and Cleckheaton in the west, to Birstall in the east and Birkenshaw in the north. Third, the conveyance refers to economic arrangements whereby Batt's tenants in Gomersal, Spen and Cleckheaton were bound to grind their corn at his mills. The site of the windmill is unknown, though Spen Mill is of course well documented (see chapter 6). The only surprise is that an important manorial mill was so far from the centre of the 'manor'. Mills often appear to have been sited on boundaries because the streams on which they depended for power also acted as boundary markers. But a mill over a mile from the manorial seat was exceptional, especially when a substantial stream was available in the Birstall church area. As explained above, this may have been a result of the fourteenth century grant of the Birstall 'millpool' to Nostell Priory. These economic arrangements continued well into the eighteenth century.

Henry Batt both before and after his Gomersal acquisition seems to have had a sharp mind substantially motivated by greed. Various descriptions of

---

The holders of Gomersal before Batt

1200 Eschoche Bulffe/Tilly ?
|
*c.*1225 Roger de TILLY
|
*c.*1250 John son of Roger
|
Ralph son of John (alive 1270-1280)
|
*c.*1300 Robert son of Ralph
|
*c.*1340 John [II], son of Robert
|
Roger de LEEDES (d. *c.*1400)
|
William son of Roger (d. 1433)
|
Dau. Emma m. Geoffry PIGOT
|
Ranulf Pigot (d. 1466)
|
Thomas Pigot (d. 1512)
|
Dau. Joan m. 1. Giles HUSSEY
        2. Thomas
        Falkingham
        (alive 1565)
|
Thomas Hussey (alive 1565)
|
Henry BATT

Figure 17

his dealings are accompanied by the suggestion of some sharp practice. There are the often repeated accounts of his melting of the Birstall church bell for scrap (he was lay rector) and his appropriation, when trustee, of charitable funds made available to him for the creation of a local grammar school.[28] These were crimes for which his son, John, had to make amends following the findings of a commission in 1602. The commission reported that Henry had also deprived the vicar of his house at Birstall. At first sight this seems strange business for the Lord of the Manor to concern himself with, but it gains credibility when Henry's position as lessee of the rectory lands is considered. As the person chosen by Trinity College he would pay a rent to them (the term was sixty years) in exchange for the privilege of collecting and disbursing all the rectory dues, rents and levies. Obviously this put him in a position of trust as far as the finances of both the church and the local community were concerned. Where Henry was involved, funds meant for others invariably seem to have mixed with his own – a circumstance which must have been severely debilitating for a small community dependent on the honesty of a leading citizen.

Henry Batt did not behave much better in his personal relationships. When married to his second wife, Anne Popeley, he was said to have appropriated from her deeds concerning the Popeley family's title to land in Birstall.[29] In managing the manor he was said, in the same document, to have also deprived his demesne farmers of their special rights and privileges.

For most of his time as Lord of the Manor Henry also held positions in the service of superior landowners. The best example is as receiver to the Saviles of Thornhill.[30] The Saviles employed him for many years and valued his ingenuity and determination.

By the time of his death in 1572 Henry Batt had revitalized the Manor of Oakwell. However he was then residing at Haigh Hall, West Ardsley. In fact it is doubtful whether he ever lived at Oakwell. The explanation is straight-forward: Oakwell in 1565 seems to have been in the occupation of the Nettilton family (under a lease given by the Husseys) and for most of his period of residence in Gomersal Henry Batt lived at the rectory house. It is also possible that Henry lived with his second wife at the Rydings, the Popeley house half a mile to the south of Birstall church. Anne lived there in 1580 after Henry's death[31] and continued

to do so in her right of (Popeley) dower until the early seventeenth century.

Henry's importance did not lie in his contribution to architecture or philanthropy. His career provides instead a much needed reminder that Batt influence in Gomersal began long before 1583, and that the precedents which he set in his management of the estate determined the course of many subsequent events.

In 1571 he had created a settlement by which his lands went to his son. This son was the John Batt responsible for building most, if not all, of the present hall. The plan to build a new hall probably coincided with the end of tenant occupation at Oakwell, as John would doubtless have waited until the expiry of any existing lease before building work commenced. John was a 'nether barrister' who seems to have inherited many of his father's characteristics, including cunning and acquisitiveness. In the Popeley land dispute (see chapter 3) the Popeley case recites that in about 1595 he had 'entered into a composition to destroy Birstall manor by denying freeholders access to the inland'.[32] He also continued his father's policy of enclosing the wastes and commons of Birstall even though 'there was not any enclosure made of any of the wastes in Birstall until now of late years ... Henry Batte marryed the widowe of Robert Popeley'. The Popeley title to their estate in Birstall is said to have been preserved only by Robert's son tearing down Batt's enclosures.

John, of course, lived at Oakwell. Haigh Hall was let in 1573, soon after Henry's death. Some of the furniture from Haigh was brought to Oakwell Hall[33], but between his father's death and the building of the new hall John's place of residence is unclear.

John was in his thirties when he inherited in 1572 and was Lord of Oakwell until his death in 1607. The construction of the hall is sufficient testimony to his energy. Towards the end of his life however, he was referred to in the land dispute as 'diseased and far from *compos mentis*'. It may be that the early years of the seventeenth century took more than a natural toll. In 1602 the commission into his father's malpractice found against the Batts and John was forced to compensate for his father's wrongs. In fact when the rectory lease came up for renewal in 1615 the Batts did not apply. Most significantly of all, however, John's son and intended heir, Henry, predeceased him. The date of Henry [II]'s death is uncertain but John's younger son, Robert, was named in a lease of 1603 as the new heir apparent.[34] This was doubtless seen as a disaster by John who in 1581 had conveyed Gomersal and Oakwell to Henry, while Robert had been intended for holy orders.

Robert succeeded John in 1607, but he appears to have been involved in the management of the estate for about five years before this date. For most of his life however Robert was an absentee landlord, eventually as Vicar of Newton Toney, Wiltshire. It must be doubted that he made any significant contribution to the development of Oakwell Hall or the Gomersal estate, though paradoxically it was his absence and the letting of the hall to tenants which provides one of the most useful historical sources for Oakwell in this period. Henry Batt [I] had first married (before he married Anne Popeley) Margaret Waterhouse of Skircoat. Close connections between the Batts and the Waterhouses seem to have been maintained for in 1609 another member of the Waterhouse family, David, was granted a tenancy of Oakwell. Cradock even refers to David as 'of Oquel' in the 1590s. In 1611 David was followed as tenant by Lewes Waterhouse. Before Lewes took up occupation Robert's steward took an inventory of most of the furniture and fittings in the house, a document which is now of unrivalled value in indicating the contemporary use of rooms. This change of tenant in 1611 appears to be attributable to a promise made by John Popeley of Woolley Moorhouse. Lewes gave up occupation of Popeley when John Popeley promised to buy back what he saw as his ancient family seat. Lewes moved out but the promise was broken and so Lewes was then in urgent need of short term accommodation.[35] The inventory refers to shelves and floors having been laid

by David Waterhouse, and so the brothers' investment in Oakwell must have been considerable.

Another feature of Robert Batt's absence was his employment of agents under the rectory lease.[36] Remarkably, yet another Waterhouse, Jonas, was favoured and so lived at the Birstall rectory house from 1608 to 1615. When the lease was renewed in 1615 it was the Waterhouse family which became tenants of one part (the other part belonged to a man called Greenwood; division of the rectory was still apparent in the late eighteenth century).

When the rectory lease had passed from John Batt to Robert in 1607 a condition of the bequest was that another son of John, Richard, should receive the tithes under the lease from Spen, Cleckheaton and Little Gomersal.[37] This Richard lived for a time at Spen Hall,[38] again demonstrating the widespread holding of the Batt family in Gomersal. Spen was a hamlet in its own right, as it had been at least since the thirteenth century. The Batts held two houses there in 1565 and, of course, the mill, which provided a considerable source of income. In the time of Robert Batt's successor, John [II], a feoffment to one John Goodale clearly described the importance of Spen Mill and the bonds that tied the freeholder to his manorial master. As a condition of the conveyance Goodale was required to do:

> suit and service at the court of John Batte ... at all times ... when and as often as the same shall be kept upon somons ... and doing service at the water cornmill called Spen Milne yearly hereafter for ever and their grynding all the Corne Grain and Malte'... [of the land hereby granted] – A.D. 1638.[39]

Such arrangements were still in place in the eighteenth century.

As well as economic levies the lord of the manor exercised control over local life by his manorial court and personal expenditure. The accounts kept by Robert Batt's steward are useful in showing the employments which depended on Oakwell. Extraordinary expenditure included £39 in all for the building of a wall around the house – a very large sum in 1611. Ordinary expenditure included weekly payments for working the fields and coal mines of the estate. The entry for the working of coal in the second week of November 1610 showed for example:

The 10th [November] to Muffet and sewor for 235 load of coals	0 - 8 - 4
...to yonge child for heweing them	0 - 3 - 1
...to Muffet and sewer 1 day a pec to carrie upp the sowe some 5 yardes to the face of [the] cole bed and layeing it	0 - 1 - 2

To 'sowe' probably meant to erect a roof or other protective shell underneath which miners could work. The roof or shed would have been movable and shifted along as the coal was worked. The word seems to have originated in medieval military engineering.[40]

The manorial court consisted of an assembly of the lord's tenants as summonsed. Orders were made for the repairing of hedges, drains and estate roads; tenants who had taken the lord's game or removed animals, from the lord's pinfold were fined;[41] and neighbour disputes were settled.

So much for manorial administration. As long as the manorial estate remained intact and in the hands of even a half competent person the administration would have changed very little. This was the case from the sixteenth to the mid seventeenth century. Robert was succeeded on his death in 1618 by his son John, a minor. In fact John was a ward of court for many years until in 1631 he formally inherited 'Oakwell-cum-Gomersal'. But there is no indication that the estates suffered even in John's minority. On the contrary, John [II] was soon in a position to greatly embellish the hall, adding the large mullioned window now so much a feature of the southern wall, as well as improving the Great Parlour by the addition of new plasterwork and panelling. He also appears to have gained the confidence of several notable Royalist families. Indeed his sister was married to Dr. Richard Marsh, Chaplain to Charles I.[42]

It was not until John [II] was succeeded by his son William in 1652 that serious problems began to arise. Probably the fine imposed on John by the Commonwealth Parliament played its part – in 1649 he had been ordered to forego £364 (supposedly a tenth of his estate), possibly for his part in the Battle of Adwalton and other local skirmishes.[43] John may even have been forced to sell some of his lands in Gomersal to meet the fine, for at this time he is known to have sold property to William Horton of Barkisland and Richard Peel of Gomersal. To the latter he sold a 'messuage and house' in Gomersal, a property which was probably to become Peel House (see chapter 5).

William inherited at the comparatively young age of twenty, and though a man who acquired various local positions of note he always seems to have had his eyes set on Halifax and the western part of the county. It was this, coupled with the hardship caused by the Parliamentary fine, which appears to have been decisive. In 1658 he married Elizabeth Horton of Barkisland [44] and removed himself, permanently as it happened, to Howroyd, the Horton family's seat in Barkisland. By an indenture of 1657 he had already settled his lands on trusts for the benefit of himself, his wife and issue.[45] William has gone down in history as a squanderer, but it is necessary to postulate nothing more than a lack of commitment at a critical time to affairs in Gomersal.

William died in 1673. His son, William [II], survived only until 1684, when he was killed in a London duel.[46] His successor was John [III], William [I]'s third son. At the time of John's succession William [I]'s wife, Elizabeth, was still alive and contested John's inheritance. She claimed that in 1654, before William's marriage settlement, he had sold all his interest in Spen to the Horton family.[47] The argument appears to have been resolved by agreement, but not without permanently detaching Spen (including the manorial mill) from the Batt estate: in his will John [III] left Spen to his wife, Henrietta, absolutely, in order to protect the remainder of the estate. After John's death Henrietta married John Smyth of Heath, near Wakefield. Spen therefore became part of the Smyth family's estate and remained so for most of the eighteenth century (see chapter 6).

John [III] died in 1707, without issue. He had obviously tried to secure the long-term future of the Batt estate in Gomersal, but even allowing for his resolution of the Horton dispute he must have known that without children the chances of keeping the manor intact were extremely slim. His property passed according to a settlement made in 1698, to his wife for her life and afterwards to his sisters Elizabeth, Martha and possibly Judith.[48] Elizabeth was ultimately to hold two thirds and Martha one third.

It was inevitable perhaps that these holdings, owned by different families, would be sold. The two thirds holding was sold to Benjamin Fearnley and to one Joshua Wilson of Pontefract, in about 1747. Oakwell Hall and adjacent land was included in this part. Benjamin Fearnley bought out Wilson and on his death in 1756 left the whole two thirds to his son Fairfax Fearnley. It was Fairfax however who had to face the bill for the purchase from Wilson – a bill which, apparently,

he could not meet. In 1788 he was forced to sell up and died only three years later, following a period of solitude and depression.

From 1788 until the 1920s Oakwell was in the hands of absentee landlords. The owners are known[49] as are most of their tenants. For a considerable period in the nineteenth century the hall was occupied as a small boarding school, in which guise it came to the attention of Charlotte Brontë. Above all, however, the essential point to grasp is that by the nineteenth century effective manorial control, centred on Oakwell, had come to an end in Gomersal. This permitted land use and organisations in the township which might not otherwise have been possible: deep mines at Oakwell; Gomersal railway and station; and the development of extensive industrial complexes. The industrial age coincided with the demise of Oakwell and the two sat happily together. If anything good can be said of this period at Oakwell it is that in the hands of absentee landlords and occasional visitors the fabric of the hall was preserved relatively unscathed for the enjoyment of a more sympathetic age.

NOTES

1. *WYAS SMR*.
2. *YAJ* Vol 58 for 1986, 202-3.
3. Giles 1986, 197; *WYAS SMR*.
4. 'An inventorie of all Mr Robt. Batt Goods in the house att Okewell and delyvered to Mr Lewes Waterhous ... in 1611' (Foster 1954, 114-6). The 'New Parlore' contained '1 longe table from Hagg Hall' (i.e. Haigh Hall, Henry Batt's eventual place of residence).
5. *WYAS SMR*.
6. *WYAS SMR*.
7. Woledge 1978, 29.
8. See Giles Worsley 'Oakwell Hall, Yorkshire' *Country Life* 18 Jan 1990.
9. *WYAS B* PP.
10. Lancaster 1924.
11. Though berewic(k) is defined as an outlying estate, which formed part of a manor, in Faull and Moorhouse (eds.) 1981, 851.
12. *YAS* DD 70/15/5.
13. A knight's fee was the service owed by the holder of the lands to his superior feudal lord.
14. Dolfin is recorded as Rector of Birstall Church in the time of King John (Cradock 1933, 15).
15. Lancaster 1924, 17.
16. It is usual to speculate on the origin of the church. Cradock attributes it to the Liversedge family, Lancaster to the Tillys. But as the site appears to have been used for religious purposes from at least Saxon times there is really little point in speculating further until additional evidence is to hand.
17. See Brown (ed.) 1898, 43, and Slingsby (ed.) 1956. The advowson is the right to present a priest to the church; in effect the priest may be the patron's nominee.
18. Lancaster 1924, 18; Cradock 1933, 137, gives the date as 1342
19. Lancaster 1924, 18.
20. *BL* Add Ch 12639.
21. Lancaster 1924, 23.
22. Lancaster 1924, 21.
23. *YAS* DD 70/15/5.
24. Lancaster 1924, 24; Sir Roger de Leedes was at the time 'assistant' to the Sheriff of York.

25. Anon 1899, 22.
26. Lancaster 1924, 31.
27. *Thoresby* Batt Papers.
28. Cradock 1933, 140-142.
29. *YAS* DD 70/15/5. The misappropriation was between the dates of Robert Popeley's death (1565) and the death of Henry Batt himself (1572), possibly for a period of months only. Lancaster does not appear to have known who Henry's second wife was (Lancaster 1924, 33).
30. Lancaster 1924, 32.
31. *YAS* DD 70/12/1.
32. *YAS* DD 70/15/5.
33. Foster 1954, 114-6.
34. Lancaster 1924, 34.
35. *WYAS B* PP 2/2/a.
36. Cradock 1933, 139.
37. Cradock 1933, 138.
38. Scraton and Scraton 1974, 6, after Dugdale.
39. *WYAS K* DD HS/G1-15

40. See for example OED 'sow': 1486 Exc. Rolls of Scotland 'instrumenti bellici vocati le sow'.
41. Woledge 1978, 18, who, more evocatively, quotes penalties laid down for 'drawing hares', killing 'fezants' and 'partiges' or hunting 'cunnyes' within the lord's demesne.
42. Cradock 1933, 55.
43. He may have fought in 1643 at the Battle of Adwalton, near Drighlington, where the Parliamentarians were defeated. But he surrendered to their cause after Marston Moor in 1644, and when his fine came to be determined in 1649 it was reduced accordingly (Woledge 1978, 24).
44. Daughter of William who bought lands from John Batt [II]. The Hortons also owned Popeley Hall at this time (see chapter 3).
45. *Thoresby* Deeds.
46. Woledge 1978, 24.
47. Scraton and Scraton 1974, 6.
48. Lancaster 1924, 36.
49. Woledge 1978, 28-30.

Chapter 3

POPELEY

Popeley Farm is one of the few places remaining in Gomersal from which it is possible to savour the pre-industrial landscape on a grand scale. The farm stands at about 155 metres above sea level, with a sharp landfall to the north and north-east but with a gently sloping expanse of grassland to the south. To the north-east the parish church is approached by descending Garfitt Hill. Beyond the church, but along the same line of sight, is Oakwell with the moors of Gomersal and Birstall

beyond. Due north, the line of the 1740 turnpike road from Leeds to Elland is visible as it ascends to Hill Top. Across Church Lane is a succession of paddocks and fields. Most of these were until relatively recently part of the church's glebeland, and some are still denoted by the name Monk Ings. Beyond these are tofts and crofts which in the seventeenth century were taken from 'Gomersal Field' into the holdings of the larger landowners of Great Gomersal. Enclosures to the south

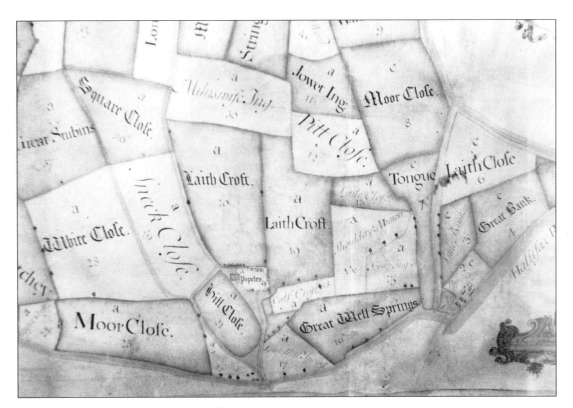

Figure 18: *Popeley in 1714: detail from Ibbetson's map*

of the farm run for over half a mile, usually bounded by low hedges or dry walls of thin stone slabs, and the slope of the land opens on to a panorama of the higher Pennines. South-westwards a medieval trackway makes its way to Castle Hill in Little Gomersal.

Buildings and Archaeological Features at Popeley

The main farm buildings at Popeley are arranged around the four sides of a square cobbled yard. A similar configuration existed in Victorian times and through most of the eighteenth century. As far back as 1714 the position of the principal buildings, namely barns, farmhouse and stables, appears to have been established much as it is today; presumably this arrangement could be traced back even earlier. Access to the farmyard has from at least the early eighteenth century been by means of the gates at its north-eastern and south-eastern corners. The approaches to both show signs of hollowing and earthen banking, probably indicating an origin well before the eighteenth century.

The farmhouse is aligned north-east/south-west, along the eastern side of the yard. It is of narrow, rectangular plan save for a larger, square block at the southern end which is set back from the eastern building line and extends about three metres beyond the western wall of the range. The building originally comprised at least two and possibly three individual dwellings. At the north-eastern end where the range is narrowest was cottage accommodation. This has now been made into one double-fronted house, though in the mid nineteenth century the section consisted of two or more separate cottages, or a house in multiple occupation (see Fig. 20).[1]

This northern end of the range is of pre-nineteenth century date and some features, notably its generous complement of windows, beg the question of its original use. It is feasible that the range was built for the home textile industry. If this was the case, the building may have initially been in single occupation, and divided later in the nineteenth century.

In addition to three sets of mullions on the western side, the range has other interesting architectural details. The stonework is well dressed and is of a higher quality than that in the more ostentatious southern block. In places, especially the first few courses, blocks are large and

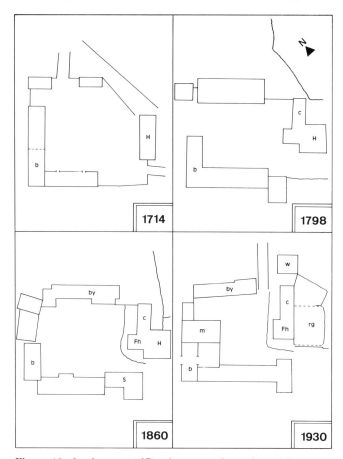

Figure 19: *development of Popeley: approximate layout from 1714*

Key:

b	*barn*	*by*	*byre*
c	*cottage*	*Fh*	*farmhouse*
H	*house*	*m*	*milkshop*
rg	*raised garden*	*s*	*stables*
w	*workshop.*		

probably recovered from an earlier building. The large gable chimney stack to the north incorporates a similar scale of work, as do the quoins. All of this work is of the early nineteenth century, or earlier.

Such dating is supported by map evidence. The form of the narrow northern end of the range is depicted in identical fashion on the maps surveyed in 1798, 1840 and 1894 (Fig. 19). Only the 1714 map shows a building of a different plan on this spot. The present form appears therefore to have originated between 1714 and 1798, and probably nearer the end than the beginning of this period.[2]

However maps pose as well as answer questions, and it is appropriate here to mention some problems of interpretation. The house shown on the 1714 map either had an outshut to the west, into the farmyard, or on a grander scale it may have had a frontage of two or three gables. An old and important house certainly did exist here, as several deeds refer to eminent local persons living at Popeley Farm from the fourteenth century onwards, culminating in 1636 with a reference to 'Popeley Hall' (see below). But how and when this building was demolished or altered beyond recognition is unclear. The 1798 map shows a projection

of about ten metres into the farmyard, at the southern end of the range. This may have been a surviving part of an earlier (hall) structure, though it too had gone by 1850.

Another question arises with the appearance on all maps between 1798 and 1894 of a very large building which butted against the eastern wall of the range. This was approximately in the position now occupied by a raised garden area still littered with stone. All relevant maps depict a building which is larger than any residential building now standing at Popeley, and we must be

Figure 21: *Popeley Farm: stone pediment east of the house*

sceptical as to whether the building was in domestic use. There is, however, evidence in favour of its having been domestic quarters; the 1851 census records, in addition to the farmer's family and labourers, the presence at Popeley of one John Taylor, a 'woollen merchant and manufacturer'. This is the same description applied by the enumerator to Joseph Swaine at nearby Brier Hall, and suggests a person of some wealth. By 1861 Taylor's place had been taken by one John Calpen, a manufacturing chemist originally from Halifax.[3] There had been a series of well-to-do residents at Popeley before Taylor, for example Thomas Walker, wool dealer, in 1805,[4] and Joseph Stainthorp, merchant, in the 1770s.[5]

Figure 20: *Popeley Farm from the west in c.1900 (KCS)*

One would have expected these men to have been living in grander surroundings than any of the houses which survive at Popeley today. In the raised garden area is a triangular pediment, hewn from a single sandstone block (Fig. 21). This could have been part of a house or an industrial building, though the fine bevelling suggests a domestic origin. In spite of this it is still impossible to be certain as to the true nature of the large building. One of the clearest descriptions of the structures at Popeley is found in particulars of sale of 1844, when the Ibbetson family, who had held the Popeley estate for over a century, put it to auction. Lot 4 refers specifically to:

> A residence called Popeley House containing Drawing, Dining and Breakfast rooms, Kitchen and Five Bed rooms, and a farmhouse attached, with two sitting rooms, Kitchen, Pantry, Three bed rooms, and one servants room, and Barn three stables for ten horses ...[6]

The 'Popeley House' described could have been the building in the raised area of garden, and the 'farmhouse' could be the square block at the end of the narrow range (which must have existed by 1844). The narrow range, providing cottage accommodation, may not have been mentioned here. Alternatively, the particulars may have exaggerated the merits of the two buildings still standing, in which case the garden building may have had some industrial or ancillary use.

The square block at the southern end of the narrow range deserves some comment in its own right. The architectural style is later than that of the narrow range to the north; the stonework is slightly coarser, the roof is of a shallow pitch and its rooms, in comparison with the range, are of more regular proportions. Its appointment and superior accommodation make it an obvious candidate for the residence of the Victorian tenant farmer.

In the mid nineteenth century a number of sources agree that the tenant was one John Thompson. At Popeley House the 1841 census records John Thompson, aged 45, farmer, with his wife and two children. The township valuation of 1840 has John

Figure 22: *Popeley Farmhouse from the east*

Thompson at Popeley, as the tenant of 'house, barn, mistals, stables, sheds, helm, stack garth and fold yard' rated at £20. The list of voters for 1840 has an entry for John Thompson of Popeley who, in addition to his leasehold lands at Popeley, held freehold property in Little Gomersal.[7]

The barns, mistals, stables and other sheds now standing have a configuration which has changed little over at least 250 years. The main difference is that whereas the 1714 map shows only two small sheds on the north eastern side of the yard there is now a nineteenth century mistal with hay loft above. The 1798 map is interesting because it shows a full range of buildings on the south western side of the yard, including an 'L'-shaped structure to the east, which projects into the field known as Laith Croft. The function of these buildings is unknown, though today the area comprises a low range for stalling cattle. Cattle rearing appears to have been an important part of the economy at Popeley from medieval times onwards. In the Poll Tax of 1379 William of Popeley, assessed at three shillings and fourpence, was described as 'landowner and franklan' [cattle dealer].[8] Then in 1487 John Popeley was recorded as making an annual gift of one cow to the church at Birstall.[9] In the eighteenth century, at the time of the probate inventory of John Taylor, a handful of cattle was still kept on the farm.

The main barn at Popeley is at the western corner and aligned with the north-western side of the farmyard. It is a high barn, built of rough, coursed sandstone, with two double doors giving through access from the yard to the fields. The first doors have clearance for a fully loaded cart while the second set has clearance for an empty cart only. The barn's roof construction is of queen post variety with purlins shaped from short, unsawn timbers. The roof is impossible to date accurately without more detailed analysis, but both the roof and the uniquely thick walls suggest that this building is at least as old as the narrow range of the farmhouse complex. It may in fact be older, perhaps of the seventeenth century, as a building of this unusual length and height appears in this position on the 1714 map.

The continuity of occupation at Popeley is one of the likeliest reasons for the lack of the earthwork remains normally found on a medieval site. Though some will have been lost to nineteenth century mine workings in the area, mine workings cannot account for the absence of earthworks close to the farmstead. Over the whole site there are only three obvious features of note. First are the gullies running along the escarpment which faces Muffit Lane. These have the appearance of lead workings but are more likely to be natural features eroded by the flow of periodic springs (the field name here is Great Well Springs). Second are the small undulations just to the south of the farm, in the field known as Laith Croft. These may indicate where tenters once stood, in the days when cloth was dried in the open air. The probate of John Taylor does refer to tenters 'in the close about the house'. Third is the impressive bridle road, over 3-4 metres wide and in places standing 2-3 metres higher than the fields below, a road which by its size, and by its depiction on the 1714 map, appears formerly to have been much more important than it is today.

There is no trace of more extensive human occupation at Popeley itself. And yet in 1619 Dodsworth listed Popeley as one of the hamlets of Birstall parish,[10] and throughout the sixteenth and seventeenth centuries the parish registers show several families living contemporaneously here. Beginning in 1591, baptisms and burials of many families other than the Popeleys were recorded. Between 1591 and 1615, Wilkinsons, Waterhouses, Walkers and Stubleys were all described as of Popeley. A similar picture emerges for the years 1625-1650, when Hemingway, Booth, Crowder, Pickersgill, Muffit and Man were all names referred to as 'of Popeley'. Popeley could therefore have been a hamlet or a large farmstead; or it is possible that some of the families actually lived in the area later called Popeley Gate, in Muffit Lane at the top of Garfitt Hill.

We might still wonder at the lives of these people. Although sharing a hamlet, they would nevertheless have had different occupations and economic standing. But the common flavour, if any, of their existence in these high fields is not a matter that is easily ignored. Of all the records which have survived from this period one of the most informative is the probate inventory of John Taylor taken in May 1721.[11]

On 12 May of that year Samuel Hodgson, Andrew Taylor and William Mason took stock of the possessions of the recently deceased Taylor. We see that in the housebody Taylor had 'one table and a forme and three chaires'. He also had a bread creel (for making oatcakes) and a clock and case. In the 'standing parlour' was a bed – a sign either of infirmity or of servants' quarters. In the 'great parlour' he had 'one ovall table, twelve chaires and a little range'. The only item recorded in 'the passageway' was 'i seeing glass' [a mirror]. In general the house was sparsely furnished. The bulk of Taylor's wealth was in cloth dressing equipment, found in that part of the house referred to as the shop. Amongst other things, he had in the shop 'i range, three presses, a pair of sheares and two shearboards'. Cloth itself however is conspicuous by its absence.

More surprising to the modern reader is the value of his possessions outside the house. In the stable were '4

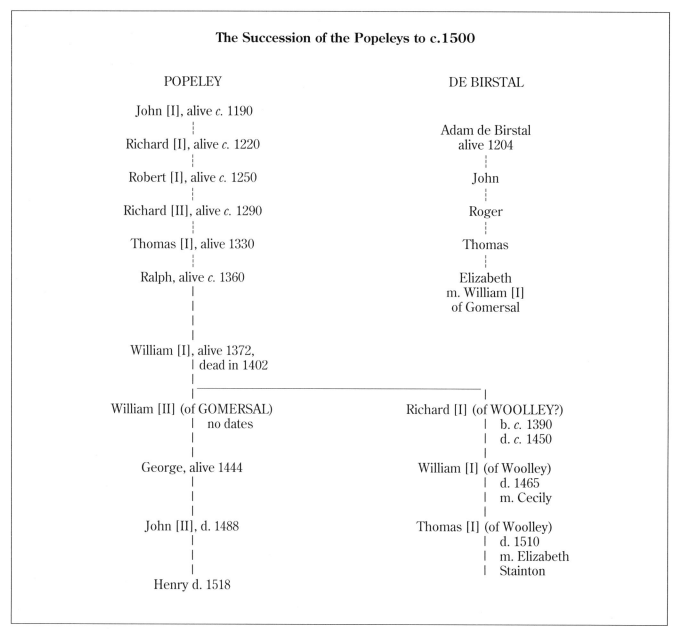

The Succession of the Popeleys to c.1500

POPELEY

DE BIRSTAL

John [I], alive *c.* 1190

Adam de Birstal
alive 1204

Richard [I], alive *c.* 1220

Robert [I], alive *c.* 1250

John

Richard [II], alive *c.* 1290

Roger

Thomas [I], alive 1330

Thomas

Ralph, alive *c.* 1360

Elizabeth
m. William [I]
of Gomersal

William [I], alive 1372,
dead in 1402

William [II] (of GOMERSAL)
no dates

Richard [I] (of WOOLLEY?)
b. *c.* 1390
d. *c.* 1450

George, alive 1444

William [I] (of Woolley)
d. 1465
m. Cecily

John [II], d. 1488

Thomas [I] (of Woolley)
d. 1510
m. Elizabeth
Stainton

Henry d. 1518

Figure 23

horses, 4 saddles, 4 pairs of iron ... 2 carts, i plow and other things belonging', valued at £30 (one quarter of his personal goods). In the barn he had 'one mow of wheat with sound straw'. In the pasture were:

> three cows and i calfe; for seed and plowing for 9 days work of wheat; for seed and plowing for 12 days work of oates; 2 days work of beans and 2 of barley.

The Popeleys of Popeley Hall

Much has been said about the visible remains and relatively recent history of Popeley. There is however another story which is still accessible in books and papers, although all outward signs of it now seem to have disappeared. This is the story of the Popeley family, a family first encountered in the late twelfth century, prominent in the fifteenth and sixteenth centuries, yet which had died out by the middle years of the seventeenth. The Popeleys were never 'Lords of Gomersal', but they were owners of important local estates, and as early as the sixteenth century were occasionally revered as of ancient lineage. Some documents suggest that at one time they were lords of a manor in Birstall.[12] We can be certain that by the late fifteenth century the family had two branches, one at Gomersal and the other at Woolley Moorhouse, near Wakefield. At least two houses in Gomersal were in their tenure: Rydings in Birstall, and Popeley Hall. As well as being a vital element in the history of Popeley, the family played an important part in the early development of Gomersal.

We first hear of the Popeley name in the early Calverley charters, in connection with land transactions on the eastern side of Bradford. At an indeterminate date – but probably during the reign of Richard I (1189-99) or John (1199-1216) – a 'Johanne de Papelaia' was witness to a grant by one Ralph of lands in 'Ulvisthorpe', in Pudsey.[13] Another witness to the same document was John de Tilly, who may already have been Lord of Gomersal manor. A little later, probably in the reign of John or Henry III (1216-1272), John de Papelay was mentioned along with his son, Richard, with John de Tilly again a co-witness.

But the Calverley charters do not provide all the early evidence. We know that as early as the year 1204 the Popeley family held eighty acres at Popeley which were not part of the Tilly estate.[14] In addition, a thirteenth century charter in the British Library [15] has one Robert de Papeli as witness to a grant by 'Richard son of Christian de Parva [Little] Gomersale'. This Robert was presumably the same person who witnessed a grant of property in Denby, in Henry III's time.[16] In 1285-6 another Richard Popeley, probably the grandson of the Richard mentioned above, witnessed both an inquisition into the affairs of Robert Tilly and a grant to the Prior and Convent at Nostell.[17] On All Saints' Day 1293 Richard was also a witness to the grant of a lease of land in 'Berstal'.[18]

Fragments such as these are sufficient to show that the Popeley family was in existence throughout the thirteenth century, and it cannot be coincidental that they usually refer either to the Gomersal area or to people interested in Gomersal such as the Tillys. It is fairly certain that even at this early date the Popeleys were based in Gomersal. This is supported subsequently by the dealings of one Thomas Popeley, who is first mentioned in a deed of 1316.[19] On 29 October 1328 he was witness to a grant of 'a messuage with buildings thereon' in Gomersal, and in the following April he witnessed (with one Thomas del Spen amongst others) a release of lands in 'Hecmundewyke'.[20] This Thomas also appears in a lease dated 11 September 1334 by which lands, tenements, woods and common in 'le Spen near Gomersal' were granted to one Richard de le S[pen].[21]

Other occasional references to the Popeleys are encountered throughout the fourteenth century. For example one Robert Popeley was a juror at the inquisition post mortem of Henry Duke of Lancaster.[22] It is only as that century draws to a close, however, that the documents begin to supply evidence about the lives of the Popeleys themselves, and a fascinating story unfolds.

Unusually, we are introduced to this story in a document produced in the early seventeenth century. The document is a legal note prepared by a seventeenth century lawyer who was seeking the advice of counsel. The subject of the lawyer's enquiry was the strength of his client's claim to the 'moores and wastes' of Birstall.[23] In this note, the origin and descent of the Popeleys is chronicled at length – for it was a Popeley who was the lawyer's client. In examining dealings in land in Birstall some three hundred years before his own time, this seventeenth century intermediary argued that a 'manor of Birtsall' was once held by Adam de Birstall, distinct from the manor of Gomersal.[24] At that time, the early thirteenth century, the Popeleys were said to have held eighty acres at Popeley, in Gomersal. This was in their own right, not as feoffees or lessees of the Tillys. The 'manor of Birtsall' passed after Adam to his descendants, first to his son, John, then to John's son, Roger and finally to Roger's son, Thomas. The manor then seems to have come to the Popeley family, making them the second largest landowners in Gomersal, for the document continues:

> it appeareth that aboute the 47 yeare of Edward 3 [1373] the lands and inheritance of Thomas Birstall ... came to 3 daughters ... one was marryed to one William Popeley ... one other to John son of Richard Hessell and the third otherwise ... but William Popeley by purchases obtained the other two parts and so had all Thomas Birstall's manor and lands.[25]

There was certainly a William Popeley alive at that time, probably a descendant of that Thomas Popeley mentioned in the early fourteenth century. William witnessed deeds as far apart as 1372[26] and 1401.[27] Moreover, in a deed of 1374, about the year of his succession to Thomas Birstall's lands, there is confirmation of William's own transactions: Agnes, described as formerly the wife of one Thomas Rogerson of Birstall, made a grant to William Popeley of 'all her messuages, lands, meadows and tenements in the vill and territory of Birstall in the township of Gomersal'.[28] Witnesses included Roger de Leedes (the new 'lord of Okewell'), John de Nevill and one John de Stubley.

As might be expected, in the years following his succession to his father-in-law's lands William appears to have been one of the wealthier inhabitants of Gomersal. At the time of the Poll Tax of 1379 'Willelmus de Popeley' was the only person resident in Gomersal not assessed at the basic 4d. levy[29]; he was charged 3s. 4d. William was married and described as a ffranklan [cattle dealer]. Doubtless this was a superior occupation when compared with other agricultural work. His standing is indicated by the fact that he was first witness to the will of the Vicar of Birstall, Roland Davy.[30]

According to the seventeenth century source William died in the year 1402. We have no confirmation of this, but a date in the early years of the fifteenth century does tally with information found in other sources. William left a son called Richard, who was under age on his father's death, and two trustees had been appointed by William to hold his lands until Richard came of age. The trustees were 'Liversedge, Vicar of Birstall and Bollinge, Vicar of Kirkbye'. Richard came of age in 1408, though not, apparently, without a struggle to preserve his inheritance. For example, concerning the commons of Birstall, there is a record of five separate transgressions by 'Leedes then Lord of Gomersal':[31]

1. That he erected Iron Smethyes on the commons which stood in or near Birstall
2. That he broke the soile of the commons
3. That where he had formerly 12 pence of wapontake fyne for 24 oxgangs of land in Birstall, after selling of an oxgang he still had augmentid this to 12 shillings
4. That he had destreynid the freeholders of the Manor of Birstal wrongfully as they were not freeholders of the Manor of Gomersal
5. That he augmentid the rent of a tenement called the Rydings from 6 pence to fourteen pence

However, Richard was served well by Liversedge throughout this period. Cradock dates Liversedge's ratification as vicar to 15 October 1397, and it is clear that he subsequently proved himself to be at least as able in estate management as he was in spiritual life. In addition to restoring the fortunes of his own, de Liversedge, family[32] he handed over the Popeley estate substantially intact.[33]

Once of age Richard proved well able to handle his own and other affairs. As early as 1414 he was executor under a will,[34] and in 1417 as the recipient of a grant of lands in 'Erdisley' [Haddesley], North Yorkshire, he was already referred to as esquire.[35] But his real contribution to the growth of Popeley influence and prestige came in 1424, with his appointment as royal receiver at Pontefract Castle.[36] He held this position until at least 1432[37], during which time the Popeley connection with Woolley and other estates in the Wakefield area were established. In general he seems to have increased the Popeley family's possessions and extended the range of its dealings.

A deed of 1437-8 records the formal transfer of land at Popeley to William and Cecily, son and daughter-in-law of Richard.[38] Presumably the transfer was from trustees of some kind as Popeley seems to have been in the Popeley family for many years by this time (see, for example, references in the land dispute). In the same year William re-settled or mortgaged the land to a number of notables, including Richard, Duke of York, and John, Duke of Norfolk.[39] These deeds contain the earliest known references to a 'capital messuage' at Popeley, and are strong evidence for the existence of a substantial house on the site, in addition to any cottages which there might have been.

One of the most interesting documents of this period is an indenture of 1444.[40] It records the resolution of a dispute between William (Richard's son) and one George Popeley, over the ownership of Popeley and other Gomersal lands. From the recitals in the deed it is clear that there had been considerable conflict between the two; George was alleged to have taken 'certayne catell' belonging to William and John Stubley, and was ordered to 'restore to the said William of Popelaye oon hors and oon and twenty shepe'. More importantly, the deed records that the two protagonists were each awarded a half of Popeley for life. George was not described in the deed as another son of Richard; he and William were more likely to have been cousins. Nor do we know whether George outlived William; though after William's death in 1465, George's line is said to have inherited the whole of Popeley and so this is a strong possibility.

Richard had died in the middle years of the fifteenth century. It seems that it was during his lifetime that the two distinct lines of the Popeleys emerged – one still in Gomersal, the other, and eventually the more important, in Woolley Moorhouse.[41] We have to wait until the late fifteenth century for indisputable evidence that the shift to Woolley had occurred, but the origin of the break is traceable to Richard's time.

William continued to improve the family fortunes. In 1448 he was appointed bailiff to John, Duke of Norfolk 'for all his lands and tenements in the vills of Gomersall, Heccundwyke, Birstall and Clerkheaton ... to hold [all monies] therefrom ... rendering a due account and a pound of pepper at Christmas'.[42] He had also received a significant grant of lands in these same vills in the previous year.[43] In an award of 1463 however this William was described as 'some tym of Popeley', from which it seems that Richard's successor may already have left the old Gomersal seat.[44]

William was dead by 1465, for in a deed of that year Cecily, described as the 'late wife of William Popeley' surrendered her dower lands to their son Thomas.[45] Cecily gave up her interest in return for a payment by Thomas of £4 annually. This deed is significant historically because it names the part of the Popeley estate which comprised her dower. The lands were described as 'the tenements called Rydings in Gommershall and the tenements called Castell Howse in the Parish of Birstall'. William's branch of the family therefore still had interests in Gomersal, but he chose to devise them in dower, an indication that they were already becoming peripheral to the main body of his estate.

Popeley itself had probably been inherited by the other line of the family, which appears after this time to have been confined almost entirely to Gomersal.

The move away from the township by the Woolley Moorhouse branch is finally confirmed during the time of Thomas, William's heir. Thomas married Elizabeth, daughter of Laurence Stainton of Woolley and inherited the Stainton lands in Woolley. In a deed of 1492 Thomas Stainton, Laurence's brother, surrendered to Thomas Popeley and his wife all claims in 'Wolvelay Morehouse'.[46] This may be an indication of the approximate date of Laurence Stainton's death and this Popeley line's break with Gomersal. Before the break they were described as Popeleys of Gomersal and Woolley; afterwards, even though still owning lands throughout Birstall parish, they were referred to as Popeleys of Woolley only. The point is illustrated a generation later when, in 1509, a bond was made between Henry Popeley 'of Popeley' and John Popeley 'of Woolley'.[47]

An earlier deed, of 1490, shows that the Popeleys of Woolley were receiving a twenty shillings annuity out of Popeley Hall, further evidence that they did not own the old Popeley seat in Gomersal. There is clear evidence, recorded in Preston's notes,[48] that at about the time of the first William Popeley's death Popeley Hall itself had been retained by the Gomersal Popeleys and a payment out of the hall reserved to the Popeleys of Woolley. Preston quotes a source named Cresay who, in the early seventeenth century, said:

> Upon perusal of Mr. [Robert] Popeley's writings I do find that upon an award made between his ancestors [of the Woolley Moorhouse line] and the ancestors of Christopher Popeley [of the Gomersal line] in the 3rd year of Edward IV [1463] ... Popeley Hall with the lands thereto belonging was awarded to the ancestor of Christopher ... and that there was reserved to the ancestor of Robert Popeley and his heires a rent of 20 shillings with a clause for distress.

From the above it seems that an agreement was reached towards the end of the life of William [I] of Woolley Moorhouse by which the Gomersal Popeleys retained Popeley subject to a small annual payment. In exchange, William [I] of Woolley no doubt secured a better title to the remaining Popeley lands in Gomersal, such as Rydings and Castle House.

The Popeleys of Gomersal

We have traced the Woolley line from Richard [I] of Woolley to Thomas of Woolley, but details of the Gomersal branch of the family in the same period are less certain. In the deed of 1463 in which William [I] of Woolley was said to be formerly of Popeley (above), the other party was one George Popeley, described as 'cousin to William Popeley'; Richard [I] of Woolley therefore appears to have had a brother. This is supported by the entry for Popeley in Flower's Visitation of the North of 1584, where George's father, William [II] of Gomersal, was said to have had a brother named Richard.[49]

George had a son and heir named John. This John left a will, attested on 1 January 1487 at St. Peter's Church, Birstall, and proved on 14 August 1488.[50] In his will he left twenty marks to his daughter, Anne, the bulk of his estate to his eldest son, Henry, and the residue to three younger sons. Little is known of Henry. In 1489, the year following his father's death, he made a grant of some lands in York to one Robert Mauleverer.[51] In 1509 he gave a bond of 100 marks to his contemporary John Popeley of Woolley.

From Henry the Gomersal line's inheritance came to his son, Edward. Once again there is evidence that the head of the household was resident in Gomersal. First is the now lost stained glass window in Birstall Church, recorded by Dodsworth.[52] This showed the Popeley crest of three eglettes above a Latin inscription which read:

> Pray for the good fortune of Edward Popeley and his wife Anne, who had this window made in A.D. 1525.

Other elements in the armorial symbolism have been interpreted as those of the Wentworth family but are now thought to be those of the Mering family of Tong.[53] Edward did in fact marry Anne Mering of Tong and without doubt the connection of Wentworth is with the Popeleys of Woolley, not the Popeleys of Gomersal.

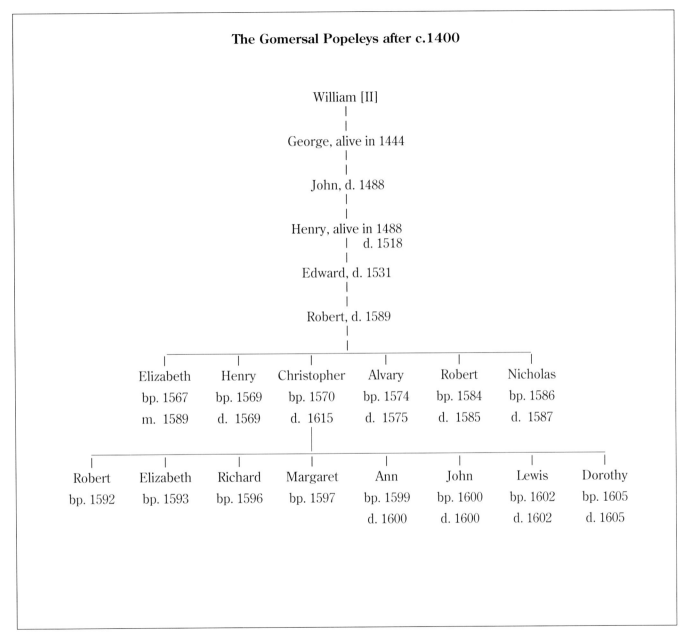

The Gomersal Popeleys after c.1400

William [II]

George, alive in 1444

John, d. 1488

Henry, alive in 1488
d. 1518

Edward, d. 1531

Robert, d. 1589

Elizabeth	Henry	Christopher	Alvary	Robert	Nicholas
bp. 1567	bp. 1569	bp. 1570	bp. 1574	bp. 1584	bp. 1586
m. 1589	d. 1569	d. 1615	d. 1575	d. 1585	d. 1587

Robert	Elizabeth	Richard	Margaret	Ann	John	Lewis	Dorothy
bp. 1592	bp. 1593	bp. 1596	bp. 1597	bp. 1599	bp. 1600	bp. 1602	bp. 1605
				d. 1600	d. 1600	d. 1602	d. 1605

Figure 24

Other evidence that Edward Popeley lived in Gomersal includes a deed of 1525 in which he witnessed a grant of lands in Little Gomersal.[54] This is followed by a deed of 1527 in which he was described as 'Sir Edward Popeley of Gomersal, gent.'.[55] An Edward Copplay was recorded in the Lay Subsidy of 1524, holding £10 of land in Gomersal[56] and it has been suggested that this was in fact Edward Popeley.[57] Finally, Edward was described as of Birstall Parish when his will was proved on 21 April 1531.[58]

Edward was succeeded by his son, Robert, a man who has often been confused with his near contemporary and namesake Robert Popeley of Woolley. Robert of the Gomersal line was alive during the middle years of the sixteenth century and did not die until well beyond his sixtieth year, in 1589. His death was recorded in the early parish registers of Birstall church, where he is described as Robert Popeley of Popeley. This terminal date is of great assistance because we know that Robert Popeley of Woolley was dead by 1565. All transactions of a Robert Popeley which fall between these two dates are likely therefore to be those of Robert of the Gomersal line. These include numerous lawsuits which, when taken, together suggest that by the second half of the sixteenth century the Popeleys of Popeley were in financial difficulties.

Unlike John Batt of Oakwell – another contemporary – Robert seems to have been *compos mentis* until the very year of his death. In 1588 he was party to a lease of the fields known as Great Ing and 'Dobbroyd' (see Fig. 28), to one John Gomersall of Little Gomersal, yeoman.[59] Robert was there referred to as 'of Popeley, gent.'. He was party to another deed in a similar capacity in 1587.[60] In the subsidy list of 1588 he was taxed at £5 for lands, the second highest tax for lands in Gomersal.[61]

Flower's Visitation of 1584 came to an end with the life of Robert. At the time the record was made his wife, Elizabeth, was already dead without bearing children.[62] No second wife was mentioned in the Visitation but one is implied by the reference to Elizabeth as his first wife. This is confirmed by his will, where reference was made to a wife named Alice. In fact the parish registers record several children of one Robert Popeley of Birstall born between the years 1567 and 1587, and the names accord with those whom Robert mentioned at his death. For this reason, and for its general historical value, the rather short will of Robert Popeley is worth reproducing in detail:

> In the name of God Amen the seaven and twentie day of October in the one and thirtieth year of our Sovraigne Ladie Elizabeth ...
> I Robert Popeley of Popeley in the Countie of Yorke gentleman, sick in bodie but of whole and perfect remembrance praise be God ...
> I give unto Christopher Popeley my son two straw beddes at hamblethorpe [?] and all my wayne and plowe geare there ...
> I bequeath unto my said sonne one great brasse potte and one great Chyst with all my evidence and writinge therein contayned concerning my lande ... And also one longe table in the hall at Popeley with the formes and stooles thereto belonging and also one stand bedde in the [ ] chamber ... and all my waines plowes and husslement ... at Popeley.
> And I give and bequeath all my other goods and chattels to Alice my wife and Elizabeth my daughter to be divided equally betwixt them ...
>
> Christopher Popeley executor [63]

Robert's son and heir, Christopher, had been born on 28 December 1570 and succeeded in 1589. His life was not a happy one. It is perhaps as well for Robert that he did not live to see the events of 1590 to 1610, for even by the standards of the time, the Popeleys' experience was a tragic one.

Christopher's wife was named Mary. The parish registers record that they had a son in 1592, a daughter in 1593, another son in 1596 and a daughter in 1597. But we hear no more of these children in the registers and the presumption must be that they died in infancy. After 1597 four more children were baptised: two sons (John and Lewis) and two daughters (Ann and Dorothy). In contrast, their details are all too clearly recorded – all died in their first year.

Christopher himself died in 1615, without surviving issue. So ended the original Popeley line. Popeley Hall and fields may have been in the family's possession until this time, though there is evidence to suggest that Popeley Hall had been lost to the Popeleys some years before Christopher's death. We can be certain however that the estate never found its way to the Popeleys of Woolley Moorhouse. As mentioned above, that family received an annuity from Popeley Hall in the fifteenth and sixteenth centuries, and at the close of the latter century appears to have been interested in acquiring the freehold. The Woolley family's main interests in Gomersal were at Castle Hill and Rydings. For all that they owned large estates, they did not have the original seat of the Popeleys.

Ownership of Popeley after Christopher's death came to one William Horton of Barkisland. The evidence for this is contained in a deed of settlement dated 3 May 1636 in which, along with many other properties, he settled on his son:

> all that capital messuage and tenement called Popeley Hall and all the houses edifices barnes buildings tofts crofts and orcharde ... in the Township of Gomersal ... now in the severall tenures or occupations of Nathaniel Boothe and John Gomersal.[64]

The devolution of Popeley Hall immediately after Christopher's death is unknown, but in the absence of any evidence for a blood relationship between the Hortons and Popeleys the presumption must be that the property was sold. The Horton family still had Popeley Hall in 1676. By the early eighteenth century however it had found its way into the ownership of the Ibbetson family, a wealthy merchant family from Leeds. It was Henry Ibbetson, probably the first Ibbetson to own Popeley, who commissioned the map of 1714 (Fig. 1).

The Popeleys of Woolley Moorhouse

Thomas Popeley and his marriage to Elizabeth Stainton of Woolley have already been mentioned. The marriage produced a son and heir named John, the great-grandson of that Richard who, as royal receiver for Pontefract, may have precipitated the Popeley move to Woolley. Hunter records that John married one of the Neville family of Liversedge, but little else is known. There is even some confusion over the date of his death, with Preston giving the date as 1541 (after Hunter) and some archival sources suggesting 1532.

From John the succession passed to his son, Robert. Evidence about the family, and of its activities in Gomersal in particular, then becomes more plentiful. Robert married Anne, daughter of Thomas Wentworth of Bretton in about 1541.[65] Together they had at least eight children. These included Ann, who in 1569 was to marry one Henry Nettilton of Birstall; Dorothy who married in 1587, also at Birstall; and a son and heir, John [II]. We know that John [II] was born in the year 1549 because he was sixteen years old at the time of his father's inquisition post mortem in 1565.

The inquisition provides a fairly detailed overview of the whole of Robert's estates in Gomersal and elsewhere. He is said to have died possessed of 'two messuages, 30 acres of land, 10 acres of [?] prati. 8 acres of pasture and 6 acres of wood in Gomersal'.[66] One of the Gomersal messuages was called 'Riddings', and was held in a form of free tenure (socage) from Thomas Hussey, the then lord of the manor (see chapter 2). This was similar to the modern freehold. The other messuage referred to was probably Castle Hill in Little Gomersal.

Robert's will, drawn up several years before 1565, makes further interesting reading. It recorded items other than his lands and, unlike the inquisition post mortem, conveys something of the man's personal tastes and surroundings:

> To my son and heir my great standyng bedsteyd in the chamber [at Woolley] ... the best countere in the hall ... one iron chymneye in the kitchyne ... one silver spoyne ... and I will that Anne my wife shall have the ordre custody and marriage of the said John my son ... and 23 shillings yearly of rent at Popeley ... to the parson of Watlewes [? West Laithes] one baye nagge.[67]

Robert's widow outlived him by over thirty-five years, dying in 1601. Her dower came specifically out of lands in Cleckheaton, Heckmondwike and Gomersal. But she was not a widow for long, for in 1572 she married Henry Batt, the new lord of the manor. In a grant of 1572 she was referred to as 'Anne Popeley widow intended wife of Henry Batte of Birstall'.[68] Doubtless Henry saw profit in an association with a family which held so much land in Gomersal. Any advantage eluded Batt however, for he died the following year. In a lease of 1580 Anne was described as 'widowe, late wife of Henry Batte, gentleman, deceased'.[69] The lease is particularly valuable as it shows that Anne was living at the 'Ridinges' (thus attesting the existence of a medieval house on this site) and refers to her eldest son as John Popeley of Woolley. It seems that Anne lived at Rydings from the time of her first husband's death in 1565, perhaps only with intermittent sojourns at the house of her second husband. She was also described as of Rydings in another lease, of 1579, and in her will of 1600, proved in the year 1601, she was said to be 'dwelling at the Ridings in the Parish of Birstall'.[70]

John [II], son of Robert, was the last notable Popeley of Woolley. He probably controlled the family estates from the late 1560s, after his father's death, until his own death in 1616.[71] In a curious document of the early seventeenth century he even appears to have entered into an arrangement to regain Popeley Hall for the Popeleys of Woolley.[72] Then in 1603 he used a legal device to change the holding of the family estates, procuring a freehold, ostensibly to enable him to give good leases to his children, for small rents. In the following year he did in fact grant a lease to his second son, Francis; and in 1611 he revoked a lease already granted to his four daughters, presumably to vary the lease's terms.[73]

John [II] had at least two wives. The first was Mary, daughter of one William Bate of West Lathes.[74] According to Hunter, John's next wife was called Jane, though the Birstall Parish Register records a Mr John Popeley marrying an Elizabeth Savill on 7 May 1614. It may be that there are two John Popeleys referred to

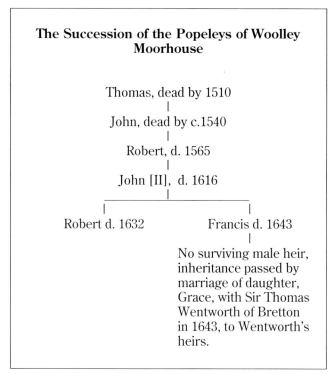

The Succession of the Popeleys of Woolley Moorhouse

Thomas, dead by 1510
|
John, dead by c.1540
|
Robert, d. 1565
|
John [II], d. 1616
|
Robert d. 1632   Francis d. 1643
|
No surviving male heir, inheritance passed by marriage of daughter, Grace, with Sir Thomas Wentworth of Bretton in 1643, to Wentworth's heirs.

Figure 25

here, for it is certain that John [II] of Woolley was survived by a wife called Jane. This Jane married William Baildon of Baildon before April 1618, by which date she had secured her dower in John's lands and had given them back to John's heir, Robert.[75]

John left eight children: Robert, Francis, George, Gervase, Elizabeth, Ann, Jane and Dorothy. In his inquisition post mortem he was said to have held, amongst other things:

> one capital messuage called Woolley Morehouse (alias Stainton Hall), the manor of Birstall which contained 24 bovates, and a messuage called Ridings consisting of a house garden and orchard and another messuage called Castle House Hill consisting of a house and 16 acres of land, both in Gomersal.[76]

The inquisition did not record the type of interest which John had in these lands, but the 'Baildon deed' already mentioned clearly shows that by this time the holdings were freehold. This deed also confirms that Gervase, John's youngest son, was in occupation of Rydings.

In obtaining the surrender of his stepmother's dower Robert must have been put to some expense. Perhaps it was this which accounted for his sale of Rydings, in the same year, to one Edward Armitage.[77] Whatever the reason for the sale this was not an auspicious beginning for the inheritance of the Popeleys of Woolley. After 1618 they appear to have held only Castle Hill and several dispersed plots of land in Gomersal.

In 1620 Robert married Martha Cutler of Stainborough Hall. Documents reveal occasional transactions in the 1620s, but little of note as far as the Popeleys were concerned. A half interest in Rydings (then owned by Edward Armitage) was sold to John Greene of Liversedge by about 1627[78] splitting the ownership and heralding the long association of the Greenes with that property. Gervase Popeley, the occupier, had died in 1623 and was buried at Birstall Church on 25 June 1623.[79]

Robert died on 8 March 1632.[80] His inquisition post mortem, taken at Barnsley in 1634, shows that he had a son, John, born eleven months before his death. This John however lived only sixteen days longer than his father, dying on 24 March. Robert's lands were thus in trust for his wife, Martha, reverting after her death to Francis, Robert's brother and next of kin. Their main holding in Gomersal by this time was the Castle Hill estate, though Francis had lived in Little Gomersal itself after his marriage in 1620. There is no evidence that members of the family lived at Castle Hill.

Francis had married Elizabeth, daughter of John Gomersall of Little Gomersal, in 1620. This was only a year after the death of her father, who had left to her a large house in Little Gomersal, called Nether House, as well as half of the remainder of his estate (see chapter 4). In 1629 a deed described Francis as 'of Little Gomersal, gent.',[81] and after his wife's death in 1632 her half of the Gomersall estate passed to the Popeleys. Francis commemorated his wife by the excellent requiem brass now lying in the church at Birstall (Fig. 26). Elizabeth is depicted in a shroud, flanked by her two surviving daughters, Grace and Dorothy, and with a dedication which reads:

HIC JACET IN SPE RESVRRECTIONIS ELIZABE=
THA UXOR FRANCISCI POPELEY GENEROSI,
MVLIER SINGVLARI VIRTVTE DVAS RELI=
QVIT FILIAS MONVMENTVM HOC MARITVS
POSVIT CHARISSIMAE MEMORIAE PIAE CONIVGIS
OBIIT TRICESIMO DIE MENSIS DECEMBRIS
ANNO 1632

(Here lies in the hope of resurrection Elizabeth wife of Francis Popeley Gentleman, woman of singular virtue leaving two daughters. This monument her husband placed to the cherished memory of his devoted partner. She died on the 30th day in the month of December 1632.)

There is no evidence that Francis remarried. In 1636 his elder daughter, Dorothy, died, and Francis himself died in 1643 at the age of sixty-nine. The Woolley inheritance thus came to his only surviving child, Grace. In 1643 she married Sir Thomas Wentworth of Bretton, and their children inherited the lands of both Elizabeth Gomersall and Robert Popeley, as well as those of Wentworth. A

Figure 26: *The Popeley brass at Birstall Church*

Figure 27: *The tomb of Francis Popeley
at Birstall Church*

marriage settlement shows 'Castle House Hill, with
houses and buildings' to have been part of the
Wentworths' property. And so it remained until sold at
auction in 1833.[82]

The final years of the Popeley family were captured in
fine detail by a monument to Francis Popeley, which is
now located high in the tower of Birstall Church. The
nineteenth century antiquarian, William Carr of Little
Gomersal, saw it at the time of the church's rebuilding.
An entry in his diary reads:

> 1868 April 18th at Birstall Church to copy the inscription on
> the monument of Francis Popeley which in the destroyed
> church stood against the south wall in the aisle near the

porch. The new church is yet unflagged and the monuments
which have been moved into the tower for re-erection are in
much confusion. I found this monument with some difficulty.
It is a slab of black marble – the lettering gilded – flanked with
pilasters & Jacobean ornaments.

It read:

"In this church lies the bodye of Francis Popeley of
Morehouse esquire beinge onelie heire male of the familie of
the Popeleys wh. formerlie lived at and weare owners of
Popeley Hill. He married Elizabeth one of the daughters and
co-heires of John Gomersall of Little Gomersal gentn. had
issue by her John, Dorothie, Elizabeth and Grace – which said
Grace onelie survived her father, being his sole heire was
married unto Sir Thomas Wentworth of Bretton Kt and Bart.
Hee was a kinde husband a dear lovinge father, a good
neighbour and loyall subject & dyed a true sonne of the
Church of England y. 22nd day of October in the 70th year of
his age and yeare of our Lord 1643 –

Here i[s] gone the pattern & epitomy
Of temperance justice and true loyalty."[83]

Popeley in Context

As with all histories, it is easy to be sentimental about
the Popeley story and therefore exaggerate its
importance. Given no more than a sober imagination
and the factual information uncovered so far however, it
is reasonable to consider the legacy of the family as one
of the most significant in Gomersal.

We may begin with Rydings. There is indisputable
historical evidence for a house of this name in Birstall as
early as the fifteenth century. It was certainly in the
general area of the house which still bears that name,
and is likely to have been on the same spot. The present
house does incorporate re-used late-medieval timbers in
its roof, as well as having some seventeenth century
features.[84]

Architectural remains at Popeley Farm show no clear
trace of the undoubted medieval occupation of that site.
There are interesting buildings of the eighteenth and
nineteenth centuries still standing but these do almost
nothing to illustrate the site's early history. The real

potential is archaeological. There has probably been intensive settlement here for at least five centuries, and investigations below ground could reveal medieval building alignments, datable pottery, as well as stonework and other artefacts which are sufficiently durable to withstand the acidic conditions encountered in Pennine areas. Not too long ago the prospect of significant medieval remains at Oakwell seemed remote, but now they are accepted as an obvious characteristic of the area. Similar archaeological potential exists at Castle Hill and Castle Hill House, Little Gomersal.

Nor should we forget the integral part which the Popeley estate played in the medieval landscape in Gomersal. Take away the road and settlement overlay of the last two centuries and we find that the area now occupied by Popeley Farm played a central role in all aspects of daily life in the township. An important local road also ran from Oakwell, to the Church, to Popeley and from there to Castle Hill, and Liversedge beyond. It probably pre-dated Listing Lane, as remains of strip fields recorded on nineteenth century maps clearly respect this road whereas they do not respect Listing Lane itself (see chapter 4). The road will have had many uses but one of the more notable was for direct access to what was initially the only church in the parish, at Birstall.

Finally, enclosure is another feature of the Popeley area which seems to have originated at an early date. At the time of the minority of Richard Popeley (c.1400) we hear that the lord of the manor was encroaching on the commons of Birstall and that by the early seventeenth century the Popeleys themselves had attempted such enclosure. Popeley Farm and other Popeley land in Gomersal, including Castle Hill and Rydings, was probably enclosed at least as early as the mid seventeenth century. From this time onwards it must have formed an easily identifiable estate in Gomersal, providing many local boundaries and landmarks. In fact the field boundaries of Popeley Farm as depicted on the 1714 map are almost identical to those visible today.

NOTES

1. Census 1841 and 1851.
2. See Appendix 1 for details of maps cited.
3. Census 1861.
4. *WYAS K* DD/HS/G/1/152.
5. Cadman 1930, 53 and 158.
6. *WYAS L* HS/unlisted.
7. *WYAS HQ* QE13.
8. Goodall 1953, 94.
9. Cradock 1933, 26.
10. Clay (ed.) 1904, 56.
11. *Borthwick* Probate inventory of John Taylor 12 May 1721; *WYAS SMR.*
12. *YAS* DD 78/15/5.
13. *BL* Add Ch 16581.
14. *YAS* DD 78/15/5.
15. *BL* Add Ch 12631; Goodall 1953, 69.
16. *YAS* MS 986.
17. Brown (ed.) 1898, 43.
18. *BL* Add Ch 12633.
19. Brown (ed.) 1914, 69.
20. Brown (ed.) 1909, 88.
21. *BL* Add Ch 12637.
22. Rusby 1891, 36.
23. *YAS* DD 70/15/5; the authors transcribed this document with many reservations before discovering in the Bradford archives an earlier transcript by William Preston which confirmed their own (*WYAS B* PP). The original is in a poorly written and part Latinized script and on the cover is inscribed 'The descent of the Popeleys and how they came to have the Manor of Birstall ... Note to take advise of counsel for the wastes of Birstall'.
24. This Adam is said to have held two carucates in Birstall which were exempted from the fine levied at York in 1204. He was probably a contemporary of the first John and Richard Popeley.
25. As also given by Hunter 1831, 385.
26. Brown (ed.) 1914, 88.
27. Clay (ed.) 1932, 97.
28. Clay (ed.) 1932, 98.
29. Persons richer by far held estates in Gomersal, e.g the de Leedes family, but they were either recorded in their place of residence or were exempted. The returns of 1379 also record one 'Robertus Poplayman', probably a servant of William Popeley.
30. Cook 1915, 241-2; Cradock 1933, 217.
31. The purpose of the seventeenth century document was to illustrate that the commons in question belonged to the Popeley

family (of Woolley) and not to the Manor of Gomersal. There does not seem to have been any dispute about the facts; the question related to the right of the de Leedes family to behave in this way. The rent referred to in point 5 would not have been what is now known as a rack rent or even a ground rent. It is more likely to have been a small charge on land by which the holder acknowledged some very remote and limited rights of the lord of the manor. Rydings may have been the subject of a grant to the Popeleys in the twelfth century or earlier.

32. Peel 1893, 43.
33. A grant of lands in Clifton was made to Richard in the same year by John Vavasour of Deningley (Armytage 1881, 78) and may relate to the beginning of Richard's majority.
34. Plantagenet-Harrison 1879, 446.
35. Walker (ed.) 1924, 68.
36. Ellis 1895, 83.
37. Morkill 1891, 232.
38. Clay (ed.) 1932, 44.
39. Clay (ed.) 1932, 44.
40. Clay (ed.) 1932, 44-6.
41. *WYAS B* PP
42. Clay (ed.) 1932, 99; 1940, 70.
43. Clay (ed.) 1932, 99.
44. *WYAS B* PP 2/2/a.
45. Clay (ed.) 1932, 100; *WYAS L* HS unlisted. The right of dower was traditionally one third of the deceased husband's real property (land). His widow had an interest in this third for the remainder of her life, after which it reverted to the husband's heir. Here, Cecily has foregone her interest in her husband's lands in return for a payment by the heir of £4 annually for life.
46. Hunter 1831, 385.
47. *WYAS B* PP Box 2/2a.
48. *WYAS B* PP 5/ix.
49. Dendy (ed.) 1921.
50. *Borthwick* Vol 5 folio 336.
51. Dendy (ed.) 1921, 40.
52. Clay (ed.) 1904, 56.
53. Dendy (ed.) 1921, 40.
54. Clay (ed.) 1932, 101.
55. Cradock 1933, 44, after *BL* Harleian 527.
56. Cartwright 1873, 48.
57. Goodall 1953, 129.
58. *Borthwick* 1514-1553 App 1 folio 2.
59. *YAS* DD 70/B11/10.
60. *WYAS B* PP 5/ix.
61. Goodall 1953, 136.
62. 10 August 1561, burial of Elizabeth wife of Richard Popeley of Popeley (BPR).
63. *Borthwick* Vol 26A fol 8.
64. *WYAS B* HM C/69.
65. *YAS* DD 70/7.
66. *WYAS B* PP Box 5/vol ix, a transcript of the original.
67. *WYAS B* PP 5/ix.
68. *YAS* DD 70/1.
69. *YAS* DD 70/12/1.
70. *WYAS B* PP 2/2/a, after the original.
71. *YAS* DD 70/7.
72. *WYAS B* PP 2/2/a.
73. *YAS* DD 70/12/2; DD/70/12/5.
74. Hunter 1831, 385.
75. *YAS* DD 70/7/10.
76. *WYAS B* PP transcript of original.
77. *WYAS L* Acc 976.
78. *WYAS L* Acc 976.
79. Anon 1902, 158; BPR.
80. *YAS* DD 70/15/6.
81. *YAS* DD 70/7/12.
82. *WYAS L* Acc 976.
83. *WYAS K* DD/CA/6.
84. *WYAS SMR*.

Chapter 4

LITTLE GOMERSAL AND CASTLE HILL

The landscape of Little Gomersal provides the key to understanding its history. When the developments of the last 150 years are stripped away, features of a late medieval village become clear. Until the middle of the nineteenth century, change in the village had been very slow; many field names and boundaries had remained the same for centuries. Little Gomersal was a relatively small settlement in the middle of acres of farm land, and lacked the exceptional buildings found in Great Gomersal. However there were, and still are, several noteworthy buildings, along with a pattern of lanes and tracks several hundred years old. This evidence on the ground is as important as that found in documents, and the two together provide a picture of the village's early history.

The late medieval village

When the first edition Ordnance Survey map of Gomersal was drawn up between 1847 and 1851, there had been little development to hide the shape of medieval settlement. In fact the areas south of Gomersal Lane and west of Nibshaw Lane had changed so little in 250 years that the fields shown on an estate plan of 1619 (Fig. 28) were almost identical to those mapped by the Ordnance Survey. Many of the fields south of Little Gomersal were long and narrow, clear indication of the pattern of a great arable field of the Middle Ages. Known as the Langfield, this open field stretched from the village centre down to Eddercliffe in Littletown, its strips running down the hill. With enclosure, which occurred perhaps in the sixteenth century, new fields were made to follow the existing lines of the strips. Footpaths in this area still trace the route of old tracks which gave access to individual holding in the Langfield.

There is further evidence of medieval land division west of Castle Hill. Here strips ran east-west from the ancient

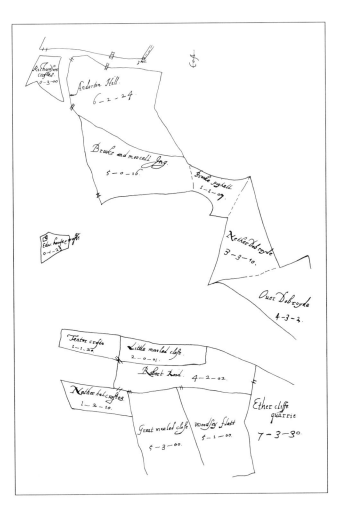

Figure 28: *Survey of John Gomersall's estate by Robert Saxton 1619: plan of the southern fields (YAS DD 70/9/17 reproduced by kind permission of Lord Allendale).*

track between Popeley and Littletown. Listing Lane bisected this field at a later date. The field pattern revealed by other old maps also suggests that arable farming took place to the east of Quarry Road, and as far north as Craven Lane. These strips too were crossed by a new road, though much later, when the Holme Lane End and Heckmondwike turnpike was built in 1824/5. The open arable fields did not extend below Nibshaw Lane towards Spen; that area, which was enclosed before 1600, does not show traces of having been cultivated in strips in earlier times, and could have been open moor (see chapter 6).

The centre of the medieval settlement was the triangle of open ground which still provides a focal point in Little Gomersal. In medieval times this would have been a green surrounded by crofts, small cottages with gardens. Traces of these plots can still be identified in part between the green and the top of Gomersal Lane. Across Gomersal Lane from where the Wheatsheaf now stands was a field called Tentercroft, where woollen cloth was laid out to dry. The first record of that field name is on the estate map of 1619, when most of the people in Little Gomersal would have worked in the woollen industry for at least some of the year.

At a short distance from the village centre was a small outlying settlement at Low (or Nether) Fold. This was on the right-angled bend of Lower Lane where Gomersal House now stands. The fold's main building was Netherhouse, a house of some importance and probably the largest in the village in the sixteenth century (see below). There was also a dwelling called Overhouse, the exact location of which is unknown, though the most likely sites are either Little Court or Royds Farm. John Gomersall (d.1619), one of the largest land-owners in the neighbourhood, owned both Netherhouse and Overhouse, choosing to live in the former.

As late as 1800 the four roads into Little Gomersal – Upper Lane, Lower Lane, Gomersal Lane and Nibshaw Lane – passed through open country. Upper Lane and Lower Lane border land which was probably a medieval common. The area now bounded by Nibshaw Lane, Spen Lane, Upper Lane and Crow Trees was common pasture or moor, used by everyone in the medieval village for grazing their animals; the track or footpath giving access to this land was until recently called Moor Lane. The moor is now completely built upon and Moor Lane has been renamed Shirley Road.

Main roads have long by-passed Little Gomersal. There was little reason for travellers to call at a small settlement which possessed neither church nor manor house. In 1675 the village appeared on Ogilby's atlas map of the York to Chester road, but was depicted only as small rows of cottages at a distance from the highway. If ever Gomersal Lane and Upper Lane formed a main route, it must have been long before 1675, and before Spen Lane became the main road from Leeds to Halifax.

Early documents

The earliest document found which refers to Little Gomersal is a twelfth century grant of land for a dowry. In this, one Richard son of Suan gave to Simon, son of Robert de Hescastun, a bovate of land in 'Litlegumarashale' along with seven acres within the hedge of Brocrodes, a toft in the water, and woods and liberties attached to this estate.[1] The parties to this deed may not have lived in Gomersal. The area known as Brookroyd was on the Liversedge boundary near Nellroyd, and was later owned by the John Gomersall who died in 1619. It is possible that the bovate in the village itself was land to the west or south of Little Gomersal which later passed to the Gomersall family.

The next recorded transaction does refer to a local inhabitant, Richard son of Christian de Parva [Little] Gumersale. In the thirteenth century Richard transferred to his sister a half acre of land in Gomersal. The plot was described as being adjacent to the land of Robert son of Simon de Gumersale, and one of the witnesses was Ely son of Simon of Little Gomersal.[2] These men could have been forbears of some of the sixteenth and seventeenth century Gomersalls who owned so much land in the village. Goodall also refers to some local inhabitants in the thirteenth century mentioned in a grant by Hugh son of Elias of Little Gomersal, though the land transferred was not specified.[3]

In the fourteenth century, Elias de Birton of Gomersall gave a gift to his elder daughter Joan, of:

> a messuage in Little Gomersall and half an acre of land abutting thereon, lying on the west side of the land of Roger de Ledys, and half an acre of land lying on Sowhwelrod on the south side of Roger the knight, also half an acre of land lying on Longlands on the north side of the land of Roger de Ledis, knt. ...[4]

'Sowhwelrod' could have been one of the closes named Pighill in the Gomersall family settlement of 1619 and Longlands was presumably the Langfield.

In the 1379 Poll Tax list for Gomersal Elias de Birton appeared as Elias Britton. Willelmus de Gomersall was the only person on the list who had the local surname.[5] It is not until the early fifteenth century that a series of documents starts to show the Gomersall family as significant landholders in Little Gomersal, and it becomes clear that these were predecessors of the John Gomersall who lived at the turn of the seventeenth century. For example, in 1401 John son of Simon of Little Gomersall granted to one William Gomersall of Little Gomersall part of Cleffoghbanke (called in 1619 Cliff Edge Bank). This area was described as abutting other lands owned by William, including a field called Okwellsyke – which was also part of John Gomersall's Little Gomersal estate in 1619.[6] A second grant, of 1412, gave permission to a John de Gomersall to enclose lands at Nelleroyde with a fence, ditch or hedge. The owners of Nellroyd at this time were still William de Ledes, lord of the manor, and Joan his wife, though it was eventually to come into the ownership of the Gomersall family.[7]

A clearer picture of the lands held by the Gomersall family emerges from a deed of 1448 by which the John Gomersall of the day granted to his son and heir, Thomas:

> all the lands and ten[emen]ts in Little Gomersall which had descended to him by hereditary right and purchase, namely Cheyf plase or Hed plase, Aloth Stayr, Magcroft, Goydhyrdcrofte with the barn built [thereon], Morhouserod, Nellerod, Brokrod, Tubyrdpigyll, Dodgedoxtpyxyll, Morellhyng, Hussteyd, Halcrofte and Estrod ...[8]

Allowing for a certain eccentricity in the spelling, most of these fields can be identified. The list includes closes which in the early seventeenth century were called Godardcroft, Nellroyd, Brookroyd, Dobroyd Pighill, Morell Ing, House Croft, Hall Croft and Eastroyd. It is clear from the fifteenth century deed that the Gomersalls' estate ran at least from Low Fold in Little Gomersal to Rawfolds. This deed apparently lists the fields in a topographical sequence. The House Stead and Hall Croft appear next to Morell Ing in the list, suggesting that the hall or main house of the Gomersalls was situated at Low Fold at this early date (as Morell Ing is known to have been the field below Lower Lane and next to Low Fold). It is highly probable, therefore, that Low Fold has contained a large and important house for more than 550 years.

None of the deeds after this were as comprehensive in their coverage of the Gomersalls' estate. Some of the subsequent documents show that the family held land in other villages and also rented land in Gomersal from other owners.[9] It seems that another branch of the Gomersall family lived in Brotherton, near Ferrybridge, for in 1450 John Gomersall granted to his daughter, Margaret de Abbay, a 'messuage called Godardcrofte' in Little Gomersal. He had been given this land by another John Gomersall, of Burton Salmon near Brotherton.[10] Twenty years later, a Thomas Gomersall of Little Gomersal was recorded as owner of lands in 'Byrton Salamon by Brotherton and Westhadylsay [West Haddlesey, near Ferrybridge] and also in the vill of Doncastre and Wilsden in Bradforthdall [Bradford] ...'.[11]

Three deeds of the early sixteenth century shed light on relationships in the main branch of the Gomersall family.[12] The head of the family was William Gomersall, alive in 1519 but dead by 1525, with a son and heir also named William. Another son, Edward, held some of the family's property on a sixteen year lease. The younger William's son and heir, John, married Agnes Rayner, daughter of Richard Rayner of Liversedge. A sizable property settled on the couple in 1525 was described as 'a messuage with appurtenances lately built in Little Gomersall, with the lands, meadows and pastures adjoining, of the yearly value of 20s. net ...'. John was also confirmed as heir to the family's other possessions in 'Litillgomersall, Byrtonsalmon, Hadilsay, and Brotherton and elsewhere in co. York ...'. Considering their wealth, however, it is curious that no member of the family appeared on the Lay Subsidy list for 1524 in Gomersal; perhaps they were taxed on their property in another township.[13]

The will of this last-mentioned John Gomersall 'of Lytyll Gomrsall', dated 27 May 1544, has survived among the Beaumont estate papers.[14] It is a conventional will which does not give information about the extent of the family's property, as John left everything to his son, apparently his only male heir: 'I wyll that Thomas my son be my full hayre of all my landys after my decesse ...'. There is also a reference to fulfilling certain agreements with Edward Gomersall 'my unkyll'. Otherwise the main interest in this will is in its language and form:

> I bequeath my sawll to god almyghty to ar blessyd Lady marie and to all the saints in hevyn and my body to be beryd in the church yard of byrstall of the Holly apostyls petr & paule ...

Full of catholic sentiments, it is a reminder that Henry VIII's Church of England had been only very recently established.

Netherhouse, Overhouse and the Gomersalls

John Gomersall, the last male in the main branch of the family and presumably son of the Thomas mentioned in the 1544 will, died in February 1619. He owned several houses in Little Gomersal itself and over 150 acres of land to the south and west of the village.[15] His own residence, called Netherhouse, was probably on the site of today's Gomersal House. Very little else is known about Netherhouse. There does not now appear to be any building at Low Fold which could have been there when John Gomersall was alive. The main southern range of the present Gomersal House dates from about 1850 and may have been built by Dr William Carr, owner in the second half of the nineteenth century. Behind this range, and fronting on to Lower Lane, is a collection of buildings in roughly dressed stone. The drip moulds around the windows and kneelers which adorn these buildings all appear to be nineteenth century additions, again perhaps by Dr Carr, but the bulk of this construction is in an eighteenth century vernacular style. Especially notable are the heavy sills and mullions to the windows on the western elevation (Fig. 29). West of the house is another domestic building with an old warehouse or workshop attached (Fig. 30). Both are well preserved. The warehouse has flat-faced mullion windows, such as are usually found in industrial buildings of the late eighteenth or early nineteenth centuries. The domestic building, probably originally a farmhouse, shows all the signs of an early or

Figure 29: *Gomersal House: western elevation*

Figure 30: *Gomersal House: domestic buildings with workshop*

mid eighteenth century date. It may even be depicted on the Ibbetson estate map of 1714 (Fig. 1). It certainly appears, along with the warehouse, on the Ibbetson map of 1798 (Fig. 31).

There is no external evidence that any of the present buildings at Low Fold existed before the eighteenth century. The idea must be considered that John Gomersall's house of 1619 was a timber structure which did not long survive him. Had it been of stone, doubtless some fragments would have been incorporated into later buildings. In the absence of archaeological or architectural evidence, a handful of documents provides all the information that is presently available.

As outlined above, there was almost certainly an important house at Low Fold in 1448. Whether this was the same building in which John Gomersall lived up to his death is unknown. A list of the rooms and contents of Netherhouse does survive, however, as an inventory was taken of Gomersall's possessions for probate purposes in February 1619.[16] It is clear from this inventory that Netherhouse had a hall, parlour, buttery, maid's parlour, kitchen and little kitchen, an entrance porch and four chambers over the main rooms. There were also stables and other small rooms used for storage, and a

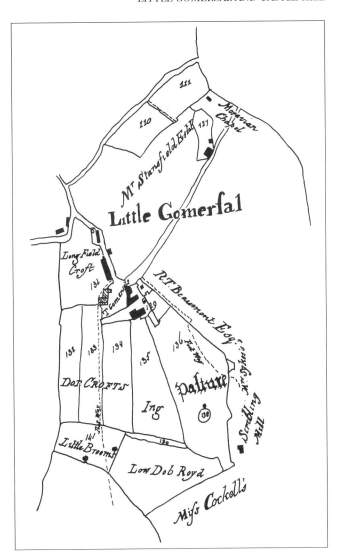

Figure 31: *Low Fold in 1798: detail from Ibbetson's estate map (WYAS L DB/M 670/4 reproduced by kind permission of Dibb Lupton Broomhead and Prior, solicitors)*

considerable value in livestock and farming implements. The best room was the parlour. The hall contained only tables, buffets, chairs and fireplace, and was probably used for dining; the parlour held items of luxury and show, including a 'green carpet on a table', a feather bed and coverlets, a Bible and other books, and various pieces of pewter and silver. The value of John Gomersall's clothing and money alone totalled £6 13s. 4d. and shows him to have been a wealthy man.

The estate was divided between his two daughters, Alice, wife of John Horsell of Eggborough, and Elizabeth, as yet unmarried. We do not know whether the Gomersall family then held land near Ferrybridge, but clearly there were still connections, as Alice had married and moved to that area. A survey of Gomersall's lands in Little Gomersal was taken in 1619 by Robert Saxton, son of the famous map-maker Christopher Saxton. Saxton listed the fields which John Gomersall had owned at his death, dividing them into three sections. The lands to the south of Little Gomersal, sixty acres in all, from Royds Farm to Eddercliffe and from Lower Lane to the Liversedge boundary, were inherited by Elizabeth Gomersall. (Though those fields immediately south and west of Gomersal House were excluded, being in separate ownership; they were later part of Ibbetson's estate.) Elizabeth also had the Netherhouse itself, and another house and croft whose tenant was one Edward Gomersall. Alice Horsell took the northern part of the estate, sixty-three acres of land including fields between Gomersal Lane and Mount Pleasant, others to the west of Nibshaw Lane, and possibly the area between Upper Lane and Lower Lane. The Overhouse, at that time tenanted by Robert Sunderland, and a house called Wilbey House, occupied by another John Gomersall, along with a neighbouring cottage, were also in Alice's share. The third lot, twenty-seven acres of land at Brookroyd and Nellroyd, was divided between the sisters. One plan survives, of Elizabeth Gomersall's inheritance, the south part of the lands surveyed (Fig. 28). This plan is considered to be too roughly drawn to have been the work of Saxton himself.[17]

Figure 32: *Royds Farm Barn from the south east.*

As outlined above, the most likely position of Netherhouse is on the site now occupied by Gomersal House, or very close to it. Overhouse (or Upper House) is harder to locate. It may have been where Little Court now is, or at Royds Farm or on Upper Lane. It is likely that Royds Farm was part of this estate, as John Gomersall owned most of the surrounding fields. The present Royds Farm is a late eighteenth century house

Figure 33: *Royds Farm Barn: timbers of northern bay*

Figure 34: *Little Court, then called Upper House, c.1900 (KCS RH4/55)*

Royds Farm barn is believed to be the oldest building in Little Gomersal. Little Court is almost as old, though it was greatly altered in the nineteenth century. The name itself is also relatively new; early this century, Little Court was called Upper House (Fig. 34) which could itself be a modernized version of Over House. The stone chimneys and west doorway give a clue about the age of Little Court, a mid seventeenth century house which has been compared in its layout to Mazebrook Farm, (dated 1654).[18] Originally Little Court consisted of a main block facing south, which contained two rooms, the housebody to the west and a parlour to the east. The housebody could have been heated by a firehood, as the present fireplace there is of later date. The parlour retains its seventeenth century fireplace. Behind the parlour was an outshut, though the features of this are now barely recognisable. Behind the housebody was a wing which may have accommodated the kitchen, and there is still a large seventeenth century fireplace on the north gable wall. The main door to the house can still be seen, in the west wall between the rear wing and the housebody. Although surveys have not revealed anything older on the site, it is possible that Overhouse stood there or nearby, and that Little Court was a rebuilding of the old house. If Overhouse was sold by the Horsells soon after 1619, it is feasible that new owners would have rebuilt it in the mid century. A probate inventory survives of the goods of one Edmond

but traces of the foundations of an earlier building can be seen in the farmyard. This older house, projecting in front of the present one and standing slightly to the west, was depicted on nineteenth century maps. Moreover, the barn at Royds Farm has a timber frame of at least seventeenth century date and could be the only existing building in Little Gomersal to have been owned by John Gomersall. The barn has an aisle to the rear, is of three bays, but was formerly longer. The posts are set on padstones and the structure encased in thin coursed rubble beneath a stone slate roof. Old as the barn is, some elements, for example an arched truss now carrying trenched purlins, provide evidence of re-use from a late medieval building (Fig. 33).

Brooke of Little Gomersal, who died in 1676. He lived in a sizable house, which could have been Little Court. Brooke's residence had a housebody, north and south parlours, kitchen and buttery, a chamber over the house, south chamber and corn chamber, a cellar, brewhouse and the usual outbuildings. It was well-furnished and his possessions were assessed at the considerable sum of £269.[19]

Figure 35: *Upper Lane House: window inscribed 1626*

If the room in the rear wing of Little Court had been a north parlour, with a kitchen and buttery housed separately, this inventory could indeed refer to the same house.

Another possibility is that Overhouse was on the top side of Upper Lane, perhaps where Upper Lane House now stands. This house, which is also nineteenth century in appearance, is in fact much older as can be detected in the roof line and gable elevation. A date of 1636 on a window in the eastern wall may well be original (Fig. 35).

The end of the Gomersalls

The names of John and Alice Horsell do not reappear in Gomersal history after the division of lands in 1619. Whether Alice's portion was kept intact, or sold off in parts, is not clear from subsequent records. Much more is known about Elizabeth and her descendants. Elizabeth, who was baptised at Birstall in May 1590, stayed in Little Gomersal after the death of her father, and probably lived at Netherhouse for the rest of her life. She married Francis Popeley of Woolley Moorhouse in November 1620. This was an advantageous alliance for both of them, as Elizabeth was the owner of substantial property in Gomersal, whereas Francis would have been considered of a higher social standing than the Gomersalls. The Popeleys were minor gentry whilst the Gomersalls were of yeoman stock (though Francis Popeley's tombstone tactfully refers to his father-in-law as a 'gentleman'; see chapter 3). Neither bride nor groom was in the first flush of youth, being respectively thirty and forty-six when they married. Francis was a younger son, and can hardly have expected to inherit the family estates. He did so however, very suddenly, in 1632/3 when his older brother and the brother's son died in quick succession. If the brass memorial plaque erected to Elizabeth's memory by Francis can be relied upon, the marriage was a happy one (see Fig. 26). It was also fruitful, though two of their four children died within a few days of their birth. Elizabeth herself died in December 1632, and her eldest child, Dorothy, in 1636 at the age of fourteen. That left only the youngest, Grace (born 1628), who lived to be seventy. Grace was married first to Sir Thomas Wentworth of Bretton, then to Alexander Montgomery, Earl of Eglington. The granddaughter of John Gomersall, yeoman, therefore ended her life as a countess.

This series of marriages and deaths had important implications for the later history of Little Gomersal and the development of its landscape. Because so much property became concentrated in a few hands, a large estate devolved upon the heirs of Thomas Wentworth. The lands which had been inherited separately by Elizabeth Gomersall and Francis Popeley stayed virtually intact as one large estate until split up in the Beaumont sale of 1833.

Francis Popeley died in 1643 and his daughter married Wentworth in the same year, so Netherhouse probably fell vacant at about that time. Cadman says that the Rhodes family occupied Gomersal House for two hundred years until the mid nineteenth century;[20] this fits in with other evidence. A Jeremiah Rhodes was certainly renting several fields around Low Fold from the Ibbetsons in 1714, as shown on their estate plan

Figure 36: *Little Gomersal from the south c.1900: Gomersal House is on the left, with the dryhouse cottages behind (KCS RH1/41)*

(Fig. 1). Dr William Carr also noted a connection with the Rhodes family in his diary of 1868: 'Mr William Rhodes from whom I bought Gomersal House (wh. he had purchased from the Ibbetsons in 1842) told me of an exchange of lands in Gomersal between the Beaumonts and the Ibbetsons during his father's lifetime. Jeremiah and Henry Rhodes the grandfather and father of W. Rhodes lived here as tenant to the Ibbetsons ...'.[21] This exchange of property appears to have involved a very small area of land and probably took place in about 1800. The William Rhodes who sold Gomersal House to Carr was a colliery owner who also owned Listing Lane Mills. It is uncertain whether the Victorian rebuilding of

Gomersal House was carried out by William Rhodes or by Dr Carr, though it was most likely the latter as the style is later nineteenth century (see Fig. 36) and Carr is known to have made substantial alterations.

Castle Hill

Castle Hill, a settlement a short distance to the south east of Little Gomersal village, has two features which arouse special interest. One is the promontory of land which falls away steeply to the Liversedge boundary. The other is the name itself, established long enough to be found in records of the Middle Ages.

The promontory consists of what appears to be an abruptly terminated natural spur, surmounted by an artificial mound. Goodall speculated that such a prominent spot could not fail to have attracted the attention of early inhabitants of the district, that it was strengthened by earthworks of the prehistoric period and was later the site of an 'Anglian' settlement.[22] However, whilst it is true that Castle Hill appears partly man-made, there have been no archaeological investigations to confirm earthworks either of the age Goodall suggests or of the medieval period. The present house and outbuildings are situated about 200 metres west of the end of the spur, and no evidence has emerged of any ancient encampment there or elsewhere on the hill.

But Castle Hill's significance should not be understated. The fact that it is visible from many parts of Spen Valley, and that it is on an old boundary, mean that it is likely to have been an ancient meeting place or even a small settlement. A medieval road passed the buildings and skirted the hill on its way from Popeley to Knowler Hill. Castle Hill seems to have been a thriving hamlet, separate from Little Gomersal, in the early modern period, and in the last century it was the centre of various industrial activities.

Documentary references to this area begin in the thirteenth century. The sister of Richard son of Christian de Little Gumersale was identified in one charter as Angela or Agnes de Oterescastell[23], and another charter names Richard de Otyrkastell as grantor of lands in Gomersal to Richard Popeley.[24] It is likely therefore that Castle Hill contained a settlement at this early date, from which these people took their names, though the first mention of a house on the site did not appear until 1346. In that year a grant of land by Robert Morrison and his son Richard was 'given at the Castill'. The property at that time included a 'messuage built, called Castill by Popelay, with all the lands, meadows, woods, common of pasture, and all other easements ... belonging'.[25] The name Morrison recurs in 1387, when Robert's widow Isabel, and Alice, widow of William

Speght, renounced their right to dower 'in a certain messuage ... called Castell, Gomersall' in favour of Walter de Kyghley.[26]

The hill was still called 'le Castell within the vill and bounds of Gomersall' in 1436, though the term Castle House was becoming established. 'A messuage called Castel howse', says a deed of 1450, which goes on to specify the 'repair [of] houses, enclosures and hedges of the said messuage ...'. In 1465 'Castell Howse' along with Rydings (near Birstall Smithies) and other property in Gomersal was the subject of a dower settlement in the Popeley family.[27] In about 1600 the place was usually called Castle House Hill, and in modern times its name has been Castle Hill.

The connection with Rydings re-surfaced a century later when Castlehouse was let by Anne Batt and her son John Popeley in 1579. Anne, widowed for the second time, was living at 'Ridinges within the Townshippe of Gomersall' (see chapters 2 and 3). The Castle Hill property had descended to John but Anne retained a life interest as widow of the previous owner and was a party to the lease. Castlehouse was described as a 'messuage, tenement and farmehould' in the tenure of a lessee, John Lyvsage [Liversedge] alias Castlehouse, a clothier. It was let, along with other houses, buildings, gardens and land at the site, for eleven years at 9s. 10d. a year. The fact that John Liversedge also had the name Castlehouse suggests that he and his family had occupied that house for a considerable time. This is also the first firm evidence of woollen cloth manufacture at Castle Hill.[28]

It is possible to trace some of the Liversedges of Castle Hill in the published Birstall Parish Registers between 1558 and 1687. The baptism of Edward, son of John Liversedge of Castlehouse, took place in March 1567, and after this came numerous references to the family, until the year 1614 when Edward died. His son, another Edward, was buried at Birstall in 1616. After this there was only one more reference to the family – in 1630, when Ann Liversedge, a widow, of Castlehouse Hill, was interred.

Between 1618 and 1687, the name which occurred most frequently at Castle Hill was that of Mann. That their residence does not seem to have overlapped with that of the Liversedges suggests that they took over the main house there from the Liversedges. In addition to these two families, about twenty-five other surnames were mentioned in the seventeenth century parish registers at Castlehouse Hill. Some of these were odd references to people who happened to die during a short residence, but others show continuity of tenant families over twenty or thirty years. For instance, there were Hepworths at Castle Hill from 1649 until at least 1685, and one Adam Scaberd lived at the hill from about 1625 until his death in 1652. These residents could have been under-tenants, or may have worked for the main tenant either as agricultural labourers, as domestic servants or as woollen cloth makers, or in a combination of these roles.

Another Popeley lease, of 1629, names inhabitants of Castle Hill as William Lether, John Man, William Parks, William Fletcher and Wilfray Walker. This deed, in which Dorothy Popeley of Little Gomersal, the elder daughter of Francis Popeley, took the property from her uncle Robert Popeley of Woolley Moorhouse, was presumably a legal device designed to confer some benefit upon Dorothy, who was a child at the time. She probably lived at the house inherited from the Gomersalls (see above) and certainly was not resident at Castle Hill, then described as 'all that capitall messuage and farme called Castlehouse hill'.[29]

From a tax return of 1641 still more information about the inhabitants of Castle Hill is available. This return is merely a list of names of all tax-payers in the Gomersal township – several hundred people in all – but they seem to have been grouped in neighbourhoods.[30] The list for Castle Hill appears to have included:

> John Man the elder and his wife Alic[e]
> Robert Man and his wife Ann
> John Man the younger
> Samuell Man
> Susan Man
> Willm Lether and his wife Annas [Annis]
> Adam Skawbard and his wife Mary
> Willm Soothill and his wife Jennet

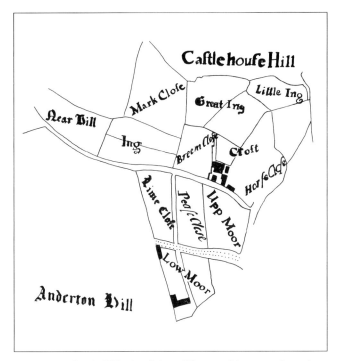

Figure 37: *Castle Hill: detail from Wentworth's estate plan of 1721 (Bretton BEA/C2/MPD6/1 reproduced by kind permission of Lord Allendale and the Bretton Estate Archive, Bretton Hall, Wakefield)*

All these were assessed for tax at the standard rate of 6d., whereas better-off people in the township paid 12d. or 2s. This suggests that there was no family at Castle Hill at this time who could be described as of the gentry or even of the yeoman class.

It has been assumed by two local historians that members of the Greene family of Liversedge lived at Castle Hill.[31] However, other than references in the parish registers for 1599 and 1600 to a William Green at Castle House, there is nothing to connect that family with the place – though the Greenes certainly owned Rydings for a considerable period in the seventeenth century.

Castle House cannot be identified in the Hearth Tax returns of 1684, so it is possible that there was not one grand house there in the late seventeenth century but that the big house of former years had been divided and sublet, if in fact it still stood at all. There is a dearth of information about Castle Hill in the early eighteenth century, relieved only by a faded map of Wentworth's estate in 1721 (Fig. 37). This map shows buildings grouped in a very similar form to the present day lay-out. What is now a drive into the rear of the property was then the main road from Popeley. It is highly likely that the house faced in that direction, westwards, on to a yard bounded by other cottages and workshops. If so, the building was 'turned round' in the nineteenth century when a new façade was added to the back of the old house and a landscaped garden and drive created in front of it. This drive leads to a road which did not exist in the eighteenth century, the turnpike which cut through the fields between Six Lane Ends and Gomersal in 1824/5.

The present house at Castle Hill appears to date from no earlier than the eighteenth century. Small window openings in an extension to the rear block may be re-used elements of an early eighteenth century structure but the main body of the house is probably of the mid eighteenth century and later. Of the two blocks which make up the double pile arrangement, the rear is undoubtedly the oldest. In the western wall it has heavy window surrounds relatively close to one another. There is also a large central doorway which at the time the block was built was probably the main access to the house. The visitor would have approached the house from the west, having passed along a cart way which ran between several outbuildings. In contrast, the front block was probably planned and built between 1800 and 1840 as a deliberate attempt to escape the farmyard clutter to the rear. The tall, imposing doorway is still a notable period feature, enclosed by a heavy classical porch on plain columns. Originally the ground floor windows were simple sash windows, like those upstairs, thereby enhancing the symmetry of the building (Fig. 38).

Figure 38: *Castle Hill House from sale particulars of 1882 (WYAS L HS/unlisted reproduced by kind permission of WYAS Leeds)*

In the early nineteenth century a merchant called Thomas Rhodes lived at the house; he died in 1802. Rhodes was the father-in-law of James Burnley and grandfather of Thomas, William and another James Burnley.[32] Rhodes also had a son, Thomas, who succeeded him as tenant of Castle House and the surrounding land. Thomas Rhodes was still there in 1833 when the property was described as a dwelling house, weaving shop, barn, stable, mistal and garden in the Beaumont sale particulars.[33] It was not put up for auction, being sold by private treaty along with other property for £1,600. Through the new owner, James Ellis, Castle House came into the possession of the Burrows family, who lived there for almost half a century. Ellis did not live long after buying the Castle Hill estate, and the property passed to his daughter Rachel, wife of Josiah Burrows.[34] Burrows was a maltster, carrying on business at Castle House, and also farming 110 acres. The 1851 census returns show a sizable establishment at what was now called Castle Hill House; the sons of the family included John Ellis Burrows, manager of a woollen factory; William, who worked for his father; and James, a grocer's apprentice. A daughter, Elizabeth, lived there with her husband,

William Birks, a brewer, and their son. In addition there were two servants and two farm labourers in the main house. In the adjoining cottage lived a house servant, the children's nurse, a maltster's labourer and two other farm workers. The house was clearly at the centre of a number of related activities, farming, malting and brewing. It is said that a windmill existed at Castle Hill at this time, and was demolished in 1873[35], but no supporting evidence has been found on contemporary maps.

When Rachel Burrows died in 1881, under the terms of her father's will the estate had to be sold. In the sale documents of June 1882 a description of Castle Hill House in its Victorian heyday can be found and an excellent drawing shows the house before the present bay windows were added[36] (Fig. 38). The estate was broken up into small lots, but the main house was sold along with the maltkilns and storerooms, and five cottages in the yard at the rear. It was after this sale that Castle Hill Road was laid out and land in the area began to be developed.

Little Gomersal in the Eighteenth Century

The eighteenth century village had hardly changed in form from medieval times. Little Gomersal still consisted of a handful of cottages grouped around a green, with two or three larger houses on the outskirts. Most of the population was engaged in agriculture and woollen manufacture, and the bulk of the land remained in the ownership of two large estates. From about 1713 until 1843, the Ibbetsons of Leeds owned the fields around Low Fold, Popeley Fields and part of the Hill Top area. The Wentworth family of Bretton and their successors the Beaumonts held the combined estates of the old Gomersall and Popeley families, which stretched from Union Mill in the east, south to Castle Hill, and west as far as Nellroyd. This was not dispersed until 1833. Both Ibbetsons and Beaumonts let out all their Little Gomersal land to tenants and sub-tenants, and it remained almost entirely in agricultural use. There was little scope for any other kind of development.

The main changes which did take place in the eighteenth century occurred in the area between Upper Lane and Lower Lane. By the mid century some or all of these closes had come into the ownership of a family called Charlesworth, who were cloth-dressers and merchants. Thomas Charlesworth leased land to the Moravian Brethren for their first chapel building in 1751. His son Martin, of Lower Lane House, is said to have been the owner in 1757 of Lower House, the Newhouse and three others called the Lane End houses.[37] The terrace of three brick dwellings now called Sisters' Houses was named Lower House on mid-nineteenth century Ordnance Survey maps. One of the Sisters' Houses, the westernmost, was probably built before 1757, and it may have been Charlesworth's Lower (or Lower Lane) House. The middle house of the terrace, taller and differing in style from the other two, appears to date from the end of the eighteenth century and could have been built to accommodate Moravian sisters, though it soon became a private residence. The three houses are all of brick with stone quoins and stone roofs. The middle house is of three bays, the others of four. All have sash windows and doorways with fanlights, architraves and small cornices (Fig. 39).

Figure 39: *Sisters' Houses, Lower Lane (KCS RH1/51)*

Cadman claimed a date of 1798 for all three houses, and said that they were used as sisters' houses from then until 1811[38], but this information could be correct only for the middle house. A close study of the houses during recent restorations has confirmed that the easternmost house was the last one to be built, and was probably a Victorian addition, an attempt to balance the terrace by creating a mirror image of the mid-eighteenth century building to the west.[39]

The Charlesworths remained wealthy and important until after the turn of the nineteenth century, and a William Charlesworth lived at Brier Hall in 1822.[40] Ibbetson's estate map of 1798 showed most of the area between Upper Lane and Lower Lane in the ownership of a Mr Stansfield – probably David Stansfeld Esq. of Leeds, who sold his Gomersal property in about 1810. The Moravian chapel was marked on this map, and the Moravians were shown to own land across Quarry Road, including the site of their present graveyard.

The development of the Moravian community was probably the greatest change in Little Gomersal during the eighteenth century. The Moravians were a German Protestant sect which had founded a branch in London

Figure 41: *The present Moravian Church*

in 1738. At that time they were close to John Wesley and the early Methodists, but a separation came about in 1740 as the Moravians could not accept the ordinances of the Church of England. The Moravian brethren established a settlement at Fulneck in 1743 and went on to build several others in Yorkshire, of which Little Gomersal was one of the earliest. It was founded in 1751 and was declared a settlement in 1755.[41] A picture survives which gives some idea of the early chapel and adjacent houses (Fig. 40).[42] This original church, with its tall arched windows, resembled in style the one at Lower Wyke. It is said to have been built largely by voluntary labour, and had galleries and floors added between *c.*1770 and 1790. Music was played here with stringed instruments, from 1786.[43] The Moravians ran schools in Little Gomersal: a girls' boarding school from 1792 until 1902, and a boys' school perhaps as early as 1758.[44] The location of this boys' school is unclear, as no buildings were shown behind the church on the Ibbetson map of 1798 where the boys could have been accommodated.[45] It may have been a day school which was held in the church itself. The girls' school was built at the same time as the manse, in 1793; these were placed at either side of the church and give a symmetrical appearance to the block.[46] Behind are a number of two- and three-storey cottages dating from

Figure 40: *Moravian Church and houses before the rebuilding of the church (KCS JJS/CO54/0185)*

Figure 42: *Eighteenth century houses forming part of the Moravian settlement*

the late eighteenth or early nineteenth centuries, all of them part of the religious settlement, and probably built to house some of the pupils and teachers. The present church dates from 1868-70, a considerable enlargement of its predecessor. Red brick was used for both churches, the manse and the girls' school.

Changes in the nineteenth century

Like other local villages, Little Gomersal did not begin to emerge from its traditional rural landscape and pattern of life until about the second quarter of the nineteenth century. The breakthrough came with the release of land in relatively small plots, making possible some industrial development which was modern and technological compared with the domestic cloth-making and agriculture which had previously employed most people. Also significant was the opening of the Holme Lane End and Heckmondwike turnpike in 1824/5; the section between Hill Top and Six Lane Ends was almost entirely new, cutting a swathe through Popeley Fields. This meant that the steep medieval tracks of Listing Lane, Gomersal Lane and the Popeley road were no longer the only routes into and out of Little Gomersal.

Before 1790 there was little in the village which could have been described as an industrial building, other than the cottage workshops of handloom weavers. In Lower Lane, between Low Fold and the village proper, was a long narrow building, which at the beginning and end of its life was a terrace of cottages; in between it was used as a dryhouse, presumably for drying wool and woollen cloth.[47] Between 1790 and 1833, the only large development was the building of Castle Hill Mill by Col. Beaumont (see chapter 7); it was not until after Beaumont's death and the sale of his land in Little Gomersal in 1833 that other more successful and enduring textile factories appeared in Little Gomersal. (Butts Mill, often described as being in Little Gomersal, was actually on the main Leeds-Halifax road and can hardly be considered part of the village.)

The major movements in land ownership took place in 1833, when the Beaumonts sold their Little Gomersal possessions, and in 1843, when financial embarrassment also forced the Ibbetson family to sell up. Quarry Mill was built upon Beaumont's Lot 9, and Union Mill on Lot 6; both of these were well-established woollen mills by the time of the Ordnance Survey in 1847-51. The freeing of land ownership also allowed holdings to be further broken up and resold, and during the second half of the nineteenth century Little Gomersal acquired many new houses and a few small streets on these divided plots. Naturally much of the Beaumont and Ibbetson land remained in agricultural use, in many cases owned by former tenants.

The old common land north of the village, that encompassed by Nibshaw Lane, Spen Lane and Crow Trees, had already been enclosed, probably in the eighteenth century. About fourteen acres there were sold in 1810 by David Stansfeld to three Little Gomersal men: William Hirst of Butts Mill; Benjamin Sykes, a surgeon and apothecary; and Jonathan Fox, cardmaker.[48] Other land in the area was also changing hands at this time. By the middle of the century the fields near Upper Lane and Quarry Road had become home to the Little Gomersal colliery, five smaller coal pits, two chemical works, a National School and a large house called Field House. Serving these various developments was a number of intersecting lanes and tracks. Upper Lane Mills, used for cotton spinning, was also established there by 1890.

The introduction of these diverse industries to the village must have changed the lives of Little Gomersal's inhabitants dramatically, with a much altered environment and new ways of working, particularly a shift away from employment at home. It was not until a century later though, that large-scale house building led to an agglomeration with Hill Top and the rest of Gomersal.

NOTES

1. *BL* Edg Ch 639. A bovate in Yorkshire was normally an area of between 8 and 15 acres (though see Faull and Moorhouse (eds.) 1981, 240-1).
2. *BL* Add Ch 12631.
3. Goodall 1953, 69.
4. Clay (ed.) 1932, 97.
5. Goodall 1953, 94.
6. Clay (ed.) 1932, 98.
7. Clay (ed.) 1932, 98-9.
8. Clay (ed.) 1932, 99.
9. Goodall 1953, 58-9.
10. Clay (ed.) 1932, 100.
11. Clay (ed.) 1932, 100.
12. Clay (ed.) 1932, 101-2.
13. Goodall 1953, 129.
14. *Bretton* BEA/C2/B7/19.
15. *YAS* DD 70/9/11 and 12.
16. *YAS* DD 70/9/9.
17. Evans and Lawrence 1979, 136-7.
18. *WYAS SMR*.
19. Hanson 1923, nos 75 and 76.
20. Cadman 1930, 118-9.
21. *WYAS K* DD/CA/6.
22. Goodall 1953, 191-2.
23. *BL* Add Ch 12631.
24. Goodall 1953, 191.
25. Goodall 1953, 191.
26. Clay (ed.) 1932, 98.
27. Clay (ed.) 1932, 118, 46, 100; see chapter 3.
28. *YAS* DD 70/1.
29. *YAS* DD 70/6/23.
30. *YAS* DD 70/1.
31. Goodall 1953, 163; Thompson 1925, 171.
32. *WYAS K* DD/HS/J/8.
33. *Bretton* BEA/C2/B21/1.
34. *WYAS L* HS 976.
35. Cadman 1930, 126.
36. *WYAS L* HS.
37. Cadman 1930, 119 and 181.
38. Cadman 1930, 182-3.
39. For information about Sisters' Houses we are grateful to Mr John Holroyd and Mr Steve McGlynn.
40. Baines 1822, 509.
41. Cradock 1933, 74-6; Cadman 1930, 180-4.
42. Thought previously to have been a depiction of Gomersal Hall (Cookson 1988, 40).
43. Lloyd 1955, 1-5.
44. Lloyd 1955, 7.
45. *WYAS L* DB/M/670/4.
46. Lloyd 1955, 6.
47. See Ibbetson maps of 1714 and 1798, and Ordnance Survey; this building can be seen behind Gomersal House in Fig. 36.
48. *WYAS C* FW:179/1 and /3.

Chapter 5

GREAT GOMERSAL

The area from Hill Top to Moor Lane formed the heart of what was known as Great Gomersal. It is still rather majestic, with a broad turnpike running north to south, high boundary walls and many stands of mature trees. The general impression is that of a quiet retreat. Most of these features are of nineteenth century origin: the turnpike was completed in 1826, successor to a much older road; the walls and trees usually belong to one of several large houses of the period, or to older houses, such as Pollard Hall, which were protected by their owners from the increasing intrusion of the main road. But this is not a complete picture. Nineteenth century developments were generally original and permanent; nevertheless they occurred against the background of an earlier settlement pattern and alongside several houses dating from at least the seventeenth century. Many of the latter were yeoman establishments, standing at the head of a medieval field system and with agricultural buildings nearby. These earlier features have survived much better than in many towns and villages of the West Riding, contributing as much as the eighteenth and nineteenth centuries did to the appearance of modern Gomersal.

Origins

Until recent times Great Gomersal was a dispersed settlement. Its population was not small but it was distributed over a wide area, both along the ridge of the hill and to the west. The pattern is not as dispersed as that found in the Calder Valley (where settlements are really scatters of farmsteads) but Great Gomersal possessed no obvious nucleus. Today, the area where Moor Lane joins Knowles Lane seems to be the village centre. But most of the development along Moor Lane is of nineteenth century date; Hill Top, where the main road from Leeds to Elland left the village, may have been equally prominent before this time. Moreover,

most public building graced neither Hill Top nor the Moor Lane area.

Although relatively dispersed and lacking a centrally located church or manor, the present layout of the

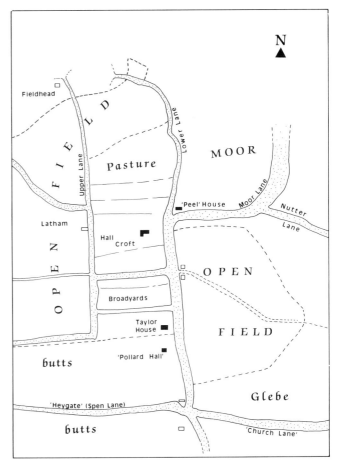

Figure 43: *Great Gomersal: possible layout of the medieval village*

61

village, like that of Little Gomersal, owes a great deal to land use in the medieval period (Fig. 43). Narrow land divisions on the western side of Oxford Road were very probably crofts which supported the domestic activities of medieval farmers. Place names between West Lane and Birdacre, such as Croft and Broadyards, are especially evocative of the open field system.[1] Just to the north of West Lane is the most likely site of the 'manor house' of Great Gomersal.

The village's medieval open field must have occupied a large proportion of the land west of Latham Lane. Here are several hundred acres laid out in broad strips, many names of which appear in sixteenth and seventeenth century documents. There is insufficient land elsewhere in the village to accommodate the fields of an agricultural settlement; and there is no question that arable farming was practised in Great Gomersal on a considerable scale.

A more contentious issue is the extent of the open field. From seventeenth century references, it appears that the fields east of Oxford Road were either part of, or comprised the whole of, what was known as 'Gummersall Field'. This area may also have been open field, as far as its boundary with the Oakwell estate. The demesne land of Oakwell manor must have extended as far west as the fields known as Park Oaks; and other land in this area, called Breaks and Scotland, was given on lease by the Batts in the mid seventeenth century.[2] Immediately to the north of Gomersal Field, the large tracts between Moor Lane and Knowles Lane (and, further eastwards, traversed by Moor Lane) were 'wastes', that is unenclosed moorland where communal grazing was available. To the south were the main church glebelands. A contrasting pattern of larger, irregular fields is still discernible in this area. Then we come to Church Lane (which may have had a medieval origin) and the Popeley lands, discussed in chapter 3.

In short, the basic plan of the village was probably as depicted in figure 43. The cottages and crofts occupied land between what is now Grove Lane (formerly Dark Lane) and, to the north, the junction of Drub Lane and Latham Lane. Roads to the east and west of these crofts, namely Oxford Road and Latham Lane, were, respectively, the front lane and back lane of the village.

In Birstall, and on the Popeley lands, enclosure of moors and open field took place in a limited fashion as early as the fifteenth century (see chapter 3). Sometimes law suits were begun to have the new boundaries removed, though presumably some altered boundaries would have gone unchallenged. Similar piecemeal enclosure probably occurred in Great Gomersal. There is, however, no evidence of comprehensive enclosure before the seventeenth century, and even then the documents are slightly ambiguous. The clearest suggestion is found in the dealings of the Taylor family, concerning their lands in the Cliffe Lane area (see below). This land, however, may have been beyond the southern boundary of the open field. A survey of Sir Thomas Norcliffe's lands taken in 1649[3] is perhaps more informative. It lists over twenty fields, many lying to the west of Oxford Road and possibly taken from the open field. But it goes on to say that 'Gummersall Field' was divided into a number of 'gates', or strips, suggesting that it may still have been in open cultivation. Norcliffe is said to have had four and a half gates. Other residents, most of whom seem to have lived adjacent to the field, between Moor Lane and the church glebelands, had the rest.[4]

An important question is the degree to which Great Gomersal was a distinct manor in the late medieval period. Much later, in 1805, the Sigston family acquired the largely decorative title of 'Lords of the Manor of Great Gomersal', but its origin is unknown. Given that the manor of 'Oakwell-cum-Gomersal' seems to have encompassed the whole township of Gomersal, including large tracts of Great Gomersal (see chapter 2), the only possibility worthy of serious contemplation is that a sub-manor existed. There was a substantial estate in the village, centred on the area now occupied by Gomersal Hall. In the late sixteenth and early seventeenth centuries this was held by Sir Thomas

Norcliffe of Carlinghow;[5] by the early eighteenth century it had passed to the Hewitt family of Craven. However, neither of these owners described themselves as lords of a manor in Great Gomersal. When the survey of Norcliffe's lands, made in 1649, talks of lands 'in the Lordship of Gomersal' it is probably referring to the lordship of the whole township, which at that time was still with the Batts. It is possible that the Sigstons introduced the notion of a local sub-manor in order to lay claim to the common land lying on either side of Moor Lane, although the deed transferring land to them suggested that a 'lordship or reputed manor or lordship of Great Gomersal' had existed before 1805.[6] The Sigstons did build speculative housing on this former common land in the early nineteenth century, though these were not the first houses on Moor Lane.

It is equally uncertain whether there was ever a medieval house in Great Gomersal which could correctly be called a manor house. If there was, it was most likely situated in the vicinity of Gomersal Hall; it was part of the large Norcliffe estate and in the nineteenth century was said to be a house of some antiquity. Plans drawn early that century show a house of hall and cross-wings arrangement, a style in use in the seventeenth century or earlier. The only other possible candidate for manor house is Peel House, which was called such by Pevsner. He does not cite any authority for this proposition, although Peel House does incorporate some late medieval timber framing and may, in part at least, be of the requisite age.[7]

Several Estates: 1550-1850

Whether or not a sub-manor existed, by the late sixteenth century there were several significant landowners in Great Gomersal in addition to the manorial lord at Oakwell. The best documented are the Taylor and Norcliffe families, both of whom acquired many acres of farmland, and a number of houses, as freeholders.[8]

One of the earliest references to the Taylors is in 1537, when one 'Robert Morreson of Scoles' conveyed a property in 'Gomersaule Magna' to a Richard Taylyor.[9] The property included a house, garden and croft, at that time occupied by one Thomas Fernley. In 1546, Richard Taylor was released from some manorial obligations (presumably in respect of the land recently acquired) by Sir Charles Brandon. In 1550, Brandon then conveyed to Taylor

> a parcel of land in the east of Fosden Clough near the way leading from Heygate Lane [the high road, possibly the medieval name for Spen Lane] to nether bawson cliff.[10]

Only about an acre of land seems to have been conveyed, but the deed is significant in that it locates the property accurately, and suggests that by the sixteenth century the Taylors were already acquiring an estate to the west of Oxford Road. Lower Bawson Cliffe was a name still in use in the mid nineteenth century, when the Gomersal valuation and tithe maps were drawn; it was shown to the north of Cliffe Lane, opposite the latter's junction with Fusden Lane.

In 1577, one James Hemingway of Gomersal, a clothier, sold to Thomas Tailer (probably Richard's father), described as a chapman [merchant], more lands in both 'nether and over bawson cliff'.[11] Moreover, Hemingway is said to have bought the lands from Thomas Hussey, sometime lord of the manor at Oakwell, and it seems likely that the fields had only recently been released from the manorial holding. Cradock believes that Hussey may have sold lands to finance his part in the northern rebellion of 1569.[12]

In 1577 there were probably three Taylor brothers; in order of seniority, these were Thomas, William and James.[13] During the minority of Thomas's sons the family inheritance first came to William (died 1589), and afterwards to James. Other fields were added to the estate during James's tenure, though these were at the northern end of the village in the area known as Langley Moor. In 1604/5, Thomas's estate was, as anticipated, conveyed to his sons William and James. It comprised 'a messuage, a cottage and thirty acres of land',[14] and probably included the site of Red House. This estate was the mainstay of the Taylors' influence in Gomersal over the next three hundred years.

There was, however, a much larger holding which was also quite separate from the manorial lands. This was the estate of the Norcliffe family. The Norcliffes are first encountered in Gomersal in 1574, when one Thomas Norclyff had a daughter baptised at Birstall. In 1596, when a son was born to the same Thomas, he was referred to in the parish register as 'Mr Norclyff', a title denoting high social status.[15] By 1612, at the time of Dugdale's visitation, we are told that Norcliffe had received a grant of arms in 1606.[16] In all these documents, Norcliffe is said to be of Great Gomersal, and he was clearly one of the leading men of the village at this time.

Like the Taylors, Norcliffe benefited from the sales of Thomas Hussey. In 1565 the latter had sold a large estate to Cudbert Breare, one of his tenants in Great Gomersal.[17] Again it was a freehold sale, but this time detaching a far larger part of the manorial lands than did the sale to the Taylors. The Breares held the estate until 1579/80, when John Breare sold it to Thomas Norcliffe, at the time said to be of Carlinghow.[18] The conveyance refers to:

the messuage, tenement and farmhouse ... in Gomersal ... and one lathe or barne, one oxhouse and all other houses edifices and buildings ... [including fields known as] Calf Croft, Great Wheatclose, Nether Wheat Close, Faldingworth, Wheatley, New Roide, Great Brannyecroft, Bawson Cliffe and Thornwell.[19]

This is the same Thomas Norcliffe recorded by Dugdale. By his purchase in 1579, he acquired an estate whose constituent parts are still identifiable. Wheatleys is to the north of Moor Lane; the Wheat Closes lie to the east of Oxford Road, opposite Red House; Branny Croft is along Drub Lane, and Bawson Cliffe is part of a large area lying either side of Cliffe Lane. The estate, therefore, was extensive, an idea supported by a survey of the lands of Sir Thomas Norcliffe (grandson to Thomas Norcliffe of Gomersal) taken in 1649. Sir Thomas had moved to Langton, North Yorkshire, but

still owned over thirty fields in Gomersal amounting to 137 acres (including eighteen acres in Birstall).[20]

The survey of 1649 is worth considering in a little more detail. First, it refers to 'the Hall, barne and mag crofte ing'. Mag Croft Ing is just to the north of West Lane and within the grounds of the present Gomersal Hall. There can be little doubt that the hall referred to is an early predecessor of Gomersal Hall. It is very likely that the Norcliffes had lived here when in Gomersal; by the time of the survey, however, it was tenanted by Thomas Taylor and one John Birkhead. Secondly, especially when considered along with surviving tax lists of the period,[21] the survey is a rich source for the names of Gomersal residents living at the centre of Great Gomersal (where most of Norcliffe's lands were situated). Taylor and Birkhead are listed at the hall; others recorded as holding land in Gomersal Field, though not as tenants to Norcliffe, were Mr Peele, Widow Fearnley, James Talor, Mr Pollard and Widow Kitson. The tax list of 1641 has entries for all these people, and records the Taylors immediately after the Birkhead family, lending weight to the statement in the survey that those families were in joint occupation of Gomersal Hall.

James Taylor and his sons William and Thomas 'the younger' were apparently living at the hall in 1641, as they were recorded next to the Birkheads in the tax list; as far as we can establish, the list was arranged in topographical order. By 1649 James Taylor may have moved, probably to the old house known to have existed next to the Red House site. The Thomas Taylor who lived in Gomersal Hall in 1649 was probably not James's younger son, who had been given property at Latham on his marriage in 1646; it may have been one of two other Thomas Taylors recorded in Great Gomersal in 1641.

Sir Thomas Norcliffe, unlike the Taylors or the first Thomas Norcliffe, was an absentee landlord. The 1649 survey was taken in preparation for a sale of the estate to one Matthew Hewitt of Linton-in-Craven, North Yorkshire. A conveyance of 1652/3 recited the familiar list of field names, a 'house' still in the occupation of the

Taylors and Birkheads, and six cottages.[22] This seems to have ended the Norcliffe family's association with Gomersal.

The new owner does not appear ever to have lived locally. He is not mentioned in the tax lists, Birstall Church pew lists or the Birstall parish registers. This did not prevent him acquiring further property in the village, including a field called Breary Royd and a place known as Fearnley Farm whose location is now uncertain. He also bought several 'lands' lying in 'Great Gomersall Towne and Moore Lane beginning at the house of William Webster unto the stone causey leading between Halifax and Leeds at the way out of Gomersall'.[23]

We do not know how long Hewitt retained his Great Gomersal estate. From an eighteenth century copy of the original Norcliffe survey, it seems that he and his heirs were still in possession well after 1700. The estate certainly remained intact through the eighteenth century. A remarkable map of 1732, by John Topham, shows that most of the lands acquired by Matthew Hewitt continued as part of the same holding (Fig. 44). The map does not refer to the Hewitt family and so we cannot be sure that the lands were still in their ownership by this date; in fact, they may by then have been owned by a family called Terry. The executors of one Leonard Terry, a York woollen draper who had spent his last years in Gomersal, sold the property in 1805 to the Sigstons.[24] Interestingly, the estate carved out of the Manor of Gomersal by Hussey in 1565 remained substantially together into the mid nineteenth century. Along with the Taylor lands, it was one of the earliest estates to stand apart from the holding of the local lord.

Other sales did occur, however, in the 1640s and 1650s when John Batt was making amends for his early support of the Royal cause. One such was a small but valuable property sold to Richard Peel (the first of that name); another may have been the site and grounds of Pollard Hall.

In the mid seventeenth century, the Batt family still had lands throughout Gomersal, as even a cursory examination of their

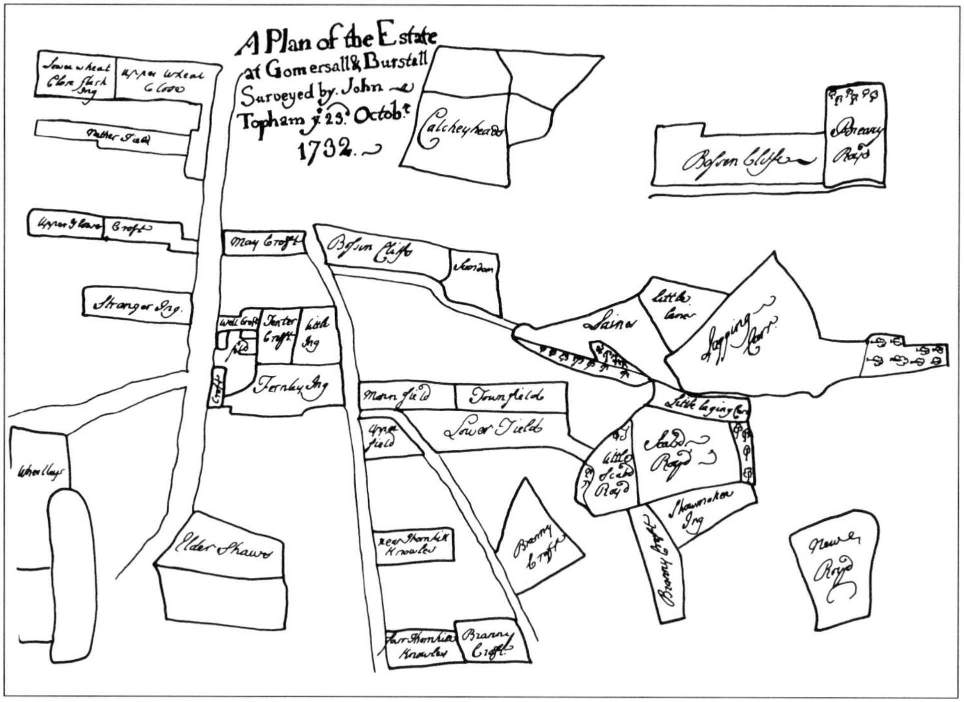

Figure 44: *Estate Map by John Topham 1732: the lanes running top to bottom are the forerunner of Oxford Road (which continued into Knowles Lane, with Moor Lane branching off to the left); and Latham Lane, with Ferrands Lane and Drub Lane branching off right. Gomersal Hall is between the two main lanes, below Well Croft. (YAS MD 132/B4 reproduced by kind permission of the Yorkshire Archaeological Society).*

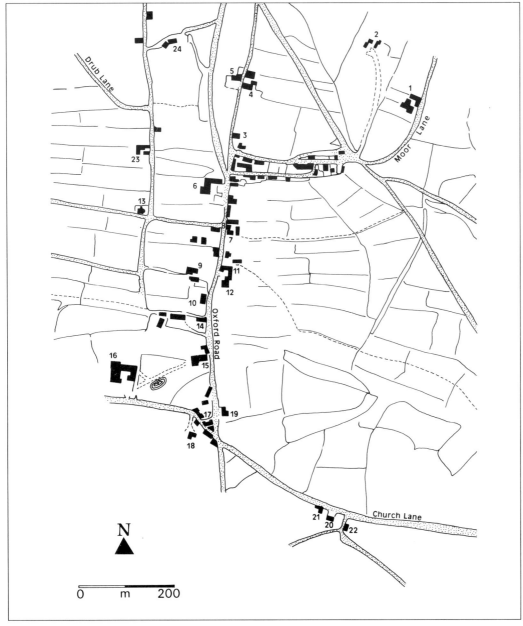

Key:

1. Moor Lane House
2. Wheatleys
3. Peel House
4. Low House
   (Richmond Grange)
5. Tenlands
6. Gomersal Hall
   (before c.1860)
7. Sigston House
8. Cross House
9. Broadyards
10. Mechanics' Institute
    (Public Hall)
11. Grove Square
12. Grove Chapel
13. Gomersal
    Methodist Chapel
14. Red House
15. Pollard Hall
16. Cloth Hall
    (Gomersal Mills)
17. Gomers Hall
18. Hill Top House
19. The White Horse
20. Laneside Farm
21. Laneside House
22. Gomersal
    Workhouse
23. Latham Hall
24. West House

N

Map D: Great Gomersal: location of principal buildings

surviving estate papers testifies.[25] But they cannot have dominated the township in the way that lords of the manor often did at that time in other Yorkshire villages, especially on the arable lands in the east of the county. Whatever the position in the late medieval period, by the mid seventeenth century several sizable and relatively independent landholders were to be found in Great Gomersal. This was in addition to the glebelands and Popeley, each already covering extensive areas to the south. All of these landholders were better placed than most to take advantage of the religious and political upheavals which had occurred, and the social and economic changes which were to follow. The effects of these new circumstances upon Great Gomersal are best appreciated by studying the wealth of new building which dates from the period.

Buildings 1650-1850

There is a wide range of architectural remains in Great Gomersal, from imposing houses and chapels to early industrial buildings and cottages. Like Cadman, we have arranged our survey in a topographical form, beginning with Peel House, often considered the centre piece of the village, and moving on to the various buildings along Oxford Road, as far as Hill Top, and from there to Fieldhead, Laneside and other outlying parts.

Figure 45: *Peel House: southern elevation*

Peel House

Peel House is one of Gomersal's best known sights, its photograph gracing many books and articles on local and textile history. It is at the junction of old routes, in the very centre of the medieval settlement. A few yards away were Gomersal Hall and most of the cottages of the medieval village.

The present appearance of the house is seventeenth century, but it is very likely that an older building stood on the site. A survey in 1979 revealed parts of an earlier structure.[26] The previous house was probably timber-framed, and of the early or middle sixteenth century, though it could have been an aisled house built of stone. This older house was of at least three bays and part of it spread further west than the present house.

There are now two doors on the front of Peel House; the western one is the original door of the seventeenth century building. The house is built of coursed rubble, more vernacular in style than some grander local halls, but nonetheless the impression is imposing. The front has three gables, each with two-light mullions in the angles, similar to those at Pollard Hall. The transomed mullions of the ground floor have a continuous drip mould running over them, rising over a higher west window.

The house was extensively altered internally in the nineteenth century. However, some fine original features survive, including a plaster ceiling in the eastern parlour, which incorporates heraldic shields, several large female figures, and a date of 1651. The main front door opened into a housebody, the largest room; this retains its fireplace, with an elaborately carved wooden surround and overmantel.

Like Pollard Hall, Peel House takes its name from a seventeenth century inhabitant. Peel was a common name in the parish register, but the first reference to Richard Peel of Gomersal was not until 1640, when a daughter of his was baptised.[27] Richard Peel and his wife Mercy were in the Great Gomersal list of taxpayers in

1641, taxed at two shillings, indicating their relative affluence.[28] In 1649 Peel bought the 'capitall messuage' of which he had been tenant, for £690 from John Batt of Oakwell.[29] It is most likely that he had lived there since his arrival in Gomersal in 1640 or just before. The sale document named the previous tenants as Samuel West and Jane West. These Wests can be found in various documents of the early seventeenth century, though nothing more is revealed about the house in which they lived. In 1626 a son of Samuel West of Gomersal was buried at Birstall; Samuel West himself was listed as a tenant of John Batt in 1630;[30] finally, Mrs West, widow, of Gomersal, was buried on Christmas Day 1637 and that was probably the end of the Wests' connection with the village.

The date of 1651 in the plaster ceiling suggests that Peel transformed his house soon after buying it from Batt. Peel was of the yeoman class and was involved in both cloth-making and farming. The house became a centre of both these activities. Richard and Mercy Peel had six children, the fourth being another Richard (1645-1699). After Mercy died in 1658, Peel quickly remarried. His second wife was also Mercy, a widow from Adwalton called Mercy Brooke. Some of the financial agreements survive from the time of this marriage, and Peel looked set to benefit financially from the match as Mercy

Figure 46: *Peel House: western gables*

Brooke had considerable property in her home village. After the death of the elder Richard Peel in 1668, Mercy retired to Adwalton. An arrangement was made whereby Richard Peel the younger, her stepson, received £230 by mortgaging her Drighlington house and fields; in return he was granted a lease on the property for which he would pay her £12 a year.[31] This device was the means of guaranteeing an income for Mercy in her widowhood. It also provided cash for Peel, who was in debt for most or all of his adult life, possibly as a result of his father's extravagance in building Peel House. This house, with ten hearths, was second only to Oakwell Hall in the township in the number of fireplaces it had in 1684.[32] It had been built with great attention to personal comfort, as shown by the number of separate apartments, most of them heated. This was quite a modern arrangement at the time.[33]

Like his father, Peel was engaged in both textiles and agriculture. He took a seven year lease on four fields called 'Parke Oake Ings and Munke Ings', between Birstall Church and Oakwell, in 1681. At £25 a year this must have been an extensive holding. The agreement referred to him as a 'cloathworker'.[34]

The younger Richard Peel's matrimonial experiences echoed those of his father. His first wife Ann (or Agnes) Brooke bore him four children; the youngest, George (baptised 1672, alive 1725), was his heir. After Ann's death in 1674, Richard was soon remarried to a woman of the same name. This Anne (or Anna) Liversige, a widow, whom he married in Halifax in 1675, outlived him. A son, Richard, was born in 1676 but must have died young as he was not mentioned in his father's will.[35]

Richard died within days of making this will in April 1699.[36] The will and an inventory of the contents of his house taken in the same month show two things. First, the house was comfortably, even luxuriously, furnished with items which would have been found in few Gomersal homes of the time – linen, pewter, silver, a clock and mirrors. Secondly, Peel was in so much debt that he could not leave his house to his son; it had to be sold to pay off a large mortgage.

In Peel's inventory the housebody was the first room described. Its contents were:

one table long with two forms; one litle square table; two great Inlade chairs; Four other chairs; one Long settle and a Childes chair; One Clock; Six sett cushions and two woven cushions; one Range 2 end Irons with 2 Curtaine Rodds and 2 Curtaines; one Old Musquett and one old sword.

The dining room held a number of tables, some with carpets on them, cushions, chairs and a 'seeing glass'. The upper parlour had a bed and various tables and chairs. Peel's own lodging room was well equipped with chests, cupboards, boxes, cushions and curtains. Other chambers were over the housebody and above the dining room, and a fourth was called the Little Chamber. There were three cellars, one of which adjoined the dairy; a pantry, kitchen and back kitchen, and two servants' rooms. These latter, a maidservants' lodging room with two beds and menservants' room with three beds, were some of the few rooms in the house which lacked hearths.

A further room called the chamber over the kitchen was not used as a bedroom but provided storage for some of the large quantity of foodstuffs which such a household would have needed to keep over winter. A number of arks, or great chests, held oatmeal, beef, bacon, meal, horse corn and salt.

The tools and equipment of Peel's trade were kept 'i'th shopp' and adjacent premises, presumably behind the house. Above the cropping and finishing shop was a loom chamber, and Peel also had a dyehouse. The shop held cloth presses with boards and papers, cropping shears and shearboards for cloth finishing. In the chamber above were pieces of blue and black cloth, 'a cloth i'th Looms', other looms, weft yarn and a cloth press.

Possessions outdoors included farming equipment – carts, ploughs, animals, troughs and so on – and a pair of tenter frames to dry woollen cloth. The crops sowed in the fields were thirteen days' ploughing of oats, six of hardcorn, three and a half of peas and two of beans. There was also £5 worth of 'manure in the fold'.

Peel's movable possessions were estimated to be worth £252. Added to that was £70 for debts owing. However the will showed a picture which was rather less rosy.[37] Peel was able to leave some estate outright to his son George – a house in Pinfold Lane (probably Moor Lane) which had been let to Erasmus Fallon, and two fields called the Further Toft Ing and Thornhill Knowle. Everything else was to be sold, his debts settled, and £250 set aside, firstly to provide for his widow and after her death to be divided between various family members. Peel had been anxious that George should not be forced to sell his part of the legacy to settle debts which the father and son had incurred together in their business partnership. He said that any such joint debts must be paid from the £250 so that George did not lose his property. Peel signed the will on 6 April 1699 and had died within three weeks.

The following year, 1700, saw the sale of Peel's estate. Four houses, four cottages, 25 acres of land, 10 acres of meadow and 20 acres of pasture and common were sold as one lot to Daniel Greenwood of Northampton, Doctor of Physic, for £840. Of this, £600 was immediately paid

Figure 47: *Low House: window details on northern elevation*

over to the heirs of William Greene of Liversedge, gentleman, to discharge the mortgage on the property. Greenwood, who bought other land in Gomersal in the same year from George Peel and his wife Mary for £100, remained an absentee landlord. It seems that much of Greenwood's Gomersal estate was let back to Peel and to John Taylor. George Peel may have continued to live in Peel House until 1725 or later. After that date, the houses and land passed to the ownership of Greenwood's heirs, and were recorded in the estate of one Lancelot Rolleston of Nottinghamshire in 1814.[38]

The 1841 census showed a cloth manufacturer called Thomas Pearson as resident of 'Peel's House'. But by 1861 the old house had moved down-market and was sub-divided and subjected to piecemeal alterations. Part of it was home to a cardmaker and his family, and another part to a washerwoman, an elderly widow who was described as the 'keeper of a mangle'. It must have been during these years that some of the internal alterations took place. On the 1890 Ordnance Survey map, Peel House appears to be divided into three. It was said to be 'occupied as two Dwelling Houses by Mr Thomas Tetley and others' when sold as part of The Wheatleys estate in 1900.[39]

In spite of such vicissitudes, Peel House is still a very evocative piece of seventeenth century architecture. For an indication of what might have happened had the pressures on it been greater, one has only to consider the remains of a house some two hundred yards to the north, on the eastern side of Knowles Lane. Here, in the yard to what is now a factory complex, stood another seventeenth century stone house, Lower or Low House, later known as Richmond Grange. The stonework was superior to that of Peel House and similar mullion sets are preserved in various places, sometimes displaced from their original positions (Fig 47). But only the façade and a few courses of internal stonework now survive. The southern elevation was rebuilt, probably in the eighteenth century (Fig. 48), and on the western side a warehouse of about 1800 (similar in form to that near Gomersal House, Little Gomersal) was keyed into the old structure. In recent years the whole interior of

Figure 48: *Richmond Grange, formerly Low House: southern façade (KCS RH4/48)*

the house, including a massive wall post, was removed to make way for open plan offices.

For many years Peel House must have been the only notable house at the head of Moor Lane. This lane was important both as a drove road to the communal grazing lands and as the main northern way out of the village. A map of 1809 (Fig. 49) shows Moor Lane to have been very wide, following a line which was still visible on the Gomersal tithe map and the first edition Ordnance Survey. The disposition of cottages along the lane is also of interest, in that they follow no particular alignment and are set at a distance from one another. There was no attempt to create a uniform street frontage. In fact, the pattern of development on the north side of the road was random, still visible in the position of early nineteenth century cottages there. Earlier writers believed that the Sigstons were responsible for this 'ribbon development'[40] but the cottages are of very different styles and look to be a little older than of the early years of the nineteenth century. The Sigstons probably acquired the property when some building had already taken place on this land.

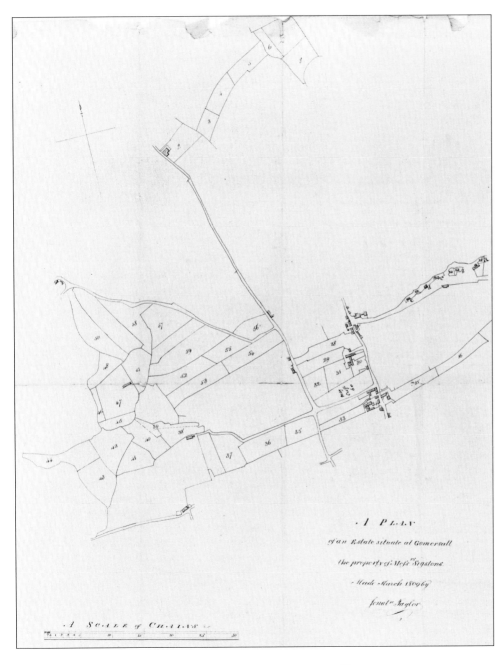

Figure 49: *Sigstons' estate in 1809; Latham Lane runs north-south, with Drub Lane and Ferrands Lane off to the west. Plot 30 includes the old Gomersal Hall and Plot 34 has buildings on the site of what is now Croft House. To the east, a number of cottages have been built on the rather loosely defined area of Moor Lane (WYAS K KC52 Sigston 2/2; reproduced by kind permission of WYAS Kirklees).*

Figure 50: *House on the north side of Moor Lane*

Figure 52: *Piecemeal development on the south side of Moor Lane. Number 2 is the double-fronted house on the right of the picture*

Figure 51: *Number 20 Moor Lane*

Figure 50 shows a typical example of the vernacular building style on the northern side of Moor Lane. Coursed rubble walls support stone slated roofs. Sills, lintels and other door and window surrounds are of flat-faced, single pieces of stone.

Of course, an estate map was never intended to show all the property in an area but only that owned by the person who commissioned the map. In 1800 some of the

present day houses on the south side of Moor Lane were also standing. One of the oldest here is number 20: the window surrounds and stone coursing closely resemble those of some of the cottages on the northern side of the road (Fig. 51). Number 2, opposite Peel House is equally worthy of note. Its raised ('rusticated') quoins and flat mullions are evidence of a date between about 1780 and 1820 (Fig. 52).

On the southern side houses used similar materials to those on the northern side of the road, but occasionally with more refinements. Number 6 Moor Lane, for example, is of well-dressed stone and has a fanlight above the door and a bay window. It was probably built in about 1840. Numbers 8 and 8A are slightly earlier, possibly of about 1820, and are clearly more modest. Numbers 10-18 were all built at about this time, by a landlord called Hirst.[41] It was in the early nineteenth century, therefore, that Moor Lane acquired its terraced appearance on the south side.

At the lower end of Moor Lane is a row of cottages built at right angles to the road (numbers 72-78). At one time in their history these were known as 'Shoddy Row' and comprised eight back-to-back dwellings. Why they should be set at right angles to the road is a mystery, though it might indicate that when the block was constructed the eastern end of Moor Lane was not considered part of the street frontage. Perhaps the name 'Shoddy' betokens a link with wool recycling. There is a taking-in door in the northern gable. In style the whole row is very similar to the Workhouse on Church Lane (Fig. 11), and it may also date from the late eighteenth century. For their height both buildings are very wide, a design which provided the maximum amount of space. It is possible that materials were brought in through the door in Moor Lane and moved down the whole length of the building. This suggests that people living in separate dwellings may have worked communally in the attic or first floor of the building. Such a business presents a very great contrast to that of Francis Beaumont, who

built the large wool warehouse across the road (now Stevenson's dance school) in about 1825.[12]

Several other buildings at the eastern end of Moor Lane deserve a brief mention. First is a semi-octagonal single storey house, now with a rear extension (number 84). This may have been a toll house for the turnpike traffic on what is now Bradford Road, though it stands back a long way from the road. It seems more likely to have been the lodge to a large house in grounds behind, obliterated when the railway was built in the closing years of the nineteenth century.

Across Bradford Road is another house with all the appearances of a toll house. It was, however, the gatehouse to a large house known as Wheatleys or Wheatleys Hall, built in about 1805 on a field of that name for Thomas Walker of Popeley.[13] The gatehouse is a single storey building in dressed stone. It has recently been refurbished and extended. The main house (now demolished) had more than twenty rooms, bay windows on the south side and was enclosed by large gardens. In 1876, when Cudworth was writing, Wheatleys was in the hands of William Ackroyd, a wealthy worsted spinner from Birkenshaw. In 1900 the house was auctioned and some well-drawn plans prepared.[14]

Figure 53: *Moor Lane in about 1900; on the right is the Primitive Methodists' Chapel (KCS)*

Another large house adjacent to where Wheatleys stood was Moor Lane House, now known as

Gomersal Park Hotel. Judging from its style, it is probably of a slightly earlier date, being simpler in plan and of more coarsely dressed stone than its neighbour. It was nonetheless a significant house in the nineteenth century, when it was owned by the Wormald family. Ellen Nussey died here in 1897.[45]

At the top of Moor Lane is the Shoulder of Mutton public house, the site of a pub and butcher's shop from at least the eighteenth century (see chapter 8). Where the lane meets Oxford Road another row of stone cottages begins. Most of these have experienced fewer alterations than the Shoulder of Mutton, and they provide a good indication of what local domestic architecture looked like in the early nineteenth century. In most cases, the backs of these buildings have changed the least and still possess their original mullions and window surrounds. Most are likely to pre-date the turnpiking of 'Oxford Road' in 1824-25 by the Holme Lane End and Heckmondwike Turnpike Trust. At the southern end of the frontage (number 372 Oxford Road) a couple of old cottages and a weaving shed-cum-workshop are noteworthy. An archway is preserved in the west wall; this was probably once a cart entrance or door where wool was taken in.

Sigston Fold

Sigston Fold was a group of four houses and a great barn in roughly square formation, situated opposite the end of West Lane. Two of the houses have been demolished and the other two much altered, yet the fold retains some of the atmosphere of the old village. As one writer put it, these houses were 'fairly representative of Gomersal as it was in the beginning of the present [nineteenth] century' when the residents of the fold were cloth merchants or manufacturers, Sigstons, Crowthers and Gumersalls.[46] The Sigston connection with these houses dated back into the eighteenth century, though that family had not been responsible for the original buildings.

The main house in the group is still called Sigston House, but the datestone which adorns it is of 1634, long

Figure 54: *Sigston House: southern elevation*

before the Sigstons came to Gomersal. Surviving timbers suggest that the house was rebuilt from an older one. Along with many of the other seventeenth century yeoman houses in the village, Sigston House is at right angles to Oxford Road, and faces south, although it seems never to have had a door on that side. The date 1634 and initials NK are set in an ogee mounted lintel above the central door in the rear wall. This door led into a single storey part of the house, the outshut. There was some logic in having the main door at the back of this house, as it gave access to the fold and ancillary buildings.

Major alterations took place in the mid eighteenth century, perhaps when the Sigstons moved into the property. The outshut was raised to provide more space, and it has been speculated that the roof at the front was heightened at the same time, as the upper windows on that side are eighteenth century in style, contrasting with the seventeenth century mullions in the ground floor (Fig. 54). There were probably always two storeys at the front, however.[47] Because of the raised outshut, the angle of the roof is very different from how it would have been originally.

Sigston House was probably divided into cottages in the nineteenth century, though it is now a single house again. It has suffered some alterations more recently, notably a red tiled roof in place of the original stone slates.[48]

The second house in the fold, now known as Cross House, has also been subjected to drastic modernization, but is now (1992) being rebuilt in a seventeenth century style. The datestone says 1691, but is misleading as it is an import to Gomersal by the new owner of the house. Recent building work has not revealed evidence of any older structure on this site; all the indications are that this was a new house in the mid seventeenth century, although the possibility of an earlier dwelling there cannot be ruled out.[49]

Cross House is a two storey stone house facing west towards Birstall; the main door seems to have been on this side. The orientation of the building, at odds with the general practice in Gomersal at a time when most houses faced south, may explain its name. It was also across the lines of strips in the Gomersal field. There is confusion about the building's original plan because of the amount of later alteration.[50] However, it clearly included the surviving parlour on the south and a large hall with open stairs approached from the main door. A

Figure 56: The barn in Sigston Fold

single storey outshut at the rear probably did not run the full length of the house. It is likely that some rebuilding occurred in the Victorian period when Cross House was divided into cottages.

The third house in Sigston Fold adjoined the great barn and stood on the side of the main road, facing the back of Sigston House. A gable outline can be picked out on the barn's end wall. A photograph has survived from around 1900, which shows that this, believed to be the original Cross House, held the datestone which is now set in a roadside wall on the site (Fig. 55). The stone bears the initials IK and a date of 1659. This Cross House had been converted into a shop by the time that the photograph was taken, and large windows inserted in the gable end, but it had obviously been a yeoman house in the seventeenth century. It bore the familiar features of chamfered mullions, continuous dripmould and single storey outshut to the rear. A small arched window in the west wall resembled that at Egypt Farm. This was the building called Cross House by earlier writers.[51]

Figure 55: *The former Cross House, now demolished (KCS)*

Across the main road, on the corner of West Lane, stood the fourth house, sometimes called Poplar Farm. This building, probably of the early eighteenth century, was demolished in the 1980s. Cadman says that it was once the property of James Boden and was sold at auction after his death in 1775.[52]

The barn in Sigston Fold is large and plain in style, though the central bay projects slightly. At either end, at first floor level, are circular window openings. Massive arched doorways front and rear gave access and egress to loaded carts (Fig. 56). There would have been plenty of room to manoeuvre a cart from the road into the barn, as Sigston Fold was open; the boundary wall which now divides it is relatively new. The barn, with stone quoins and a stone slate roof, is probably eighteenth century. It may be the only part of the fold actually built by the Sigstons.

It has long been speculated that Sigston House was built by Nicholas Kitson, and the original Cross House by another member of his family, probably a John Kitson (as a carved I generally stood for J).[53] The Kitsons of Gomersal seem to have been an offshoot of a prominent Cleckheaton family; there were Kitsons in Cleckheaton and Liversedge in the sixteenth century, the main branch settling at Syke Fold, Liversedge, early in the 1600s.[54] Kitsons were tenants of Popeley properties in Cleckheaton at that time, and a reference to Kitson House, Cleckheaton, owned by Francis Popeley, is to be found in the 1634 pew list for Birstall Church.[55]

The first firm link between these Kitsons and Gomersal is found in a deed of 1589 when fields called Clarke roids and le legge were transferred to John Kitson senior of Cleckheaton, and Nicholas his younger son.[56] A generation later, in 1627, John Kitson senior and John Kitson junior appeared on a list of freeholders in Oakwell manor, though it is impossible to tell from this whether it was houses or land which they owned. On the same list a Nicholas Kitson (who is unlikely to have been the same man mentioned in 1589) was shown as tenant of thirty acres in the manor.[57] An equivalent list for 1630 had John Kitson and Nicholas Kitson as Gomersal freeholders.[58] In 1630 Nicholas Kitson of Gomersal was fined for refusing a knighthood. From this it could be inferred that he was a wealthy man, as

the offer of a knighthood was really a tax on the better-off.[59] In the 1634 pew list of Birstall Church Nicholas Kitson was recorded as paying for a stall for his 'hill ten[emen]ts' and further seats for 'hall ten[emen]ts'.[60] Nicholas and his wife Elizabeth were also the only Kitsons listed in the Great Gomersal section of the 1641 tax list. As with other wealthy people in the village, the amount of tax paid was not specified.[61]

Nicholas had died by 1650.[62] He left two sons, John (baptised in 1636, and who in 1662 was a churchwarden at Birstall), and Thomas, both of whom lived in Gomersal. It was probably this John who built Cross House in 1659; Thomas may have inherited the Sigston house from their father. In 1663 the brothers were involved in an exchange of lands when Thomas gave John two closes called Brearyroyds along with £54 and received land in Gomersal called Littlemoors.[63] John then seems to have mortgaged three closes called Brearyroyd to the Batts of Howroyd in 1670 and again in 1679.[64] Both brothers appeared as householders in the 1672 Hearth Tax, John Kitson having three hearths.

John's eldest son, another John, made an advantageous marriage in 1690 to Mary Scatcherd of Morley. The Kitsons of Gomersal, though well off, were always referred to as yeomen. They were apparently farmers, and no record of their being clothworkers or merchants has been seen. Mary's father Matthew was also sometimes described as a yeoman, but elsewhere was said to be 'a rich man' and son of 'an opulent merchant'.[65] A pre-nuptial agreement was drawn up in 1690, when the old John Kitson's house (presumably Cross House) and twenty acres of land were pledged to the younger John and his bride. If there were no children of the match, the property was to revert to the younger John's brother, Nicholas.[66]

The elder John Kitson, builder of Cross House, died in 1715, an old man of nearly eighty. His will made provision for his widow and younger son, Nicholas, and small bequests to five married women who were apparently his daughters. The main part of the estate went to his elder son, John. The probate inventory dated November 1715[67] confirms that his house was a farmhouse and there is no reference to any textile activities there at the time. That the document does relate to the original Cross House is likely, though the owner of the present Cross House says that the number and type of rooms tally with those in his house. The main rooms described were the housebody, furnished with chair, tables, cushions, a brass clock and case; a Great Parlour, containing cupboards and a desk with various chairs and buffets; a Little Parlour with chests and bedding; a North Parlour, and two chambers. It appears that there was also a kitchen, a milkhouse and a laith (barn), with the usual farming equipment and animals. John Kitson's valuables included a silver cup and spoon, and 32 lb. of pewter. The total value of his goods was estimated to be £38 14s. 6d.

The younger John Kitson appears to have made his home at Syke, on the Liversedge/Cleckheaton boundary. He was described as a gentleman in a 1721 deed relating to his late father's property in Gomersal.[68] This deed is informative about both the Kitson family and the house, presumably Cross House. Members of the Scatcherd family held the elder Kitson's legacy in trust. It consisted of a messuage in Gomersal 'wherein John Kitson the Elder in his lifetime did inhabit and dwell and all the Outhouses Barnes Buildings Foldsteads Gardens and Orchards ...' along with several closes of land, including the Hall Ings, Breary Royd and Bawson Cliff. Hall Ings is a field adjoining the present Cross House, adding further difficulty to establishing just which house was referred to in the document. The tenants named in the deed were Charles Bellfield, Benjamin Crowther and John Blackburne; one of these men was probably occupying Cross House. John Kitson of Syke had a son, Joshua, apparently unmarried, and a daughter Anne, described as a spinster. Another daughter, Mary, the wife of William Brooke of Wyke, had died leaving three daughters who were to be John Kitson's heirs if Joshua did not have children. What became of John's brother Nicholas, or of his uncle Thomas, is not known.

It was in about 1715 that Joseph Sigston came to Gomersal, but it is not likely that the Sigstons moved into the 1634 house until the middle of the eighteenth century or later, when William Sigston had become head of the family. William and his sons gradually bought up much property in the immediate area. In 1803 they acquired the site of Croft House, which at the time contained a house and several cottages let to Joseph Woodhead and others, along with the field behind which stretched as far as Latham Lane. They also bought fields south west of Sigston Fold, and may already have owned the Poplar Farm buildings at the corner of West Lane.[69] In 1813 they bought a number of Gomersal properties from one Lepton Dobson, a Leeds merchant. The first conveyance included a dwellinghouse with barn, stable, cowhouse, workshop and other outbuildings, occupied by William Crowther. This was probably the original Cross House. There was also a neighbouring cottage with an under-tenant called Robert Darnbrook. The Sigston brothers paid £1,072 for this and another property, Low House on Knowles Lane, with nearby cottages.[70] A separate conveyance from Dobson to the Sigstons transferred two cottages and a close called the Town Field.[71]

William Sigston's sons Joseph and Thomas lived out their lives at Sigston House. The house was eventually subdivided and in 1840 part was rented out as two cottages to William Lee and Edward Gomersall.[72] By 1890 it had been split into three units.[73] Although still in Thomas Sigston's ownership in 1840, Cross House had been let to one John Crowther. There were under-tenants in the property, perhaps in the outbuildings as the uses included a weaving shop and wool chamber.[74]

The Sigstons of Gomersal

The story of the Sigstons is not exactly one of rags to riches, but their origins were relatively humble and they had become among the largest landowners in the village by the 1830s. The founder of this prominent family was Joseph Sigston, a Wakefield clothmaker who married Ruth Taylor of Red House c.1715-1720. Ruth, the fifth of

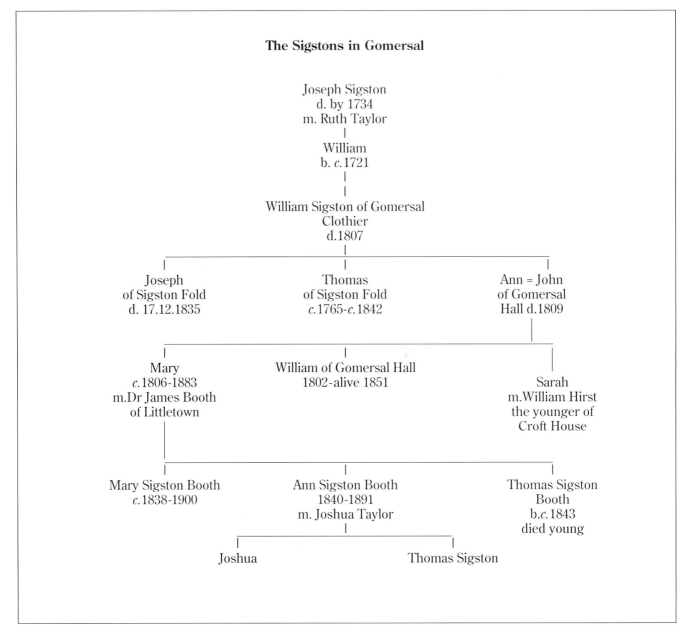

The Sigstons in Gomersal

Joseph Sigston
d. by 1734
m. Ruth Taylor
|
William
b. *c.*1721
|
|
William Sigston of Gomersal
Clothier
d.1807
|

Joseph	Thomas	Ann = John
of Sigston Fold	of Sigston Fold	of Gomersal
d. 17.12.1835	*c.*1765-*c.*1842	Hall d.1809

Mary	William of Gomersal Hall	
*c.*1806-1883	1802-alive 1851	Sarah
m.Dr James Booth		m.William Hirst
of Littletown		the younger of
		Croft House

Mary Sigston Booth	Ann Sigston Booth	Thomas Sigston
*c.*1838-1900	1840-1891	Booth
	m. Joshua Taylor	b.*c.*1843
		died young

Joshua	Thomas Sigston

Figure 57

six daughters of John Taylor (d.1713) received a modest £10 legacy on her father's death.[75]

William, the son of Joseph and Ruth, was bound apprentice to John Charlesworth of Gomersal, clothmaker and clothworker, in March 1734. The term of the apprenticeship was eight years, suggesting that William had been born in about 1721. The indenture was signed by his mother, who had been widowed and remarried, and by his step-father Thomas Teale of Hunsworth.[76] Little is known about the Sigstons in the eighteenth century, though their fortunes were growing. William Sigston, clothier, appears in a record of 1776 [77] and by the turn of the century the family's woollen business was in the hands of Joseph, Thomas and John Sigston, sons of William Sigston who died in 1807. This William was probably the same as the boy who was apprenticed in 1734.

The Sigston brothers by this time were usually referred to as merchants, and had become wealthy. They invested their money in land and houses. John, the only one of the three to marry, lived as a tenant at Gomersal Hall until 1805, when the hall and a large estate were sold by the heirs of Leonard Terry.[78] The three Sigstons bought the major part of this estate, about sixty acres, including Gomersal Hall, Owlet Hall ('a newly erected dwelling house' and workshops), Croft House, the Lordship of the Manor of Great Gomersal and a number of cottages 'built upon the waste' – the uncultivated area around Moor Lane.[79] In addition they inherited their father's dwellinghouse, Sigston House, and other property. The unmarried brothers continued to live at Sigston Fold.

John Sigston died in 1809 leaving a young family. The brothers had divided their property into three parts, presumably anticipating John's death. John appointed Thomas Crowther, scribbling miller, as trustee to look after the interests of his children William (b.1802), Mary (b. c.1806) and Sarah.[80]

The older Sigstons continued to acquire property in Gomersal, including that of Lepton Dobson in 1813 (see above), and in 1821 fields called Brandy Croft and Toft Ing from the heiress of Joshua Walker of Crow Trees.[81] Joseph died in 1835 and Thomas about six years later when nearly eighty. Their property went to John's children, of whom the eldest, William, had been described as a woollen manufacturer in a directory of 1826.[82] By 1830, however, he was said to be William Sigston esquire, lord of the manor, and his uncles were referred to as gentlemen.[83] Census returns show that by 1841 William regarded himself as being of independent means. He lived at Gomersal Hall, did not marry and died soon after 1851.

The remaining Sigston property was then divided between his sisters, who had already inherited some of their uncles' and father's possessions. Mary was the wife of Dr James Booth of Littletown. Sarah, who had married William Hirst the younger of Butts Mill, lived at Croft House. The Booths moved to Gomersal Hall and the last of them, Miss Booth, left her property to her sister's sons, who were Taylors of the Red House family. So by a curious twist, the estate of the Sigstons, built up by the descendants of Ruth Taylor, returned to the Taylor family five generations later.

Gomersal Hall

The present Gomersal Hall is the third of that name in recent times, and is some distance from the original hall. The old Gomersal Hall was on the roadside almost opposite the Shoulder of Mutton. It is said that the pump in the yard of the old hall was open to use by villagers;[84] later, a forbidding high stone wall was built to surround the hall and its grounds.

We have been unable to trace any picture of the old hall, and its style and origins are uncertain. There can be little doubt that a dwelling of some kind has existed on this site for upwards of 400 years, but the form of this house, even as late as the mid nineteenth century, is a mystery. The Ordnance Survey of c.1850 shows an 'L'-shaped range forming two sides of a square yard opening on to the road. The building appears to have grown considerably from the house of square plan, adjoining cottage and neighbouring barn depicted on Topham's map of 1732 (Fig. 44). The Gomersal Tithe Map shows a roughly rectangular building, probably with cross wings, referred to as the 'Old Hall'. Such a plan accords with houses of hall and cross wing type, like Oakwell Hall. It is possible therefore that the rectangular block depicted on nineteenth century maps was the original hall building.

As discussed above, it is probable that Gomersal Hall was the seat of the Norcliffes until *c.*1615, and that it was then divided and let out, though still providing accommodation superior to most in the village. The tenants in the mid seventeenth century were Taylors and Birkheads; the Birkhead family may have stayed on in Gomersal Hall as tenants of Matthew Hewitt and his heir, Richard, who inherited the property in about 1670 and was still alive in 1710.[85] Hearth Tax returns show a William Birkhead in a house with four hearths in Gomersal in 1684.[86]

Figure 58: *The 'Victorian' Gomersal Hall pictured in the early twentieth century*

The hall, described as 'a substantial stone house', was sold in 1805 along with other houses and land to the brothers Sigston.[87] John Sigston had been the tenant of Gomersal Hall before the sale, and his widow continued to live there after 1809, when a part was let out to Henry Horsfall for a school.[88] Pupils at this school included the poet Herbert Knowles.[89] Horsfall was still there in 1836, though by 1840 he was living at New House, New Road Side, on the new turnpike road towards Birkenshaw.[90] Some educational activity probably continued in part of Gomersal Hall, as two governesses were living there when the 1841 census was taken. The other part was occupied by William Sigston and one servant. By 1851, the hall seems to have reverted to being one private dwelling. Sigston died in the 1850s and his property was divided between his sisters, Sarah Hirst of Croft House and Mary Booth.

Mrs Booth was married to Dr James Booth of Littletown, and it was he who altered Gomersal Hall completely. The rambling old buildings on the roadside were demolished, to be replaced by a Victorian mansion set far back in the grounds (Fig. 58). The high walls around the estate probably date from this period. Dr Booth died soon after rebuilding the hall, and the 1861 census shows Mrs Booth, her three children and two servants at the new Gomersal Hall. Of these children, Thomas Sigston Booth (b.1843) died young of consumption and Ann Sigston Booth (b.1840) later married Joshua Taylor of Red House. When Mrs Booth died in 1883 a complete inventory of the hall's contents was drawn up.[91] This describes four bedrooms, a bathroom with tin bath, a carpeted staircase, dining room with mahogany dining suite, drawing room, breakfast room and entrance hall with passage, along with two kitchens, a scullery, cellar, coach house and stables. The total value of the furnishings was £714 7s. 6d.

After this the only member of the family left at Gomersal Hall was the elder daughter, Mary Sigston Booth (b.1838). Miss Booth's death was recorded by William Carr of Little Gomersal in his diary:

Oct 21, 1900 Died at her residence Gomersal Hall (so styled) Miss Mary Sigston Booth ... Funeral was only attended by her two nephews Joshua and Sigston Taylor, her companion Miss Russell and one or two servants. Though possessed of an ample fortune she had never shown any disposition to do good in the locality from which her income was derived and had lived on in selfish seclusion and died unlamented.[92]

The Taylor nephews inherited the property.

The photograph of the Booths' Gomersal Hall was taken in the early years of this century, after Miss Booth's death, when it was a family home once again. The Victorian building has since been demolished and replaced by a brick structure.

Public Buildings

To the south of Sigston Fold are two of Gomersal's leading public buildings. The first, on the west side of Oxford Road, is the building now known as Gomersal Public Hall. Originally conceived as the local Mechanics' Institute, it was built on the site of a row of old cottages called Ratten Hall. The foundation stone of the new building was laid in 1850, the bulk of construction work finished during 1851 and the whole opened in 1852.[93] Its purpose was to provide moral education of a 'non-sectarian' nature – a very popular idea at the time – and to this end it was equipped with a lecture room, infant schoolroom and library. The money was raised locally, by the subscription of Gomersal's wealthier inhabitants to a share issue.[94]

The building is of coursed stone with ashlar front beneath a hipped roof of Welsh slate. It has two storeys and five bays. The main entrance, with a heavy surround surmounted by a balustrade, is centrally placed. Both the quoins and eaves are deeply cut, indicating a high quality of craftsmanship. Unusually, the windows at first floor level are much more heavily decorated than those on the ground floor. This gives the impression of a building which is 'top heavy' and it is difficult to understand what effect its architects were trying to achieve. On the southern side and to the rear, later additions have been made in simple, hammer dressed

Figure 59: *Grove Chapel*

stone; although some of this work, especially on the south side, seems to be earlier than 1850, and it may be that some of the stone was salvaged from Ratten Hall.

For a short period in the late nineteenth century it seemed that the Mechanics' Institute would be refurbished and turned into a local authority school. This was not to be and, as new schools were built in the village, the building was put to more general public use.

The second 'public' building in this area is Grove Chapel. Built by the Independents, or Congregationalists, it is now, over a century and a half later, home to their successors, the United Reformed Church. The chapel is another fine Gomersal structure. It was built in 1825-26 and opened on 22 February 1826, following a gift of land and underwriting of building costs by James Burnley.[95] Burnley was one of the leading Congregationalists in Gomersal and it is a measure of his financial success during the Napoleonic wars that he was able to contribute on such a scale. A schoolroom (for Sundays) and a minister's house were added in 1842, at the same time as the chapel itself was enlarged.

According to Peel, this was the first Sunday school in Great Gomersal – all previous Sunday tuition had taken place at the 'Old Town School' in Moor Lane.

As chapels go, Grove is a modest example. This has, in part, been responsible for its survival during years when many larger chapels in the locality have either fallen derelict or disappeared altogether. Although we cannot echo Peel's sentiments of 1891 – 'in a word Grove Chapel has never been more prosperous than at the present time' – the chapel is still well maintained and fits in pleasantly with its surroundings.

It is of two storeys, three bays wide and five deep, with a pediment to the front (Fig. 59). Windows on the front are arched; the main entrance here is adorned with an elegant architrave. In contrast, windows on other sides of the building are set in heavier, single piece surrounds. The roof is of stone slates. The masonry, though not ashlar, is nonetheless worked to a high standard, a feature which is also notable in the construction of the Sunday school to the north. Like most chapels, Grove is unique in its details. But it fits easily into the Pennine tradition of chapel building. Very similar forms were employed in Flockton United Reformed Church (built 1802) and Thurstonland Methodist Chapel (built 1836).[96]

Finally, it should be noted that the construction of Grove Chapel was part of the Burnley family's more general exploitation of its lands in the early nineteenth century. Within the space of about twenty years, Grove Square (to the north of the chapel site) was enlarged, the chapel was completed from new and improvements made to boundaries of their property with the new turnpike road. In 1820 there was probably only a textile workshop and some now demolished cottages in the Grove area; by 1850 the area looked very much as it looks today.

There are two other chapels in Great Gomersal. The Taylor chapel, situated just to the north of Grove Square, was a private chapel of the Taylor family of Red House (Fig. 60). Unfortunately, it is now in a condition of neglect. Built in about 1800, it is a single storey building

Figure 60: *The Taylor Chapel in the last century (KCS JJS/CO54/0184)*

Figure 61: *Gomersal Methodist Chapel*

in red brick, of four bays and a central doorway with porch. A second doorway was later inserted in the window opening just to the right of the porch. In a landscape populated predominantly with stone buildings it must, like Red House, have once presented a memorable spectacle.

The only chapel not yet mentioned is that of the Methodists, which stands at the top of West Lane. Like Grove Chapel, this is another impressive monument to the blossoming of non-conformity in the early nineteenth century. After many years of worshipping at various dispersed locations, the Wesleyan community eventually built their own chapel in 1827, at the instigation of the preacher Edward Brooke.[97] The building is unusual in having a curved front, a feature which allows the rows of pews inside to describe an arc around the pulpit. Access is by way of two arched doorways which flank the main body of the building (Fig. 61). Like nearly all chapels of the period it has an upper and lower gallery, so that a large congregation could be accommodated. The stone, as at Grove Chapel, is well-dressed though not ashlar. To the rear are arched stair windows, similar to those visible in Grove Chapel, Grove Square and Castle House at Little Gomersal.

Red House

By far the greatest memorial to the Taylor family is the building known as Red House, situated on the west side of Oxford Road between Pollard Hall and the Mechanics' Institute. The house is still in a good state of preservation, though different from its original form. Ferrett has brought together much of the available historical and literary information; her work means that a more accurate interpretation of the buildings is possible.

One of the earliest references to the Taylor 'messuage' in Great Gomersal is in a deed of 1537.[98] Throughout the sixteenth and seventeenth centuries there were many more deeds, each speaking of various members of the family as residents of Gomersal. But it is not until the later seventeenth century that any house is referred to specifically – though then quite explicitly, in the will of

Figure 62: *Red House: southern façade of the mid-eighteenth century*

William Taylor (1613-1689). This William was the builder of Red House, and his will mentioned two houses of substance: the Old House and the New House.[99] A lease of 1690 granted by William's son and heir, James, speaks of the New House lying to the east of the old.[100] The latter therefore stood some distance into the present garden, probably where the rockery now is. The Old House is very likely to have been at least partly of timber construction, but it seems that no evidence has survived to support this. A record of the house's rooms and contents has been preserved, however, from which it is clear that the Old House was smaller than the new, probably with six or seven rooms in total.[101]

What remains a mystery, however, is who occupied the Old House during the early seventeenth century and earlier. It appears that William Taylor lived at Gomersal Hall with his father James and brother Thomas until the 1640s. Thomas was given a house and land at Latham at the time of his marriage in 1646. William had married the previous year, and may have moved to the Old House at about that time. Another branch of the Taylor family could have lived at the Old House before then; or it is possible that another family was there. Indeed, if the 1641 tax list is taken as a reliable guide to location, the

Figure 63: *Red House: northern elevation (after rebuilding in 1988) showing seventeenth century gables*

people living nearest to the Red House site at the time were Rowland Sawghill or Salkeld, lay Parish Clerk; and Randall Fearnley (who owned Hill Top House but did not live there). There were no Taylors in the vicinity.[102] We do not know whether the Taylor family had previously lived at the Old House, moving to the grander surroundings of Gomersal Hall and then returning in order to build Red House; or whether James and William were the first Taylors to live at the Old House, in the mid seventeenth century. It may be recalled that the 1537 conveyance to the Taylors included a house whose tenant was a Thomas Fearnley, and it is even possible that the Fearnleys remained tenants of the Taylors for over a century. In other words, Fearnley Farm and the Old House could be the same building.

It seems generally agreed that William Taylor built his new house in 1660, though he was living in the old house at the time of his death, presumably having vacated the bigger house in favour of his second son John, who had a large family (the eldest son, James, had moved to Keighley).

The New House was the one which, in the nineteenth century, became familiarly known as Red House. It has changed considerably since the 1690s of course, and it

may be helpful to imagine the building as something akin to a Peel House (Fig. 45) built in red brick. High gables are still a feature of the northern side of Red House (Fig. 63). It would have been very unusual locally for a new yeoman house of the seventeenth century to have omitted them.

Red House was not, as is often supposed, the only brick built house in Gomersal. Others include an earlier building of Hill Top House, and mid eighteenth century houses on Lower Lane, Little Gomersal. However, Red House may have been the first house of brick in the locality and with its prominent roadside position must have been especially conspicuous.

An inventory taken on John Taylor's death in 1713 shows that the New House then had five downstairs rooms, one of which was a dining room, and at least six rooms upstairs. There were also numerous outhouses, including the 'great barn', pigsty and out-kitchen. The Old House was still standing at this time and was connected to the New House by a 'little parlour'.[103] For many years therefore it must have been possible to witness the change from a predominantly agrarian way of life to that of a commercial clothier simply by walking from one house to the other. It is very telling that the inventory of 1689 lists many farm and trade implements in the house, but such items are not recorded in the inventory of 1713.

The front of Red House as it now stands is of about mid eighteenth century date (Fig. 62). The house was remodelled some time before 1750, and it seems that the alterations resulted in the sweeping away of the Old House as well as the loss of the original façade of the New House. The ageing remains of the Old House may have been removed even before 1725.

The house now standing has a well-balanced classical façade of five bays, three double sashed windows separated by two single sashes. The main doorway, formerly approached from the road by a curving carriageway, has a fanlight enclosed by an arched window. The window on the western side of this

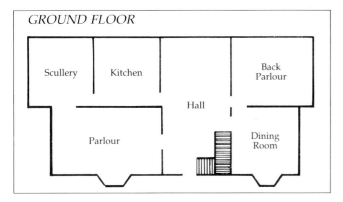

Figure 64: *Red House: ground floor rooms as set out c. 1830 (incorporating some nineteenth and twentieth century extensions)*

elevation is a later addition. The walls and chimney stacks are all of brick. In the absence of other suitable materials the roof used stone slate. Large stone quoins are also present on the east, though these were not necessary in a brick built structure. Much of the original brickwork on the eastern side is not that of an experienced bricklayer, and it may be that he did not fully trust the newfangled material with which he was working.[104] The eastern side of the house is also the only one to retain its early stone surrounds to the windows.

The rear of the house was, until recently, probably older than the eighteenth century front. Three of the gables at the rear were very likely to have been original, and therefore of seventeenth century date. Gables were very fashionable at the time Red House was built, and it is difficult to conceive of such a roof structure being adopted after 1700. When the south front was remodelled, the ridges of these gables would have been joined on to the new ridge running east-west through the southern range, and gables at the front removed. Note how the rooms at the rear of Red House retain a more cellular appearance than those to the front (Fig. 64).

Red House also had some interesting outbuildings. A barn and cart shed are still standing at the top of the garden, though in very contrasting states of repair. Both are situated for easy access to the family's main fields, in

the Cliffe Lane area. The barn has some similarities with that at Sigston Fold; they are probably both of late eighteenth century date. The Red House barn may be on the site of the 'great barn' referred to in James Taylor's probate inventory of 1713. It is also said that in the early nineteenth century Joshua Taylor's Gomersal Bank stood close enough to the house for it to be alarmed by means of a mechanical wire. The building cannot have been many yards away. A counting house and a shop or workroom (for finishing and displaying woollen cloth) are also said to to have stood very close to the house. Most important of all was the Taylors' warehouse. This is marked on the 1840 valuation map, just to the east of the cart shed already mentioned. It was a very large rectangular building – an indication of the Taylor family's commercial position in the woollen cloth industry.

As with the house, most of the outbuildings seem to have been either rebuilt or constructed from new in the eighteenth century. The years from 1720 to 1820 were ones of great success for the Taylors. This was reflected in improvements to the house but, more significantly, by John Taylor's move into the factory finishing of cloth (in the 1780s, at Hunsworth Mill) and in the family's increasing participation in public affairs. It is clear from all kinds of surviving documents that Gomersal was thriving in the late eighteenth century. The Taylors were no exception. No doubt this growth laid the foundation for the family's merchant lifestyle, typified by Joshua Taylor's venture into banking. Almost as a tribute to the high point of this achievement, Red House is now decorated and displayed as an 1830s home: the hall is bright and its fittings grained and marbled; a reproduction carpet in the best parlour imitates an older Brussels weave; stained glass windows, depicting Shakespeare and Milton, have been returned from storage in Haworth to decorate the room at the north-east corner of the house, now set out as a dining room. The portraits were known to Charlotte Brontë, as were the two paintings gracing the walls. More than most historic houses, internally at least, Red House is now a snap-shot of a particular period in history.

Having 'come of age' in the eighteenth century, Taylor fortunes and standing did not continue to grow with the same ease in the middle and later parts of the nineteenth. Their bank's failure during the commercial crisis of 1825/6 was an immediate disaster, but more important was the consequent longstanding indebtedness of Joshua Taylor and his son (another Joshua), who took it upon themselves to repay their creditors. Some families, having profited as merchants during the first phase of the industrial revolution (about 1760-1820) became successful factory-based industrialists during the course of the nineteenth century. For the Taylors however, the second phase never really materialized. They did not quite break out of domestic production, instead remaining locked in a system which was to change radically. The family still had a large estate in Gomersal and was affluent: in 1840, they probably owned more land than ever before, including new lands at Spen. But, in contrast to the Burnleys of nearby Pollard Hall, they did not apply themselves to the new commerce with conviction. The family gradually became dispersed and seems to have been incapable of unity on any important issue. Typically, following Anne Taylor's death in 1856, there was a protracted dispute over family property. The matter only resolved itself in Chancery.

Although Red House was not sold by the Taylors until 1920, their influence in Gomersal had by that time been on the wane for over fifty years.

Pollard Hall

Perhaps Gomersal's grandest house is Pollard Hall. The Department of the Environment inspector who listed it as an outstanding building accepted a date of 1659 for the major part of the hall. Most commentators, seeing the year 1659 and the initials of Tempest Pollard and his wife on the hall, have done likewise, attributing it to Pollard although there remains room for doubt.

It would take a thorough internal survey to establish exactly how and when Pollard Hall developed. A brief examination of the outside is enough to show that at least five phases of building occurred. Indeed, Pollard Hall may originally have been yet another example of a late-medieval timber-framed house, cased in stone only in the seventeenth century.[105] It is feasible that a medieval hall stood on this sheltered spot, well served with water and close to the old road which followed the ridge of the hill. There is a difficulty, however, in working out what form the medieval hall might have taken, as the present hall body stands in the only place where a cross wing is likely to have been. The stonework in this part is also newer than some other parts of the hall.

The two gables to the left, or west, of the porch appear older than the rest of the frontage and comprise the first phase of stone construction; the stone is more roughly dressed and laid in narrower courses than in the rest of the house. These gables could date from 1630 or even earlier; a good comparison in terms of quality and style is Highfield Farm House, Birstall, which has a datestone of 1612. This old part of Pollard Hall also resembles Peel House in style, particularly the two-light windows in the apex of the gables, though the stone is of better quality. If timber framing exists, it is probably in this section. The house here is double pile, though the rear elevation appears to be of later date, perhaps 1660-1700.

Figure 65: *Pollard Hall from the south*

A second building phase is to be seen in the gable containing the hall body. This has a window four lights deep by six wide, illuminating a hall which rises through two storeys and has a balcony on three sides (Fig. 66). Again there is a two light window in the gable, and the windows line up exactly with those of the western gables. However, the masonry in the hall area is of much better quality; it has deeper courses and a smooth

Figure 67: *Pollard Hall: door bearing the date 1659. The photograph was taken in 1912 (KCS JJS/CO54/0577)*

Figure 66: Pollard Hall: hall window.

finish. This gable and the porch are probably of 1659, the date in the studding of the door (Fig. 67) and on a lead rainwater head nearby. The porch may have been built in front of an original doorway. If, as Giles suggests, the hall body has a medieval origin, it was encased in stone later than the other gables. The house may therefore have been part stone, part timber, for a time – a phenomenon for which there are plenty of

Figure 68: *Pollard Hall: hall ceiling*

precedents. Alternatively it is possible that the hall body was newly built after 1650. This would be late for such a hall but not uniquely so, as we saw at Oakwell. From the coats of arms depicted, it has been estimated that the plaster ceiling in the hall (Fig. 68) dates from between 1649 and 1656.[106] It is not clear how this could fit in with the Tempest Pollard rebuilding date of 1659, or indeed whether the ceiling is original.

If the various extensions to the rear represent the third phase of Pollard Hall, the fourth is the addition of a new bay to the east of the hall. The gabled front here differs greatly in style, proportion and window levels from other gables to the west. Its stonework is similar to that of the hall body gable, but clear breaks can be seen between the masonry of the two, suggesting that the one to the east was added later. There is also the outline of what appears to have been a doorway, in the wall where the two gables meet. Structurally, it hardly seems possible that a doorway could exist here, inches away from the large window, unless the door pre-dated the window, and the window was inserted when the doorway was no longer in use.

The fifth phase comprises a projecting wing on the extreme left of the frontage (Fig. 69). This is late Victorian probably of 1889, and replaced a group of

industrial buildings which stood at right angles to the house. The new wing was built at a time when the Burnleys had transferred their textile business to Gomersal Mills and wanted to remove all traces of industry from the hall.

If any firm evidence exists of the origins of Pollard Hall, it has yet to be discovered. Before 1843, the hall seems to have been owned for the most part by families who did not live there and who rented it out on long lease. Hanson's suggestion that it formed part of the Oakwell property seems feasible, and it probably remained part of a large estate thereafter. Hanson believed that Pollard Hall was sold by the Batts, along with other Gomersal property, in about 1650. He cites the presence of the Horton coat of arms in the plaster ceiling of the hall as evidence that Pollard Hall went to the Hortons of Howroyd, Barkisland – they are known to have bought part of the Batts' Gomersal estate (see chapter 2). But the link is tenuous and, when the Hortons sold their large Gomersal estate to James Ibbetson in 1713, Pollard Hall was not among the property conveyed.[107] The hall, along with most of Hill Top and Popeley, did belong to Ibbetson in 1714,[108] but he must have acquired it from a different source.

In the absence of evidence to the contrary, the name Pollard Hall is therefore assumed to have derived from that of a tenant (or new freeholder) of the Batts, who did considerable rebuilding and extension in the seventeenth century. Pollard was a common name in Birstall parish, though the unusual Christian name means that Tempest Pollard is easy to identify in the parish registers. There were also Pollards in Tong who, in 1634, are known to have owned property in Gomersal.[109] Tempest may have been related to this family and have taken his Christian name from the Tempest family, who were lords of the manor in Tong.

Tempest Pollard's first appearance in local documents was in 1625, when an 'Infant unbaptised of Tempest Pollard of Gomersal' was buried at Birstall. A similar entry was made in the burials register for 1639. These

Pollard may have benefited financially during the 1650s from his support of the Commonwealth, whereas royalists like the Batts paid large penalties for being on the losing side.[111] Tempest Pollard died in 1673 and was buried at Birstall.

The second Tempest Pollard went on to produce eight children of his own between 1672 and 1684; the eldest was another Tempest. Tempest [II] could not have been the re-builder of the hall in 1659 as he was only fourteen at the time, though he may have been responsible for some of the subsequent extensions and alterations. The 'TMP' initials on the main door stand for Tempest and Margaret Pollard. Margaret died in 1682, aged seventy-six, 'an ancient gentle-woman', and was buried at

Figure 69: Pollard Hall: the Victorian wing soon after construction (KCS RH2/48)

Birstall where her name was mistakenly recorded as Mary in the register.[112]

could both have been children of a first marriage of the same Tempest Pollard who rebuilt part of the hall. He was recorded in the 1641 tax list as a single man, living in or near Pollard Hall; the amount he was required to pay was unstated, but he was not taxed at the standard rate of 6d. so was probably a rich man.[110] It is known that he married in that year, perhaps for the second time: his bride was Mrs Margaret Waterhouse. They had four children, two of whom survived to maturity: Tempest, baptised in 1645, and Mary, baptised in 1649, who married a yeoman called Abram Brooksbancke in Wakefield in 1667. That Tempest Pollard was relatively wealthy is confirmed by a further reference in the Birstall register, to the burial in 1652 of 'Lawrance', identified only as a servant of Tempest Pollard.

There is evidently reference in deeds of Pollard Hall to someone named Thomas Prest, and it has been mooted that this could be the TP. However there is nobody called Prest in the Birstall registers for the whole of the period 1558-1687, so if such a person were connected with the hall it seems unlikely that he lived in Gomersal.

The name of Tempest Pollard appeared in the hearth tax returns of 1684. This must have been the second Tempest Pollard, living in a house with nine hearths.[113] His son, referred to as Tempest Pollard the younger, of Gomersal, received a small bequest from Richard Peel in 1699, and was asked to assist Peel's widow and executor.[114] After that, we have not found any further occurrence of this distinctive name in Gomersal. It must be concluded that the Pollards left the hall in 1700 or soon afterwards.

The hall changed ownership in about 1713. In the following year, the Ibbetsons' new acquisitions were depicted on a colourful map (Fig. 1). The map features a bird's eye view of Pollard Hall. Details of the hall cannot be distinguished, as it is drawn from the road, end on and foreshortened by an unusual perspective. It is clear that the adjoining industrial buildings were as big as the hall; and they appear to have been in three parts. The tenant of all the surrounding fields, and presumably of the hall as well, was Joseph Goodier. We do not know whether the workshops had been there in the time of the Pollards; indeed there is nothing to say whether the Pollards were involved in the woollen trade. But it seems certain that Goodier was a manufacturer, as the buildings were of such size and prominence and unlike any agricultural building in the locality. These buildings appear, projecting far into the hall's front garden, on maps of 1798, 1847 and 1888-92, along with other, smaller, barns and sheds in the grounds.[115]

The Burnley family moved into Pollard Hall as tenants in 1752, bought the hall and Gomersal Mills in Ibbetson's sale of 1843, and finally left in about 1920.[116] Using Pollard Hall as their base until 1850, they built up the largest textile business in the village, and one of the few to survive into the late twentieth century. When William Burnley started up at the hall in 1752, he did not have a mill or factory. Some of the cloth-making processes, including dyeing and finishing, would have been carried out in the workshops at Pollard Hall. Others took place in the cottages of hand-spinners and weavers, and, later in the century, some of the work was done at Grove Square. There was a limited amount of mechanization, but power was still provided by human exertion. Later, the Burnleys were involved with the Union Mill project. They moved into their own factory at Hill Top only in 1850.

It was Thomas Burnley who bought the premises from Ibbetson in 1843. The sale catalogue described Pollard Hall as 'house, kitchen, warehouse, barn, stables, mistal, gig-house, saddle-room, cart shed and garden with dyehouse, dryhouse, spinning shop, warehouse, reservoir and croft'.[117] The existence of a dryhouse explains why there were no tentertrames around Pollard Hall at that time; it was more secure to dry cloth indoors, and problems with the weather were avoided.

The story of Pollard Hall after 1850 was one of gradual change into a fine mansion. Separated from Gomersal Mills by a high hedge, industrial buildings adjacent to the Hall were removed and the ambitious west wing completed.

Hill Top

South of Pollard Hall is the area known as Gomersal Hill Top, situated at the intersection of nineteenth century and eighteenth century turnpikes. The latter road – to the east of Hill Top known as Church Lane, and to the

Figure 70: *Laneside House at the turn of the century (KCS RH2/55)*

Figure 71: *St Mary's Church, Spen Lane, in about 1915*

west as Spen Lane – was a significant regional route for at least a hundred years before turnpiking, and the place where it crossed the Gomersal ridge must have been a landmark long before the construction of Oxford Road.

Church Lane was depicted on Ibbetson's map of 1714 (Fig. 1). On the south side, just above Muffit Lane, a collection of buildings is drawn. This is a farmstead called Laneside, the main house of which is still standing and which most eighteenth century travellers must have passed on their way along the 'stone causey' to Hill Top. Outbuildings shown on the 1714 map have long since gone. Likewise, a nineteenth century farmhouse standing just to the east of Laneside was demolished in about 1965, to make way for the housing development on Craven Lane.

Laneside House is of the second half of the seventeenth century, perhaps as late as 1700.[118] It is a two storey house of four bays, facing east. The roof is of stone slate, with copings and kneelers. The stonework in the walls is roughly dressed, though quoins are present. Two of the most notable features of the house – other than its fine cottage garden – are its splayed mullion windows and

two storey porch at the front (Fig. 70). It is these which are important indicators of date. The mullions suggest a period a little later than similar windows in Peel House and the first phase of Pollard Hall, as their chamfers are less pronounced. The porch may be a little later still; the use of larger stone blocks and a break either side of the drip course suggest that it was an addition to the original house. The porch also has a very high door surround, more commonly found in eighteenth century buildings. In comparison to Peel House and Pollard Hall a more equal proportion between the upper and lower storeys is noticeable (though perhaps a product of the difference in scale rather than a difference in date of the buildings).

In the seventeenth century the yard to the rear of Laneside must have contained all the outbuildings associated with a farmer-cum-clothier's place of work. These no longer exist; indeed most were demolished before 1850. The house itself was virtually rebuilt during the nineteenth century. Externally this resulted in the construction of new chimney stacks.

In 1805 the house was tenanted by Joshua Walker, a wool merchant [119] who later acquired land at the junction of Nova Lane and Nutter Lane, and built Oakwell House

Figure 72: *Gomers Hall: southern elevation (demolished in 1928)*

there. Walker's brother, Thomas, was tenant of the large house (now demolished) at Popeley. By 1830 Laneside was occupied by Joseph Hirst[120], and in 1840 by William Crowther.[121] In 1844, at an auction held at the White Horse, Hill Top, the freehold of Laneside was sold along with all the other Ibbetson lands in Gomersal.[122] Towards the end of the century it was home to Ellen Nussey.[123]

Across Hill Top, in Spen Lane, there are few remains of historic importance. The church of St. Mary, built in 1851 by John Dobson of Leeds, is sobering enough with its neo-Gothic tower and steeply roofed nave (Fig. 71). It is, nonetheless, a relative newcomer to the area. A house known as Marsh House existed on the site of what is now the Barrington Estate, but this has long since disappeared, as has Gomersal's own Cloth Hall (see chapter 7).

At Hill Top, a house known locally as Gomers Hall was a feature until its demolition in 1928.[124] The hall stood at right angles to Spen Lane and Oxford Road, facing south. It was a long narrow two storey building of at least five bays with a projecting cross-wing to the west. The house had tall chimneys, a two storey porch, heavy quoins and kneelers (Fig. 72). Working from photographs, it is difficult to be precise about the date of Gomers Hall. A number of alterations had been made, in particular the

Figure 73: *Hill Top: Post Office and rear extension of Gomers Hall*

insertion of larger, wooden framed windows in place of stone mullions; part of the hall was used as a shop in its later years. It was probably an eighteenth century building, though the main section could have been as old as Laneside. The porch appears to have been an addition, judging by the different quality of masonry there. At the rear of the cross wing was an extension which abutted Spen Lane above the Post Office (Fig. 73). The name Gomers Hall does not occur in documentary sources before the nineteenth century. In the middle years of that century it housed a small private school under the charge of one Sarah Mann. The origins of this hall, however, remain uncertain, though it should be noted that it stood on the former glebelands and was for many years owned by Trinity College, Cambridge.

Hill Top House

The most notable building now standing at Hill Top is the house just to the north of Spen Lane, set back in its own grounds. This is Hill Top House. It owes something to the noted Yorkshire architect John Carr (1723-1807). Although built after his death, it resembles Carr's work and may have been designed by his successor, Peter Atkinson [II]. In fact, it is very likely that money left by Carr paid for the building of the house.

The main part of Hill Top House dates from soon after 1808. It is a well-proportioned, double fronted, two storey building, plain in style and of dressed stone with ashlar quoins (Fig. 74). A delicate semi-circular fanlight contrasts with the heavy stone door surround. The sash windows are divided with glazing bars. In spite of its appearance, however, the house has never stood alone. When first built it was attached to what according to Cadman was a seventeenth century brick house, the old Hill Top House.[125] After a time this old house was demolished and replaced by a new wing. Map evidence and style of building indicate that this may have been as late as the 1840s, but the new wing was carefully matched to the main house, with identical eaves cornice, fanlight and door surround. The newer part is of two bays and stands slightly forward of the rest.

Figure 74: Hill Top House: the new wing which replaced an earlier brick house is nearest the camera

It is the stable block and other outbuildings which probably contain the oldest surviving remains. Though much altered and partly demolished, these still have eighteenth century features, and may be older than that in parts. They are predominantly red brick, with original stone quoins. A smithy referred to in a deed of 1674 could have been in this block.

The original house, known simply as Hill Top, was probably one of the earliest examples of brick building in Spen Valley. It was mentioned in a lease of 1635, when along with a barn, garden and close of land it was let to Thomas Mortimer of Gomersal, a carpenter, at £3 a year; whether it was built in brick at this time is not specified. The owners were Randall Fearnley, and from 1643 Fearnley's son Thomas.[126] The names of Mortimer and the Fearnleys are to be found in the 1641 tax list, apparently at or near Hill Top, adding substance to Cadman's information.[127]

Hill Top left the ownership of the Fearnleys, and until 1674 its owner and occupier was a yeoman called John Rooke. He sold it for 'four score and ten pounds' to William Turner of Gomersal. Included was a smithy and a close of land along with about three acres at the 'backside' of the house. Even at that time Hill Top

marked the junction of two main roads, and the site was an advantageous one for a smithy. Turner, a clothier, mortgaged Hill Top in 1691 to Mrs Elizabeth Hobson of Leeds for £100. He was unable to repay the money and lost his property in 1697 to Mrs Hobson, by then remarried to Josias Farrer of Headlands Hall, Roberttown. As married women were at that time unable to own property in their own right, Farrer became the new owner, and paid Turner £134 for his interest.[128]

The house was let to various tenants in the first half of the eighteenth century, including a Thomas Hodgson and in 1746 Richard Charlesworth. By that time the smithy had ceased to be mentioned in descriptions of Hill Top.[129] The ownership of the property had passed to Mary Midgley of Alwoodley, a relative of Elizabeth Farrer, following Mrs Farrer's death some time before May 1723. Mary Midgley married Robert Dyneley, a gentleman, who was bankrupt by 1746 when Hill Top was let to Catherine Bolderston of Mirfield, widow, at £50 a year. The term of the lease was to be the lifetime of Robert Dyneley. In this way, as it had been his wife's inheritance, it escaped sale by Dyneley's creditors. After his death she was able to sell it, which she did in 1760 to Jonathan Crowther of Gomersal, a clothdresser.

Crowther does not seem to have had any more financial good fortune than previous owners. He paid £280 for Hill Top, took out a mortgage in 1764, remortgaged it in 1767, and finding himself in further difficulties sold it in 1769 for £360. It was bought by Charles Knowles of Gomersal, a butcher and younger son of Lionel Knowles [I]. In 1784 Charles, who had moved to Tadcaster, took a mortgage on the property from Joseph Mann and Caleb Crowther, trustees of the estate of Samuel Laverack of Spen. This debt was transferred to John Rawson of Halifax in 1791 and increased to £350. Lionel Knowles [I] probably lived at Hill Top from 1769 until his death in 1779. The tenant after that was his eldest son Lionel [II], who bought the house and land from Charles in 1792 for £460, paid off the mortgage and took out another loan in 1797 from a Mr Armitage of Woodhouse.

When Lionel [II] died in 1802, the house was left to his younger son James who lived only until 1805. James' family of five young children was sent to live with different relatives as their mother was already dead. The Knowles family left Hill Top and from that time the various branches lived near their business premises at Tenlands (see chapter 7).

A new owner then took over at Hill Top. This was Charles Carr, a solicitor, son of James Carr of Birstall, another solicitor and brother to John Carr the architect. When John Carr died in 1807 his enormous fortune of £150,000 was shared between nephews and nieces.[130] How much of this fell to Charles Carr is not known, but it seems to have enabled him to move to Hill Top in 1808 (from the house known as Crow Trees at Bunkers Hill) and embark upon the rebuilding. The evidence that Peter Atkinson was the architect is circumstantial, as little is known about his early work. But Atkinson was in charge of Carr's York practice in the early years of the nineteenth century, and it would have been natural for Charles Carr to use his uncle's successor. Atkinson did work in Spen Valley, designing the 'Million Act' churches in Birkenshaw, Heckmondwike and Cleck-heaton in 1829-31.

Charles Carr continued to improve his Hill Top property. The township valuation of 1840 records a greenhouse, bathhouse, lawn, garden and shrubberies there. Carr had died before 1840, but his widow, Grace, and two sons,

Charles and William, still lived at the house. The unusual porter's lodge on Spen Lane was built as a single storey house in about 1850; another floor was added many years later. The sons also continued Carr's legal practice at Hill Top, and were still at Hill Top House in 1876 when Cudworth spoke of the house as 'surrounded by pleasant grounds, which extend down to the churchyard'.[131]

Crow Trees

There remains just to the south of Hill Top one further area worthy of comment. This is Crow Trees. Originally, three houses seem to have borne that name, for a time all occupied by members of the Swaine family of Cloth Hall Mill.

Figure 75: *Crow Trees at Bunkers Hill, now demolished (KCS RH2/56)*

The main Crow Trees, 'a very old brick house',[132] has survived, though much altered. It stands on the brow of the hill in Oxford Road (facing Victoria Road) and is now converted into flats. A large building, originally double-fronted, double piled, and of two storeys throughout, it has since been extended to the north. The original materials are now concealed beneath render, though stone quoins and kneelers are still apparent. Its chimneys and windows have been altered, adding to the difficulty in estimating the age of the building. It seems too tall a structure to be of great age, but a mid eighteenth century date is possible. The elaborate stone surround to the front door shows that this was once an imposing house; the door itself appears to be contemporary with the surround. The northern wing of the building may have been a coach house, the first floor of which is said by Cadman to have been once used as a schoolroom.[133]

Documents show that this, the main Crow Trees, was the home of Joshua Walker, gentleman, who died in 1783.[134] He owned various houses and land in Great Gomersal, and property in Kirkheaton. His only child left Gomersal when she married, and the house passed to one Dr Benjamin Sykes, surgeon and apothecary. Dr Sykes died in 1822, leaving one child, Martha, the wife of Edward Swaine who was a partner at Cloth Hall Mill (see chapter 7). Crow Trees was described in 1826 as a house with 'barn, stable, [work]shops, coach houses, dovecote ... garden, orchards, yards ...'. Swaine had moved into the house and used it and other property inherited from Dr Sykes to raise a mortgage of £1,500.[135] The Swaines continued to live at Crow Trees until Edward retired from business, and by 1855 he had moved to York where he died, aged ninety-four, in 1885. Subsequently, Crow Trees was let to a succession of tenants, including a schoolmaster called Williamson and – when a railway line was under construction in Gomersal in 1896-1900 – the London and North Western Railway Company.[136]

The second property called Crow Trees was sometimes known as Bunkers Hill. It stood a little below the main

Figure 76: *Crow Trees, Oxford Road: house of c.1819*

Crow Trees and was reached by a track. Its style suggests a date of the middle to late eighteenth century (Fig. 75). In the 1780s it was owned by a merchant family called Rhodes, and tenanted by one Thomas Walker.[137] Cadman says that Charles Carr lived there before his move to Hill Top House in 1808. Then Edward Swaine's brother and co-partner Joseph was there until he went to Brier Hall in about 1825.[138] The house still stood in Cadman's day, though much altered.

The third Crow Trees is the only house to retain the name. It was the newest of the three, built just before 1819 by Charles Mellor, a clerk to Charles Carr. It is a double fronted stone house and stands directly behind Charles Street. Apart from an extension to the rear and new window frames, the house is much as it would have looked in the early nineteenth century (Fig. 76). The front door looks original and is surmounted by a fine fanlight. Mellor was in dispute with his neighbour, Dr Sykes, about a wall which the doctor had built close to Mellor's new house. He retaliated by putting an ugly building (known locally as Spite Hall) opposite Sykes' house.[139] However, Mellor seems to have left soon afterwards, when maiden sisters of the Swaines lived at Crow Trees.

Figure 77: *Mazebrook farmhouse*

Some Outlying Places

A question remains over the role played by various outlying farmsteads in the development of Great Gomersal, especially those to the west of Oxford Road between Latham Lane and Cleckheaton. In some areas of northern England (for example in the higher Pennines of Yorkshire or Cumbria) settlement shows very little nucleation; the landscape tends to be one where single farmsteads are distributed thinly over many miles. When growth occurs in such surroundings, new farmsteads are not built close to the old and fields worked by a greater number of farmers; instead, new farmsteads grow up away from existing ones on land which might formerly have been considered more marginal. We cannot be sure whether outlying areas in Great Gomersal supported houses in the medieval period, or whether these areas saw the arrival of houses only after economic and tenurial change in the late sixteenth century. The latter is a strong possibility, at least for the area east of Brookhouses and Balme Mill.[140] There was certainly a significant amount of new building here in the seventeenth century: good examples can be seen at Lands Farm, Mazebrook and Egypt Farm.

Mazebrook farm house is a stone house of two cells (Fig. 77). A wing projects to the north to give an 'L'-shaped plan. The main door, to the west, has a datestone of 1654. Mullion windows to both storeys support the date of 1654 as they are similar in style to those of the earliest phase at Pollard Hall. The narrow coursing of stone also recalls Pollard Hall and, to a lesser degree, Peel House. The wing appears to be a slightly later addition to an original, two celled arrangement, as does the outshut to the rear. There is no easily observable evidence of a timber frame in any part of the building[141] and the likelihood is that no house graced this spot before the seventeenth century, though there could have been an earlier barn or cottage.

Lands Farm is smaller than Mazebrook farmhouse but equally significant in terms of seventeenth century construction. Although altered a lot, not least by the recent addition of render and a tiled roof, its original form is still sufficiently visible for the building to be of interest. Again the house is of two cells but this time with an outshut which runs along its whole length. The main entrance, on the south side, is inscribed with the date 1693. The straight lintel and narrow chamfered surround of the door, and the relatively symmetrical arrangement of window openings, lend weight to a date some fifty years later than Mazebrook. It has been suggested that a timber-framed building may have pre-dated the main block here[142] but there is no evidence available yet to support this idea.

It is Egypt Farm that has produced the most convincing evidence of timber framing. Recent rebuilding revealed all surviving timber elements of the house, including the arcade posts, a reused tie beam and roof trusses. The complete structure of the building was open to view for a short time in 1990 (Fig. 78). The wooden superstructure was certainly a very impressive sight. Unfortunately, however, it is still not possible to affirm that a timber-framed building existed here. The tie-beam which runs from the top of the arcade plate (the beam sitting on top of the two posts either side of the doorway, to the middle right of Fig. 78) to the wall opposite has a

storeys, with two main rooms at ground level and an outshut to the rear. Late seventeenth century mullion windows are also a feature of the south side (those on the north are modern reproductions).[143]

Figure 78: Egypt Farm: the timber structure revealed during rebuilding in 1990

Finally, the growth of settlement at the periphery of the village can be considered historically by looking at the Taylor family of Latham Lane. In the township valuation of 1840, Latham Hall and a strip of land to the south is recorded as the property of one John Taylor. A little further along the lane a house and field known as Gomersal Fieldhead are said to have been in the ownership of a Samuel Taylor. It is usually assumed that the two farmsteads were at this time part of the estate of the Taylors of Red House, probably as the inheritance of a second son. However, documents do not support this and a separate branch may have split from the main family line, perhaps as early as the mid seventeenth century.

mortise at the wall end, indicating that it was once supported by another post. Indeed it is now supported by the wall, but in a place where the wall is weakened by the presence of a window. However, from other mortises in the beam, which also had no obvious relationship with the present building, it seems likely that the tie beam is from an earlier structure. The positioning of the beam over a window is a perplexing but not unknown architectural feature. Even after stripping the roof and north wall, it is difficult at Egypt to speculate on much more than the reuse of several medieval timbers.

What Egypt farmhouse does have, like Mazebrook and Lands Farm, is evidence for substantial building in the seventeenth century. Again the house is of stone, two

In his will dated 1765, William Taylor of Fieldhead appointed his sister Ann Taylor executor and devised to his nephew William a share in his Latham lands.[144] None of the people mentioned in the will are members of the main Taylor line as depicted by Ferrett;[145] the same is true of the will of John Taylor (1818) of 'Latham in Gomersal'.[146] The house referred to as Fieldhead may be that at the very end of Latham Lane, now divided into Fieldhead House and Fieldhead House Farm but in about 1850 called World's End by the Ordnance Survey. The house is of stone and appears to be of the first half of the eighteenth century or earlier (Fig. 79). However, we know of no records of a Taylor presence at this property. At various dates in the seventeenth and eighteenth centuries the house seems to have been in the Fearnley family; in fact, a probate inventory of 1688 shows that one John Fearnley lived at Fieldhead.[147] The Taylor house must therefore have been at another location in Latham Lane, probably much nearer to the village, in the area between what was sometimes called Gomersal Fieldhead (now demolished) and the house known as Latham Hall.

Generally, we know much less about the Latham Lane Taylors than the Taylors of Red House. The former may initially have been clothiers but by the eighteenth century were more exclusively associated with agriculture. The household accounts of one Anne Taylor for the years 1727-1730 have survived. These indicate that the family may have been carriers and suppliers of horses for the various farms, houses and industries in Great Gomersal. The account for 3 October 1728 reads

Figure 79: *Fieldhead House from the south*

'63 horse loads of coal carried from a pitt'; an entry for November 1729 says that a horse was provided for Ben Fearnley's wedding; and on the 27 March 1730 the account reads 'harrowed three days work with five horses returned home not until 10 at night'.[148]

NOTES

1. The name of Broadyards was certainly in use in the early seventeenth century; *WYAS B* MM37/53.
2. *Thoresby* Batt 177.
3. *YAS* MD 132/B3.
4. *Thoresby* Batt 210; *YAS* DD 70/1.
5. *YAS* MD 132.
6. *WYAS HQ* Deeds Vol ET 654 817.
7. Pevsner 1967, 222.
8. As feoffees, in other words still paying manorial dues to Oakwell.
9. *YAS* MD 311/10.
10. *YAS* MD 311/13.
11. *YAS* MD 311/15.
12. Cradock 1933, 52; given the scale of Hussey's disposals, there is certainly some merit in this argument.
13. Ferrett 1987, 22.
14. *YAS* MD 311/38.
15. Birstall Parish Registers 13 June 1574; 29 June 1596.
16. Clay (ed.) 1907, 428.
17. *WYAS K* DD/HS/G/1/2.
18. Norcliffe hailed from Nunnington in North Yorkshire. He married Elizabeth, daughter of Robert Ealand of Carlinghow and came to live in Gomersal only after these purchases.

19. *WYAS K* DD/HS/G/1/4.
20. *YAS* MD 132/B3.
21. *YAS* DD 70/1.
22. *WYAS K* DD/HS/G/1/16.
23. *WYAS K* DD/HS/G/1/19.
24. *WYAS HQ* Deeds Vols ET and EX.
25. *Thoresby* Batt Mss.
26. *WYAS SMR* RCHME survey.
27. This and subsequent biographical information about the Peel family is derived from the Birstall Parish Registers
28. *YAS* DD 70/1.
29. *Thoresby* Batt 213.
30. *Thoresby* Batt 211.
31. *WYAS L* HS66.
32. Goodall 1953, 163.
33. Thornes 1981, 12.
34. *Thoresby* Batt 177.
35. *WYAS L* HS66.
36. *Borthwick* Inventory of Richard Peel, 26 April 1699.
37. *WYAS L* HS66.
38. *WYAS K* DD/HS/K/4.
39. *WYAS B* 1D78/68.

40. Cadman 1930, 31, and Cudworth 1876, 521; though Cadman presumably obtained his information from Cudworth's book.
41. For this information and other details of buildings in Great Gomersal we are grateful to Dr Stephen Caunce.
42. Caunce, personal communication.
43. Cudworth 1876, 521.
44. *WYAS B* 1D78/68.
45. Cadman 1930, 27.
46. Cudworth 1876, 523.
47. For this and other suggestions about the evolution of buildings in Sigston Fold we are grateful to Mr Barry O'Neill.
48. *WYAS SMR* Sigston House, Gomersal
49. A 'Croshowse' mentioned in the Birstall pew list of 1634 (*YAS* DD 70/1) and which appeared in the parish registers from 1559 was probably elsewhere, perhaps in East Bierley.
50. *WYAS SMR.*
51. Hanson 1922, no 48; Cadman 1930, 52.
52. Cadman, 1930, 52-3.
53. Hanson 1922, no 48.
54. Peel 1893, 156.
55. *YAS* DD 70/1.
56. *YAS* MD 311/25.
57. *Thoresby* Batt 210.
58. *Thoresby* Batt 211.
59. Knighthoods were almost always refused because of the expense of bearing the title; a fine was then imposed, to be paid to the exchequer.
60. *YAS* DD 70/1.
61. *YAS* DD 70/1.
62. *Thoresby* Batt 203.
63. *WYAS B* MM37/54.
64. *WYAS B* MM37/53; MM A92.
65. Smith 1886, 16 and 34.
66. *WYAS B* MM37/53.
67. *Borthwick.*
68. *WYAS HQ* Deeds Vol Q 256 332.
69. *WYAS K* KC52 Sigston Box 2 Bundles 1 and 2.
70. *WYAS K* DD/HS/C9.
71. *WYAS K* DD/HS/C10.
72. *WYAS L* DB/M 506; copy at Cleckheaton Library. Hereafter referred to as Gomersal Township Valuation.
73. O.S. 25" 232.6 Resurveyed 1888-92 Published 1894.
74. Gomersal Township Valuation.
75. Ferrett 1987, 22; *YAS* MD 292/23.
76. *WYAS K* KC52 Sigston Box 3 Bundle 3.
77. Cadman 1930, 159.
78. *WYAS HQ* Deeds Vols ET and EX.
79. *WYAS HQ* Deeds Vol ET 654 817; *WYAS K* KC52 Sigston Box 2 Bundle 2; see Fig. 49.
80. *WYAS K* KC52 Sigston Box 3 Bundle 3.
81. *WYAS K* KC52 Sigston Box 1 Bundle 4.
82. Parson 1826, 227.
83. Parson and White 1830, 467.
84. Cadman 1930, 51.
85. *Thoresby* Batt 179.
86. Goodall 1953, 163. Nothing has been found to connect these Birkheads with the family which moved into Brookhouses in the mid eighteenth century, who were said to have originated at Westgate Hill. For a history of Brookhouses see Gillian Cookson 'Brookhouses' *Spen Valley Historical Society Journal* 1992, 14-17.
87. *WYAS K* KC52 Sigston Box 2 Bundle 1; *WYAS HQ* Deeds Vol ET.
88. *WYAS K* KC52 Sigston Box 2.
89. Cudworth 1876, 522.
90. *WYAS HQ* QE13.
91. *WYAS K* KC52 Misc Box 1 Bundle 6.
92. *WYAS K* DD/CA/6.
93. Cadman 1930, 155; Ferrett 1983, 18.
94. Cadman goes into some detail on the early workings of the institute and the personalities involved. Even more detailed records are available at *WYAS K* KC122.
95. Peel 1891, 207; Cudworth 1876, 524.
96. For which see Bielby 1978, plates 73 and 78.
97. Peel 1891, 200.
98. *YAS* MD 311/10.
99. Ferrett 1987, 3.
100. *YAS* MD 292/15.
101. Ferrett 1987, 2; though the list of rooms in this inventory may be incomplete.
102. *YAS* DD 70/1; Cradock 1933, 255.
103. Ferrett 1987, 2.
104. Caunce, personal communication.
105. Giles 1986, 197.
106. Hanson 1922, no 64.
107. *WYAS HQ* Deeds Vol G 155 166.
108. Fig. 1; see Wilson 1988.
109. *WYAS B* Tong 3/196.
110. *YAS* DD 70/1.
111. Hanson 1922, no 65.
112. Hanson 1922, no 65.
113. Goodall 1953, 163.
114. *WYAS L* HS66.
115. *WYAS L* DB/M 670/4; Ordnance Survey. Burnley's bicentenary history (Anon 1952) says that the Victorian wing of Pollard Hall was built in 1860, but this is refuted by other evidence, particularly the Ordnance Survey map of 1888-92.
116. Anon 1952.
117. *WYAS K* DD/CA/7.
118. *WYAS SMR* RCHME survey.
119. *WYAS K* DD/HS/G/1/52.
120. Parson and White 1830, 467.
121. *WYAS HQ* QE13.
122. *WYAS L* HS unlisted.
123. Cadman 1930, 77; *YAS* Photographic collection.
124. *Spenborough Guardian* 27 January 1928.
125. Cadman 1930, 89.

126. Cadman 1930, 89.
127. *YAS* DD 70/1.
128. *WYAS HQ* C23/11; from which source the information in the following paragraphs is drawn.
129. Cadman 1930, 89.
130. Linstrum 1978, 373.
131. Cudworth 1876, 526-7.
132. Cadman 1930, 102.
133. Cadman 1930, 104.
134. *WYAS K* KC52 Sigston Box 1 Bundle 4.
135. *WYAS C* FW 179/7.
136. Cadman 1930, 104.
137. *WYAS C* RP 1686.
138. Cadman 1930, 104.
139. Cadman 1930, 102-3.
140. Which are at the western end of Cliffe Lane, and relating to which medieval records survive.
141. *WYAS SMR* RCHME record.
142. *WYAS SMR* RCHME record.
143. There is of course a long non-conformist tradition associated with Egypt. Both Goodall (1953, 153) and Peel (1891, 38-40) refer to Ye Closes, where Independents met from about 1670, as the site of Egypt Farm.
144. *WYAS K* KC52/34.
145. Ferrett 1987, 22.
146. *WYAS K* KC52/37.
147. *Borthwick* Grant of January 1688/9.
148. *WYAS K* KC52/32.

Chapter 6

SPEN AND SPEN MILL

Spen and Spen Mill, like Birstall Church and Oakwell Hall, were physically separated from Gomersal yet central to the lives of Gomersal people. The early importance of the mill and hamlet came about because of their links with the manor of Oakwell. Although Spen Bottoms and the mill are on the fringes of Cleckheaton, all the land from Nellroyd to Brookhouses on the east side of the river was in Gomersal township. Spen Mill was therefore mainly for the use of Birstall and Gomersal tenants of the lord of Oakwell. Spen had one of the best sources of water power in the manor. A similar mill may have stood near Birstall Church, but this had been separated from the manor of Oakwell in the early or middle fourteenth century (see chapter 2).

Spen has achieved wider fame in giving its name to the entire valley between Low Moor and Ravensthorpe. However it was purely by accident that this occurred. The valley's beck did not have one name, but took the name of places through which it flowed. As late as the mid nineteenth century, the Ordnance Survey noted a variety of names along the river's course, such as Rawfolds Beck and Balme Mill Beck. A mistake by the editor of a book in the 1860s led to the river being called the Spen, and the valley then appears to have assumed the same name. This was formalized in 1885 when a new parliamentary division was created and called Spen Valley.[1]

Until the present century, Spen was hardly even a hamlet. The mid nineteenth century Ordnance Survey map shows it to have been a series of buildings and small settlements along the course of Spen Lane. Upper Spen began at about the junction with Nibshaw Lane. Travelling down Spen Lane in the 1840s, one would have been struck by the rural aspect of this part of Gomersal. On one side, there was no development between Cloth Hall Dryhouse (opposite Nibshaw Lane) and Spen Hall; Fusden Lane did not have a single building along its way.

Figure 80: *Fusden Lane (formerly Vicarage Lane), looking towards the junction with Cliffe Lane (KCS RH5/49)*

Figure 81: *Upper Spen: tannery and cottages c.1900*

The first house on the other side of Spen Lane, below Butts Mill and Marsh House, was Spen Cottage (sometimes called Pruin Hall and now Tanfield House). The origins of this house are unclear though it probably dates from the eighteenth century. A local carpenter called James Shepley is credited with building the oak staircase and other oak panelling in the house in 1829.[2] Tanfield House has been a dame school, a grocer's shop and in the 1870s was a public house called The Gardeners Arms. The outbuilding was a weaving shop in the 1840s, containing twelve handlooms. From about 1890 Spen Cottage was the home of John Harrison, who established a tannery in a group of former farm buildings below (Fig. 81).[3] It is possible that a tannery which existed in Spen in the seventeenth century was at Upper Spen, though much more likely that this old tannery would be at Spen Bottoms (see below).

Below the tannery was a group of cottages with a brewery and beershop, later the Old Saw (see chapter 8). Spen House, dating from the late eighteenth or early nineteenth century, was the next building below the Old Saw. A grand residence in extensive grounds, it was re-fronted in 1842 by Edward Atkinson, second generation of the family of worsted spinners at Peg Mill.[4] Atkinson accumulated other property in Spen and Cleckheaton and by 1871 he was owner of the Old Saw and the fields behind it.[5] He died in December 1872; the Atkinson family still held this Spen estate at the turn of the century.[6]

The main settlement at Lower Spen in the 1840s was on Spen Lane's junction with Gomersal Lane, in what is now part of the grounds of Spen House. There were about a dozen cottages there; an eighteenth century deed refers to them as Spenhouses.[7] These buildings have long gone, though traces of their foundations can still be seen between Gomersal Lane and a line of trees a few yards into the field. Further down the lane, on the right beyond the dip, are a few overgrown remains of the house bought for Joseph Mann in 1751 (see below).

Spen Lane had been a busy main road for generations. The toll bar cottage which in the 1840s stood in the middle of the junction with Gomersal Lane, its foundations now long disappeared under tarmac, presumably dated from the turnpiking in 1740. Pedestrians had to walk through a stile to continue up Spen Lane.[8] Across the road, Spen Hall was perhaps the only place in Spen whose setting in the 1840s was less attractive than it is today, for its grounds contained a chemical works. Beyond the hall, though, stretching as far as Drub, were unspoilt acres of farm land where Sigston of Gomersal Hall went hare coursing with greyhounds.[9] Below Spen Hall on the road side was the pair of stone cottages which can still be seen today. A little lower, facing on to Spen Bank, stood a cottage which was swept away by the London and North Western Railway in 1896-1900. This last, 'straw-thatched ... with weather-beaten stone walls and small-paned windows ... approached by a flight of steps and a sloping road' was inhabited by a hand woolcomber who rented it from the Taylors of Red House.[10] The buildings below this cottage were all connected with Spen Mill.

Medieval Spen

The earliest records of Spen refer to Spen inhabitants of the thirteenth century. John de le Spen was in the area at that time, and may have lived in an earlier version of Spen Hall.[11] In the following century, it appears from deeds of 1316 and 1317 relating to Ketelesker (a field called Kettle Carr, below Nibshaw Lane) that the common pastures of Spen were in the area which now forms the grounds of Spen House. This is confirmed by a transaction of 1649 referring to Spen Green (see below). The de le Spen name again occurs in these early fourteenth century documents, in the form 'del Spen'. The men concerned were called Thomas del Spen and Robert del Spen; the former was mentioned again in a deed of c.1330-40.[12]

There is also a little information about the lands at Spen in the fourteenth century. In 1334 one Robert le Tornore of Skelton and Alice his wife leased their lands and tenements and a wood with common at le Spen near Gomersall, at seven shillings a year for Alice's lifetime. A piece of meadow called the Intake was excluded from the agreement. The lessee was John, son of Richard de le S[pen], Alice's son from her first marriage, who would inherit the lands on her death. He was effectively buying her interest in the property.[13]

Soon after this, some or all of the estate of the de le Spen family found its way into the hands of John Tilly of Oakwell. It appeared in a Tilly grant of 1342/3, along with other properties in Gomersal and 'Birkenshagh'. Tilly was said to have obtained land from John del Spen, though the exact area was not specified.[14] Property accumulated by Tilly found its way in due course to Thomas Hussey and was sold to Henry Batt in 1565. This sale included 'two messuages called Spennes with the appurtenances in Spenne and Gomersall in the occupation of Edward Broke and Margaret widow of John Wibsaye ...'.[15] It is worth noting that fields between Spen House and Gomersal Lane were called Wibsey in the nineteenth century, and that this name may have come from the family which had held the land three hundred years earlier. Spen House could be the site of the Wibseys' dwelling.

Some enclosure took place while the Batts were in possession of Spen. The Kettle Carr fields mentioned in 1316 and 1317 were sold in 1649 to Robert Raye of Gomersal. The lands were described as 'the Kettlecarrs the Kettlecarringe the three closes lyeinge nere or upon the Spen greene with ... one parcell of land late inclosed ...'.[16] The tenants of the land had been Robert Franke, gentleman, and Raye himself.

Another seventeenth century deed has emerged which relates to Spen, though there is no means of telling to which buildings it refers. In 1699 William Horton of Barkisland issued a lease to Thomas Gumersall, a clothier, for a house called Spen Closes in which Gumersall himself lived, along with other houses, barns and land.[17] The name of Spen Closes has not been traced elsewhere in Spen documents.

Spen Mill

In all probability there was a water corn-mill at Spen in medieval times. Unfortunately this cannot be confirmed either from documents or from physical remains. Early deeds relating to Spen do not mention a mill, as would be expected if such a building had existed at the time. Nor does an inspection of the site reveal any remains which can be said to be of the medieval period.

Claims have been made however that the mill at Spen existed in the thirteenth century and that it served the manor of Cleckheaton.[18] But the Cleckheaton manorial mill owned by the family of Longvilliers was almost always referred to as the mill 'of Heton'; nowhere is there mention of it standing across the township boundary in Spen, which one would have expected had it done so. Furthermore, the medieval records of Spen, such as they are, do not include any reference to land being held by the Longvilliers or their successors as lords of Cleckheaton manor, the Nevilles. It does seem likely therefore that the 'Heton' mill was actually in Cleckheaton itself, possibly on the Blacup beck at Old Robin. The large dam which still existed there in 1802 may have had much earlier origins, resembling as it did in shape, size and situation the medieval dam at Birstall Church.

The first certain reference to Spen Mill was in 1565. However the deed of that date which lists Spen properties suggests that the mill was already well-established, adding to the likelihood of a medieval foundation. The 1565 sale from Hussey to Batt included:

> a water mill called Spenne milne and a wind mill called Gomersall wynd milne, with the dams, watercourses and suits of tenants in Spenne, Gomersal and Heton Clak in the occupation of William Brere, Margaret Wibsey and Robert Norton.[19]

The site of the Gomersal windmill has been lost, though it may have been between Hill Top and the Latham area. We do not know either where Hussey's tenants lived. The tenants were people who had no option but to have their corn ground at the manorial mill. This arrangement was extremely profitable for the lord of the manor, though often expensive and inconvenient for the tenant. It seems then that Gomersal and Cleckheaton tenants of the lord of Oakwell were required to use Spen Mill after the mill in Birstall had passed to the church. People were required to travel considerable distances to have their corn milled at Spen. The lease of a cottage in Birstall in 1672 by William Batt of Oakwell specified that the tenant, William Rayner, should 'grynd all ... [his] corne, grayne and malt ... att the water corn milne of the said William Batte and his heirs commonly called Spenn Milne within the manor of Oakwell...'.[20] Only the freemen of the townships, those not bound to a lord, would be able to choose where to take their grain for milling, whether to Spen or to Oakenshaw, Hunsworth (Balme Mill) or Millbridge, all of which were medieval manorial mills. Alternatively they could do the job laboriously at home with a hand-mill.

Spen Mill was mentioned in a magistrate's notes of the Commonwealth period. In 1657 William Barrett of Gomersal was accused of feloniously entering Spen Milne and taking goods and money 'out of the milnere chest there'. A prosecution witness was William Broome of Gomersell, millner, who could have been the miller at Spen.[21] However, another name to appear at this time in close association with Spen Mill was that of Walter Speight and the likelihood is that he lived in the mill house at Spen. In 1660 Robert and John Raye acquired property from William Batt which was described as a house at Spen in the tenure of Walter Speight, with three fields which adjoined Spen Lane on the west. There was also included 'such liberty for dressing and scouring of the goyte belonging to Spen Milne as is reserved unto the said William Batte ... in the lease made to the said Walter Speight'.[22] Walter Speight's name appeared in Spen deeds as early as 1654, when he witnessed a transaction with his mark[23] and he was also said to be a Spen tenant in 1678.[24] Other deeds relating to the Spen properties in 1690 and 1695 were unclear about who was tenant of the mill; probably Walter Speight had recently left the mill in 1695. The premises then were described as 'all those two water corne mills called Spen Mills' along with streams, goits and dams, and also a house at Spen.[25] The two mills would actually be two sets of milling machinery, probably in a single building.

The deed of 1690 also referred to a tannery; it described a 'messuage at Spen with ... Tanhouses Tanyards Orchards ... now in the tenure of Taylor Widdow ...'.[26] It is most likely that this would be at Spen Bottoms and near to the beck, as tanning requires copious quantities of water.

The Spen area, including the mill, passed by marriage from the Batts to the Smyth family of Heath in 1708, and the connection with Oakwell was severed.[27] The tenant of Spen Hall and probably of the mill from before 1706 until his death in 1728 was Christopher Laverack. Laverack was a wealthy man who left goods valued at over £700 at his death, so Spen Mill at this time may have been worked by an employee or under-tenant of Laverack. However, included in the £312 valuation of his house contents and goods connected with farming and other activities, was an astonishing £160 for 'malt in the kiln'. This could not have been a household item, and it shows that Laverack was engaged in malting on a commercial basis.[28] The kiln itself seems to have been at Spen Bottoms next to the mill.

From 1744 various transactions relating to the mill are recorded in deeds now in the possession of Mr H. Hepworth (hereafter referred to as Spen Mill Deeds). The first relate to mortgages taken out by John Smyth of Heath. Then in 1746 the mill was leased for twenty-one years to one John Walker at an annual rent of £35. A new description of the premises appeared, which was to be repeated in other eighteenth century leases: '... all those three water corn mills ... called ... Spenn Milles and one drying kiln to the same belonging...'.[29] The two mills of the 1690s had become three. Spen Mill may have had to be rebuilt between these dates to accommodate the extra machinery. There is confirmation also of a miller's house at Spen Bottoms, as Walker was said to be 'of Spenn Milles'.

The name of Joseph Mann, closely linked with Spen Mill for several generations, first appeared in Spen records at this time. This first Joseph Mann was the son-in-law of Samuel Laverack, a successor to Christopher Laverack at Spen Hall. Samuel Laverack bought a cottage in Spen in 1751. It is thought that this was intended for Mann and was the building whose ruins lie just beyond the dip in Gomersal Lane, where the lane starts to climb to Little Gomersal.[30] At the time of this purchase, however, Mann does not appear to have been connected with the mill.

The 1746 lease to Walker cannot have run its full term because a new seven year agreement was made in 1754 between Smyth and John Garsed for the same property. Garsed was already living in a 'new erected ... dwelling house ... with a barn stable and other conveniences lately built upon the Mill Garth ...'.[31] A number of improvements were in progress at this time and the lease required that by the end of the following year Garsed should

> take down and rebuild the Water Wheel house at the Mills and make wider the Race and also make new the Water Wheels and also put the machinery of the said Mills into complete repair according to the most modern and best plan possible.

There was also a schedule of the mill equipment which belonged to the landlord, Smyth:

> Twenty seven picks, one mall[et?], three chizzels, one gavelock, one strickle, one peck, two half pecks, one hack, one axe, one shovle, one Gin and good ropes, one mulcture ark. In drying kiln, one Iron Grate, one Trugan, one Coldrake and wood mall, two Iron Wedges, one Walling Hammer, one Matack, one pair of pincers, one Little Hammer.

The lease to Garsed (or Garside) was twice renewed, in 1760 and 1767, though it has been claimed that Joseph Mann was already at the mill in 1763.[32] It is most likely that the Manns took over the mill some time after the death of Samuel Laverack, which occurred in about 1777; indeed, the Gomersal land tax returns show a John Garside as tenant of a farm and mill owned by 'John Smith Esquire' as late as 1800.[33]

Laverack left his estate to his two daughters, Mary Mann and Sarah, wife of Caleb Crowther, and the Manns lived at Spen Hall in the early 1780s.[34] The Manns of Spen were cousins to Dr Thomas Mann of Pearson's Croft, Gomersal, who died in 1785, and through him were distantly related to the Sigstons. Through the Laveracks they seem also to have been connected to the Knowles family of Gomersal.[35]

The head of the Mann family of Spen for almost a hundred years from 1751 was always a Joseph. One of these, at the time referred to as Joseph Mann the younger of Spen, maltster, bought the freehold of the mill in 1812 with financial backing from a Cleckheaton oil merchant called William Williamson.[36] It is just possible that Mann was milling oil seed for Williamson at Spen Mill, though the loan could have been a straightforward financial investment as far as Williamson was concerned. There is nothing to say that a formal partnership existed between the two men.

Extensive earthworks had been necessary to supply a good head of water to Spen Mill. A channel was constructed from a point in the river upstream of Providence Place; it was joined by the stream from Fusden Woods and ran on into a long, narrow dam just above the mill. The tail race ran under Spen Lane, rejoining the river beyond Peg Mills.[37] Ensuring a good supply was a constant anxiety for the operators of watermills, especially after 1800 when the number of mills multiplied. The Manns made various agreements with their neighbours to protect the water source. In 1831 Joseph Mann, then described as a corn dealer, bought land from James Sutcliffe Broadbent of Roundhill so that the channel feeding Spen Mill could be enlarged. It was also agreed that he could raise the level of the dam beside the mill by one foot, provided that he made adjustments to the weirs upstream.[38] Then, in 1833, a major diversion of the beck was carried out by Mann in agreement with George Stead, a Cleckheaton ironfounder who owned land across the river. In 1842 Joseph Mann and his sons William and Henry, said to be corn millers and starch manufacturers, arranged with the Atkinsons of Peg Mill to divert water from the tail

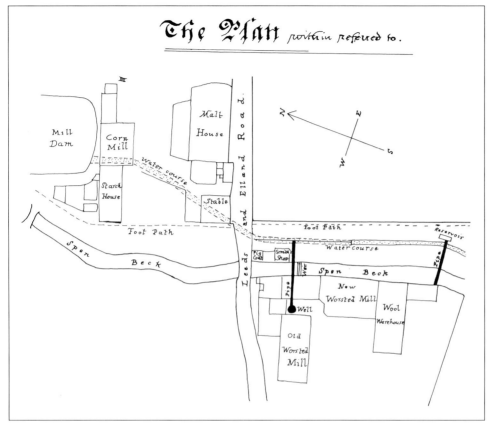

Figure 82: *Plan of Spen Mill and Peg Mill 1842 (Spen Mill Deeds)*

mills, counting house, drying kiln and gig house, malt kiln, stables ... with reservoir and mill yard'. Joseph Mann was still in charge of the business, though by 1841 he was about eighty years old and is said to have been very eccentric.[40] He lived with his sons until his death in April 1847.[41] The next census, in 1851, recorded only Henry Mann at Spen Bank House; he was a starch manufacturer and maltster employing ten men. William died in 1864 leaving everything to his brother.[42] The firm was still known as Joseph Mann and Sons in 1873 when they sent information to a parliamentary enquiry into river pollution. They were described as starch and British Gum manufacturers, producing annually 120,000 lbs. of wheat starch. Water was taken direct from the stream – 520,000 gallons each year – and they also consumed 250 tons of coal. The mill by this time was powered by both steam and water, to a total of 30 horsepower. They employed only five workers.[43]

Henry Mann sold the premises in 1876 to Samuel Blackburn and Arthur Firth, maltsters and cornmillers, both of Cleckheaton. Mann and his wife, formerly Lucy Ann Knowles of Gomersal, left Spen Bank House and settled in London where he died in 1879. Firth and Blackburn carried on the business at Spen for many years, with Arthur Firth living at Spen Bank House.[44] The reservoir is still, however, known throughout the locality as Harry Mann Dam.

race into a well in the yard of Peg Mill in return for a small annual payment – in effect selling their used water to supply the Atkinsons' steam engines! The 1842 agreement was accompanied by a plan showing details of the layout and use of buildings at both mills (Fig. 82), from which it appears that a rebuilding of Spen Mill mentioned later in the century had already taken place.[39]

At one time the miller's house may have adjoined the corn mill. By 1840, however, the Manns were living in Spen Bank House, well away from a valley bottom which was prone to flooding. The township valuation of 1840 described the premises at the mill as 'corn and starch

Spen Hall

The history of the hall has been extensively researched by one of its former owners.[45] However, the hall is an important building, and new source material has been found since the Scratons did their work, justifying a brief review here.

Spen Hall is said by the Scratons to date back about 700 years. A 'messuage' is refered to at Spen in fourteenth century deeds, but the present building is mainly of the late eighteenth and nineteenth centuries. The southern corner of the eastern range of the hall, that closest to Spen Lane, the Scratons estimate to be the only surviving remnant of a 'Tudor' rebuilding in about 1580. The rest of this sixteenth century structure was demolished and replaced by the present main hall in the middle of the last century. The oldest part of the hall as it now stands is the gable and two side walls at the end of what was a row of three cottages (Fig. 83). It has five-light mullion windows on the ground and first floors,

Figure 84: *Spen Hall: nineteenth century block*

though these differ in shape; the first floor chamfers have a convex mould down the front and could be older than those on the ground floor which are square-faced.[46] The two cottages furthest from the road, now occupied as one dwelling, may be eighteenth century, though they are listed by the Department of the Environment as having been built after 1800. They are of hammer-dressed stone with stone slate roof and two-light windows.

The main hall is a well-proportioned building of ashlar with a stone slate roof. Four bays of sash windows face on to a garden made private by a late Victorian arcade stretching south-east from the house (Fig. 84). The outbuildings, originally a stable, coach house and two cottages in the early nineteenth century, now form a single house and garage.[47]

A new discovery is the probate inventory of Christopher Laverack made in 1728. This is significant as it provides information about the house which was largely demolished last century. It also tells us much about Christopher Laverack and the activities which centred on the hall. The total value of Laverack's movable estate was estimated to be £726, though this included bonds and notes 'some good others desperate' and 'Booke

Figure 83: *Spen Hall: 'Tudor' wing and cottages*

Debts some good some desperate' with a nominal value of over £400. The actual goods of which he died possessed in 1728 were said to be worth £312, including £160 for malt in the kiln (see above). The figure also included livestock and farming equipment, and crops standing in his fields – which were of high value at the time, as the inventory was taken in August. The produce included 'wheat, oates, barley, beanes, pease and vetches'.[48] Besides small numbers of cattle and pigs for domestic use, Laverack owned nine horses and mares and three carts, which would have been used in his business as a maltster.

The contents of the hall were estimated to be worth about £50, a small proportion of Laverack's estate yet a considerable sum by the standards of the time. The list of items began with those in the kitchen, where the main furniture was a dresser, a settle, chairs and tables and the range. There was also a 'bread creell', a drying rack for oat cakes. Besides the everyday pots, pans, piggins and irons was a considerable amount of pewter: 'Nineteen puter dishes, a dozen of plates Containing Twenty Eight pounds weight – £01-18-00'.

The next room described was the 'parlour neare ye kitching' which held beds and hangings and 'a press for hanging cloaths in' besides tables, chairs, buffets and chests and a clock and case. After this were various small rooms where the work of the house was carried on – the buttery, the 'litle roome' and the milkhouse.

Upstairs were three bedrooms: the chamber at the stairhead, the Milk Chamber and the Far Chamber. Some malting equipment was stored there, including measures, 'ridles' and hoppers, though the quantity of

soft furnishing mentioned, bedding and hangings, suggests the rooms were comfortable. A 'Closett' held chairs and drawers besides blankets, sheets, tablecloths and napkins. The other rooms examined were the cellar, containing tubs and barrels, and the 'Milnhouse' which held only a hand mill, hopper, trough and an 'oke chest'. This was a small domestic mill unconnected with Spen Mill.

The Laveracks stayed as tenants of Spen Hall until about 1777 and were succeeded by the sons-in-law of Samuel Laverack. After the death of one of these the hall was advertised to let: 'House, late of Caleb Crowther, merchant, outbuildings, warehouses, dressing and press-shops, gardens, at Spen ... in the centre of the woollen manufactory'.[49] Crowther based his woollen business at the hall and may have been responsible for constructing some of the outbuildings. The malting side of the Laveracks' business had passed to the other son-in-law, Joseph Mann (see above), though the hall retained a malt kiln which seems to have been used by a later tenant, Joseph Gomersall, in the 1820s and after.[50]

After 1810, the Taylors of Red House owned Spen Hall for over a century and for most of that time it was let to tenants. Many of these lived there for only short periods, and there were several tenants at a time as the cottages were rented separately.[51] The chemical works mentioned earlier was built by one of these tenants, Alexander Dixon, before his move to Nellroyd Mill in 1844 or 1845. These industrial buildings dominated the grounds of the hall as late as 1850, though by then no longer used for chemical processing. They had been completely demolished by 1890.

NOTES

1. Goodall 1953, 8.
2. Cadman 1930, 85.
3. Cadman 1930, 85-6; *Cleckheaton Guardian* 18 Jan 1924; Harrison 1910.
4. Cadman 1930, 84.
5. *WYAS B* 1 D 78/82.
6. *WYAS C* MISC:526/9.
7. *Bretton* BEA/C3/B32/15.
8. Harrison 1910.
9. Harrison 1910.
10. Harrison 1910.
11. Goodall 1953, 219.
12. Goodall 1953, 220 and 51; Brown (ed.) 1914, 69.
13. *BL* Add Ch 12637.
14. *BL* Add Ch 12639.
15. Lancaster 1924, 31.
16. *Thoresby* Batt no 212.
17. *NYCRO* ZFW 1/18/2.
18. Goodall 1953, 52 and 221.
19. Lancaster 1924, 31; see chapter 2.
20. *WYAS K* DD/HS/G/4/1.
21. Goodall 1953, 151.
22. *Thoresby* Batt no 158.
23. *Thoresby* Batt no 174.
24. Scraton and Scraton 1974, 7.
25. *Thoresby* Batt nos 17 and 75.
26. *Thoresby* Batt no 17.
27. For a full account of the descent of Spen Hall and Mill, see Scraton and Scraton 1974; see also chapter 2 above.
28. *Borthwick* Inventory of Christopher Laverack Aug 1728 and see below.
29. Cadman 1930, 84.
30. Scraton and Scraton 1974, 8.
31. Spen Mill Deeds.
32. Goodall 1953, 221.
33. *WYAS HQ* QE13/7/19.
34. Scraton and Scraton 1974, 8.
35. Cadman 1930, 158, and see chapters 5 and 7.
36. Spen Mill Deeds.
37. Thorp's Map 1822.
38. Spen Mill Deeds.
39. Cudworth 1876, 528.
40. 1841 Census; Harrison 1910.
41. Spen Mill Deeds.
42. Spen Mill Deeds.
43. *Parliamentary Papers* (House of Commons) 1873 XXXVI pt 11.
44. Cadman 1930, 84.
45. Scraton and Scraton 1974.
46. Hanson 1922.
47. Scraton and Scraton 1974, 1; DoE.
48. *Borthwick* Inventory of Christopher Laverack, 1 August 1728.
49. *Leeds Intelligencer* 29 Dec 1794.
50. Parson 1826, 227.
51. Scraton and Scraton 1974, 9-11.

Chapter 7

THE TEXTILE INDUSTRY IN GOMERSAL

Few villages in Yorkshire can match Gomersal's long and wide-ranging connection with the textile industry. A textile centre for at least four centuries, from domestic to factory system, Gomersal can boast the remains of a cloth hall, some seventeenth century clothiers' houses, a merchant's warehouse and loomshop dating from the eighteenth century, a company mill, and the grandiose houses of nineteenth century industrialists, along with the vestiges of cotton, woollen and worsted factories.

Spen Valley was at the centre of the West Riding wool textile district, where woollen cloth-making became firmly established during the Tudor period. It was an industry whose scale varied widely; some families used only their own labour and worked in the woollen trade in seasons of the year when they did not have agricultural jobs to do – where land was relatively poor and farms small, it was common to combine the two occupations. Other men, of the class now called yeoman clothier (though this was not a term used at the time), were engaged in cloth manufacture and marketing on a large and well-organised scale. These clothiers did not have many direct employees; most of the work was done on the domestic or 'putting out' system by families paid piece rates. But the success of some yeoman clothiers can be judged from the comfort and substance of several houses built in Gomersal after about 1650.

In the eighteenth century, woollen manufacture was still a domestic industry. Until about 1780, changes were gradual and involved the growing importance of merchants and the rise of cloth halls. Much of the cloth made in Gomersal and other textile villages was sold through the Leeds market. Leeds cloth halls grew bigger and more specialized as the century progressed, and the power and wealth of Leeds merchants who bought and finished the cloth grew accordingly. Hopes that the Leeds monopoly could be broken, and that cloth

could be sold and bought locally, led to a plan that Gomersal should have its own cloth hall. The scheme came to fruition, but the hall was not a success and was soon converted to other use.

The closing decades of the eighteenth century brought innovation to the textile industry and the new methods were quickly introduced to Gomersal. The main change in the woollen trade was the transfer of some preparatory and finishing processes into factories. But wool could not be woven by powered machinery until well into the nineteenth century. A parliamentary report in 1840 calculated that there were still over 10,000 handlooms at work in the West Riding – 130 of these were in Great Gomersal, 30 in Little Gomersal and 146 in Birstall.[1]

Fulling (wetting and hammering woollen cloth to shrink and thicken it) had been carried out in mills since the middle ages, and by 1800 processes prior to spinning wool, such as scribbling, carding and slubbing, were largely mechanized. In many places water-powered factories were built, but this was difficult in Gomersal, on the ridge of a hill. The Taylors of Red House found a way round this problem by building a mill in the valley bottom at Hunsworth two miles away.[2] Other entrepreneurs in Gomersal solved the difficulty by introducing up-to-date technology in the form of steam engines. There were two steam-powered factories in the village by 1800 – Castle Hill and Cloth Hall – and a number of others appeared in the early years of the nineteenth century.

Like their competitors elsewhere in West Yorkshire, Gomersal entrepreneurs experimented with different fibres. Both Castle Hill and Cloth Hall mills were used for cotton spinning in the early nineteenth century. Some woollen manufacturers, like Thomas Burnley, were making a gradual move to worsted spinning. Although worsted cloth is made from sheep's wool, it requires a longer fibre and a different system of manufacture from that used on the coarser woollen product. Worsted spinning and weaving were carried out by machine soon after cotton production had been mechanized, and some time before machinery could be applied in the woollen industry.

One other major change which occurred in about 1800 was the involvement in textiles of a variety of speculators, people who had no previous experience in the trade. In the case of Gomersal, a number of examples illustrate the point. There was the landowner who wished to increase the value of his estate, exemplified by Col. Beaumont of Bretton who built and equipped Castle Hill Mill (though he was never active in running it). There was the speculator who let out all or part of a mill on a 'room and power' basis – like Thomas Carr of Halifax, who occupied part of the former Cloth Hall for cotton spinning and sub-let the rest to a woollen scribbler. And there was the company mill, these often built by groups of small clothiers, each investing as much as he could afford in order to gain access to mechanized scribbling and carding. Gomersal's example is Union Mill, built in 1837.

Pre-Factory Workshops

In the eighteenth century a number of Gomersal's most successful clothiers began to trade as merchants. As business grew, it was not always possible to accommodate all of the storage and finishing of cloth at the merchant's home. There was also a desire for closer control of cloth-making operations. Much work was put out to domestic spinners and weavers, and it was difficult to maintain quality, regulate the quantities of wool issued and check the size of cloth pieces returned. Some forward-looking merchants therefore began to build large workshops. These could be described as factories, in the most basic sense of the word;[3] however, the only motive power was that of man or woman, and processes were mainly carried out using traditional

Figure 85: *Grove Square: the three storey workshop on the right has been converted to houses, but features such as taking-in doors can still be seen in the stonework. A break in the masonry to the left of the corner door and windows indicates that the cottages with cellar kitchens dated 1836 were later additions.*

Figure 86: *Grove Square: northern side of former workshop*

methods. These buildings were large by the standards of the time, though not when compared to later factories; they are now very rarely found, as they had become redundant by the mid nineteenth century and were usually either drastically altered or demolished.

112

Behind two early-Victorian shops in Oxford Road is an 'L'-shaped block of seven cottages called Grove Square (Figs 85 and 86). The east range is three stories high, the north range a more conventional terrace of three two-storey cottages with cellar kitchens. This north range bears a datestone of 1836. The appearance of the square is unusual and it is difficult to categorize as domestic or industrial. It is in fact a rare survival, a workshop from the pre-factory era.

The three-storey section of Grove Square presents a puzzle. Slightly west of the angle in the square, where three-storey joins two, is a datestone of 1751. The back of the three-storey east range, facing on to Grove Lane, has been little altered, and features on that side confirm that 1751 could well be the date that the block was built. By contrast, the frontage on to the square has changed considerably, though a line of three taking-in doors, one in each floor, can still be seen. These are typical of late eighteenth century industrial buildings and appear to have been blocked when the warehouse was converted to living accommodation. Another datestone, of 1846, is inserted there, perhaps showing the date of that conversion. Other buildings also once extended south of the square, as shown by maps and by part of a demolished wall. In the middle of the last century, buildings here butted the Grove Sunday School.

According to local tradition Grove Square was part of Thomas Burnley's workshops. However, no evidence for this has ever been published. There is a passing reference in Cadman to a house behind Grove Chapel, where a boy slept in an upper room without underdrawing between 'a jinny and warping woof'. No dates or other details are provided.[4]

Apart from this story, there is some circumstantial evidence that the eastern range of the square was Burnley's warehouse, and perhaps loomshop and finishing shop. This range was built at the same time that William Burnley established his woollen manufacturing business at Pollard Hall. It ceased to be used for industry at about the time that Thomas Burnley

transformed his business from a domestic one to a factory base at Gomersal Mills in 1850. Furthermore, when Burnley became owner of Pollard Hall in 1843, the buildings there were described in some detail and included a warehouse, dye-house, dry-house, and spinning shop.[5] The wool would have been scribbled and carded in a factory (probably at Union Mill, part-owned by Burnley). A question remains, however, as to where Burnley's cloth was woven and finished. We know that he still made woollen cloth at this date – an 1851 letterhead described his business as 'cloth, blanket, worsted and yarn manufacturer'. Some of the cloth would be woven by out-workers on handlooms, perhaps even after 1850. But one would expect a manufacturer and merchant of Burnley's importance to have had his own finishing-shops and probably a loom-shop. Grove Square seems to fit Burnley's requirements perfectly – a convenient annexe to his workshops at Pollard Hall.

There is some firm evidence that Burnley was involved in Grove Square. Gomersal's township valuation of 1840 shows the buildings there to have been owned by Thomas Burnley, including one described as a warehouse which he himself used. There were also two dwellings – house and linen draper's shop, occupied by George Berry, and a house, kitchen and mistal, along with various fields, whose tenant was James Acroyd. Census returns of 1841 and 1851 do not help establish how many houses were in Grove Square, but significantly its name was recorded in the 1851 census as Warehouse Yard. There were probably three cottages occupied then, along with the two shops on the main road side, kept by a grocer and a butcher. Heads of the households in the square were a worsted spinner, a wool sorter and a whitesmith, men who could have been Burnley's employees at Gomersal Mills, though there is no suggestion that these were ever 'tied houses' for the mill's workforce.

By the time the Ordnance Survey revised their Gomersal map in 1888-92, the former warehouse had been converted to housing and Grove Square was arranged as it is today.

The Cloth Hall

Gomersal's Cloth Hall was a remarkable achievement. It did not survive for long as a cloth market, and is invariably written off by historians, generally meriting only a footnote in books on the West Riding textile industry. But the fact that it was built at all in the face of mighty opposition from the Leeds merchants says much for the tenacity and influence of those involved in the project. If evidence is needed of the fright given to the Leeds merchant community, one need only look at their response: the existing Leeds White Cloth Hall, less than twenty years old, was replaced by a new one in 1775-76 with ten times the floor space of its predecessor.[6]

The system of marketing woollen cloth through cloth halls was well-established by the mid eighteenth century, with Leeds and Wakefield the local centres. Leeds gained the ascendancy over Wakefield and had two Cloth Halls where weekly markets took place. One was devoted to the white (unfinished) cloth in which Gomersal specialised, and the other, known as the Coloured Cloth Hall, sold dyed and finished cloth. Leeds had a large and sophisticated marketing system for the cloth, but suffered from a major geographical problem in that the cloth-making areas were mainly south and west of the town. Gomersal was eight miles away over poor roads, and many other clothing villages were even further from the Leeds market. Small clothiers needed to visit the market every week to sell their cloth so that they had money to buy wool for the next piece. Generally the journey to Leeds and back would take a full day. Clothiers also complained that the Leeds White Cloth Hall had become far too small to accommodate the growing trade of the time, and they had not enough space to display the wares to their best advantage.

So a scheme was devised by a number of merchants and landowners in Gomersal to build their own cloth hall in the village. The project attracted immediate hostility from the trustees of the Leeds White Cloth Hall. They took legal action to try and stop it. The proposed hall, at the very centre of the White Cloth district, was a real threat to their business. In their turn, supporters of the Gomersal scheme enlisted powerful support in parliament.

The situation was described in a letter from Sir George Savile's steward, Edward Elmsall, to Lord Dartmouth in February 1775:

> I have inclosed yr. Lordship a plan which I received from the White Clothiers in the Neighbourhood of Birstall – These People have been used to carry all their Cloth to the Merchants at Leeds, & it is at such a great distance from great numbers of them, & for that reason so inconvenient, & so expensive, that they have a design of building a Cloth Hall at Gommersal, wch. you will see is in the Centre of the White Cloth Manufactory & Sir Geo. Savile, Sir Jas. Ibbetson, Sir Geo. Armytage, Sir Thos. Wentworth, & a great many others, Gentlemen of property, give them great encouragement to proceed in, & they have already got together materials for this purpose, but the Merchants at Leeds oppose this as it is a greater ease to them to have the Cloth delivered at their own Doors than having to ride 5 or 6 miles. The Gentlemen Merchants of Leeds are now in Town, & intend making application to the House to oblige the Clothiers to carry their Cloth to Leeds, as heretofore, wch. every bod thinks very unreasonable. Sir Geo. Savile is apprized of them, & I fancy will have an eye upon them, & the Clothiers have beg'd me to mention the affair to your Lordship, believing that you will by yourself, or Friends, assist them where the good of this branch of Trade, is so materially concerned.[7]

None of the supporters of the planned hall whose names appear in Elmsall's letter were resident in the area. All, however, were considerable local landowners who hoped that the value of their property, and the rents they received, would increase if the Gomersal project were successful. The Leeds merchants evidently had powerful friends in parliament, but so too did the sponsors of the Gomersal hall.

The trustees of Gomersal Cloth Hall were allowed to go ahead with the scheme and their chairman, John Wood, wrote to thank Lord Dartmouth in May 1775 'with Hearts full of gratitude'.[8] The foundation stone was laid on 23 March 1775, and the hall was quickly completed.[9] Built on land belonging to Sir James Ibbetson, it was a large brick building with two wings projecting from a main block, forming three sides of a square. The courtyard faced the Leeds-Elland turnpike road (Fig. 87).

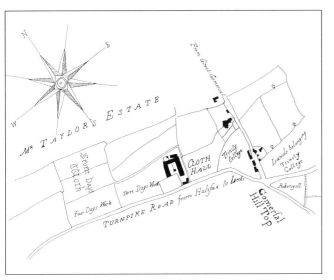

Figure 87: Plan of Gomersal Cloth Hall: detail from Ibbetson's estate map of 1798 (WYAS L DB/M 670/4 reproduced by kind permission of Dibb Lupton Broomhead and Prior, solicitors)

Local clothiers who supported the Gomersal scheme had signed undertakings that they would sell their cloth nowhere else. Strenuous efforts were made to promote the new hall across the county. A map was produced which showed Gomersal as the hub of the West Riding white cloth district with all other villages revolving around it.[10] But despite its apparent geographical advantage, the hall did not thrive as a cloth market. Little evidence has been found to say why this was so. The obvious explanation is that Leeds could offer other attractions to clothiers on their weekly visits, along with the improved facilities of its own new hall. A sustained boycott by the Leeds merchants may have been enough to end the Gomersal experiment.

The Gomersal Cloth Hall had failed. As early as March 1786 the building was advertised in the *Leeds Intelligencer*:

> To woollen and cotton manufacturers. Gomersall Hall, well adapted for a manufactory, large strong building, two wings & a place called the Headland joining wings together. In Wings 4 rooms 62 yards long, each 20 feet wide & 14 feet high. Headland 61 yards long, 20 feet wide, 14 feet high, chamber over, same size. Coal ½ mile away, water under all building, 12 feet. Populous country near Leeds ...

This enormous building must have been the largest for miles around. Perhaps understandably, it found no takers and was again advertised to let in December 1787. By August 1788 the trustees appear to have become desperate, offering for sale the materials of which the hall was built: 'bricks, timber, lead, sashes, slates, flags etc.'.

The Gomersal Cloth Hall was not demolished, but re-advertised in July 1789: 'To be lett for a term of years by private contract ... The Cloth Hall at Gomersall ... with or without about 20 days work of land lying contiguous to it ... Apply to Mr Thomas Carr, Halifax.' Carr, who was said to have been the agent of Ibbetson, took over the hall himself and converted it to cotton-spinning in about 1793, though a directory of that year still refers to a cloth hall in Gomersal: 'Not far from Birstall is a small village called Gomershall, where the clothiers have erected a large brick building for a cloth market, in hopes of bringing the merchants nearer their own homes, and thereby save expense. It was in course encouraged by the landowners, but it is doubtful whether it will answer...'.[11] Carr was described as a cotton manufacturer and had moved to Gomersal by 1794 when an agreement was drawn up for his marriage to Ellen Richardson of Thrum Hall, Halifax.[12]

When Thomas Carr insured the Cloth Hall as a cotton mill in 1801, it is clear from the description that the buildings had been put to a number of uses. He himself had moved into a house built near the hall, or perhaps converted from a part of it, and insured for £300. His steam powered factory was insured for a total of £4,200. There was also a scribbling mill adjoining his cotton mill, which was insured for £300, and five cottages abutting insured for £200.[13]

By 1803 Carr was in financial difficulty, and advertised his interest in a 'large cotton factory, now in his possession and of Messrs Crowther & Hirst. House & stable, machinery of factory, steam engine 16 horse power, 20 carding and trimming machines, 3 drawing frames, a third of another steam engine of 24 horse power'.[14]

Thomas Carr's bankruptcy was announced in the *Leeds Intelligencer* in December 1803. His interest in Cloth Hall Mill was transferred to his major creditors, a Halifax merchant family called Swaine. The business was again advertised in 1806 and 1808, but it was not sold.[15] Instead, two very junior members of the family, half-brothers Joseph and Edward Swaine, took over the mill in partnership as woollen manufacturers. They built up a successful business whose scope can be gauged from insurance policies of 1833. The East Wing of the factory was in use as a fulling, scribbling, carding and cloth dressing mill, with engine and boiler houses. The mill was steam heated, lit by lamps and candles, and divided by two brick walls from the North Wing. Teazles (used for raising the nap on woollen cloth) were dried on iron rods in the boiler house, and sheep's wool on a wooden trellised floor above. The North and West Wings were used for fulling, carding and scribbling and had their own engine and boiler houses.[16]

Joseph and Edward Swaine gave detailed answers to the parliamentary enquiry into Children's Employment in 1833. They said that they manufactured wool into cloth, throughout all its processes. Their mill was 'intended for a cloth market, which was soon abandoned', then occupied first as a button mill (a misprinting of cotton) and for the last twenty-six years as a woollen mill. Power was supplied by two steam engines, of 30 and 26 horse power. Part of the mill, which accommodated 668 worsted spindles and two woollen scribbling and two carding machines, was let out. The Swaines employed 231 people, though some of them – 16 weavers, 6 spinners, 12 slubbers, 30 croppers and 15 burlers – worked for piece-rates and employed assistants themselves. The highest average wages were earned by slubbers, at 25 shillings for a 67-hour week. The workforce at Cloth Hall Mills enjoyed a total of four

days' holiday a year, though unpaid. Swaines were more liberal than many employers of the time, in that they paid for medical assistance when an employee had an accident at work, and sometimes made up wages lost as a result of the accident. Nor did they use corporal punishment on the children who worked for them. But they saw no need for parliament to regulate children's working hours: 'The appearance of our children denotes robust health, and this we regard as the best proof that their employment is anything but injurious'. Regulation, said the Swaines, would encourage the introduction of more machinery in place of children, 'and thus add to our oppressive parish rates'.[17]

The township valuation described Cloth Hall Mill in 1840 as a scribbling, cloth and dressing mill, with engine and boiler houses, raizing shop, pearking shop, packing shop, smith and joiners' shop, burling rooms, counting house, stables, fire engine house, oil warehouse, mistal, old dye-house. reservoir and mill yard. Joseph and Edward Swaine and Co. were still there as tenants of Sir Charles Ibbetson.

When Ibbetson sold his Gomersal estates in 1843, Thomas Burnley bought the Cloth Hall Mill, Pollard Hall

Figure 88: *Gomersal Mills: most of the buildings visible date from about 1913, but it is still possible to see older parts of the mill, which may once have been houses, behind the office frontage.*

and some surrounding land. Burnley had to wait until Swaines' lease expired in 1850 before he could move his own business into the mill from Pollard Hall. The Swaines apparently continued in business as merchants after leaving the mill, though Edward had retired to York by 1855. Joseph's sons were still merchants in Leeds in the 1870s.[18]

Thomas Burnley in 1851 was a manufacturer of cloth, blankets, worsted and yarn. The mill that he took over in 1850 followed the basic three-wing pattern of the old Cloth Hall, with a few minor additions. These included four sizable reservoirs around the mill. Lower down Spen Lane a dryhouse had been built, at a distance from any other building, perhaps because of the risk of fire. Old-fashioned methods of drying cloth appear also to have been in use; two tenterframes stretched the length of a field in the Woodlands area. In the 1850s the factory's name was changed to Gomersal Mills.

In 1876 Burnleys were the 'largest ratepayers and employers of labour in the village'.[19] Thomas Burnley & Sons Ltd. was still a private company in 1915, when its value was put at £35,000 in £10 shares. At this time the company left the ownership of the Burnley family; it was taken over by W.C.Gaunt, and then in 1929 by The West Riding Worsted and Woollen Mills Ltd.[20]

Little remains of the buildings which were called Cloth Hall Mills in 1850. A large fire in 1913 destroyed most of the original mill. The present front office block appears to be one of the houses known to have stood in the yard of the Cloth Hall Mill, and could be the mill manager's house where younger members of the Swaine and Burnley families lived in the middle years of the nineteenth century.[21]

The Absentee Landlord as Factory Entrepreneur

Not everyone who built a factory had connections with the textile industry. Landowners often took a leading part in promoting mill-building – as they had tried to encourage a cloth hall in Gomersal – with the aim of improving the value of their estates. A local example of speculative mill-building by a property owner is Castle Hill (or Castlehouse) Mill, Little Gomersal, built by Col. Thomas Richard Beaumont of Bretton Hall. Perhaps because of its inconvenient location, the investment showed little or no profit, and it seems that the factory stood empty for much of its life.

The mill was in fields below Listing Lane, near to Listing Farm. It stood on the Wentworths' extensive Little Gomersal estate which came into Beaumont's ownership as part of his wife's inheritance. Castle Hill Mill, built about 1794, was one of the earliest steam-powered factories in the district.

It was first advertised in August and September 1794 as a 'large, new erected scribbling mill and corn mill, wrought by a steam engine ... scribbling mill has eight engines for scribbling and carding wool. Corn mill complete for all kinds of corn. Land near mill and several houses for owners and workers'.[22] Beaumont was aiming to capitalise on new technology which enabled wool to be prepared by steam-powered machinery. He was also offering a corn-milling service to local farmers, though no evidence has been found that the factory ever operated as a corn mill.

Similar advertisements for the mill were placed the following year.[23] It was some time before Beaumont found a tenant, but in July 1800 he issued a fourteen year lease to a Batley woolstapler, Joseph Oldroyd, at £100 per annum. The factory 'now used for scribbling and carding of wool' was let with its contents, along with three new dwelling houses, and a house, farm and 12 acres of land, previously occupied by Obadiah Porritt but into which Oldroyd had already moved. It seems that Oldroyd may have been at the mill for a few months before taking a formal lease.[24]

The fittings and contents of the mill were listed and valued at just over £1,000. Attached to the valuation in the Beaumont estate papers was a list of expenses incurred during the previous year for repairing and maintaining the mill. Some of the work had been carried out by B. Ross, Blacksmith – who was also publican at the nearby Bull's Head. These accounts show that Ross was profiting well from the new mill in his neighbourhood – and not just for the metalwork required there:

B. Ross Blacksmith work from 17th Octr 1799 to 15th Jany 1800	£	3	14	5
Ditto from 15th Jany to June 1800	£	29	10	8
Ditto Ale for Millwrights from 15th Jany to 30th June 1800	£	10	5	7
Ditto Blacksmith work from 30th July to 15th Septr 1800	£	14	2	5
Ditto Ale Millwrights from 30th June to 15 Septr 1800	£	2	14	3

At 3d. a pint or less, this represents a large volume of beer for the millwrights, men responsible for fitting and maintaining the engines, shafting and gearing in factories. Highly skilled, they were in short supply and were well paid. Millwrighting was evidently thirsty work.[25]

Joseph Oldroyd insured his mill in February 1801 for considerably more than its 1800 valuation. Besides the 'scribbling mill, stone and slated, called Castle Mill' insured for £800, he mentioned a steam engine (£100), millwrights' work (£600), and scribbling, carding and slubbing machinery (£1,000). Stock valued at £500 was included in the total of £3,000.[26]

When the lease came up for renewal at the end of 1813, Oldroyd was dead and his widow had taken over the business and property. She continued to rent Castlehouse Mill 'now used for scribbling and carding of wool' and run the farm there on a yearly agreement at £210 per annum.[27] By the end of 1818 Ann Oldroyd had

left, and Beaumont again advertised the property to let.[28] The mill was not mentioned in trade directories of the early 1820s, and could again have been unoccupied. In December 1823 Joseph and Benjamin Smith of Manchester, described as merchants and co-partners in trade, took over the whole property at an annual rent of £152. In their lease was an agreement to reimburse the Smiths for expenses incurred in pulling down and rebuilding the engine house of the mill.[29] Joseph Smith bought Castle Hill Mill in 1833 when the Beaumonts sold their Gomersal estate. He paid £2,200 for a dwelling house, cottage and garden, worsted mill of three floors 102 by 28 feet each, engine house, warehouse of three floors, stables and three cottages, and was allowed £175 reduction in the price for having added one storey to the mill.[30]

At some time during this period Castle Hill Mill was converted to cotton spinning – a firm of cotton thread manufacturers occupied it in 1838.[31] In the township valuation of 1840, the owners were given as Junius and Horatio Smith, and the tenants were the Castle Hill Mill Company; the premises included a dryhouse over the warehouse, a bleaching house, gas house, and reservoirs. The Smiths never lived in Gomersal, and the mill seems to have been run by managers.

Castle Hill Mill was offered for sale in 1844, and may have been bought by James Sutcliffe Broadbent, of Roundhill Mill, Gomersal, in 1846.[32] An 1853 directory shows the Castle Hill Twist Co. still in occupation[33] but by the end of the century Castle Hill Mill appears to have gone out of business altogether, a victim of the decline of the cotton industry in West Yorkshire, and unattractive to wool or worsted spinners when there were many other factories more conveniently situated. The mill has been demolished.

The Textile Entrepreneur

Butts Mill was built and run for forty-five years by one family who suffered spectacular reversals of fortune. After that, from the middle of the nineteenth century, it was put to a variety of uses until 1877 when the original mill was completely destroyed by fire.

The heads of the firm which built Butts Mill in 1804 and ran it until 1850 were two William Hirsts, father and son. The first reference to a William Hirst of Gomersal comes from an unlikely source; in 1795 an engineer of that name was one of a handful of West Riding men to subscribe to John Banks's *Treatise on Mills*, an early technical work. Over the next years there are many references to William Hirst, sometimes described as a scribbling miller or an engineer, and also as a merchant. It seems that these are the same William Hirst who built Butts Mill.

In 1803 Hirst had been the partner of Thomas Crowther in a wing of Cloth Hall Mill, where they employed thirty-five people carding and scribbling wool.[34] When Hirst built Butts Mill, probably in 1804, he was in business on his own as a scribbling miller. He soon bought other land in Gomersal and Spen, and was referred to in a deed of 1808 as a merchant.[35] By 1820 he had been successful enough to build himself a large house, Marsh House, in the field below Butts Mill. His son was taken into partnership, and they appeared in directories through the 1820s and 1830s as William Hirst and Son, merchants, manufacturers and sometimes woolstaplers. During this period they insured their mill for £1,800. It was brick and slated, steam heated and lighted by gas – they were said to be the first people in Gomersal to have manufactured gas.[36]

But by 1827 the Hirsts faced ruin. They were forced to deposit the deeds to their mill and house with Leeds bankers Beckett and Blayds as security against their overdraft. When William Hirst was declared bankrupt in May 1832 he owed the bank £9,280 10s. Beckett's therefore acquired his property, including the scribbling, carding and fulling mill called Butts Mill with a range of ancillary buildings and its own coal pit. Marsh House, with six main bedrooms, luxuries such as wine cellars, library and a water closet, and well laid out pleasure grounds commanding a 'fine and beautiful

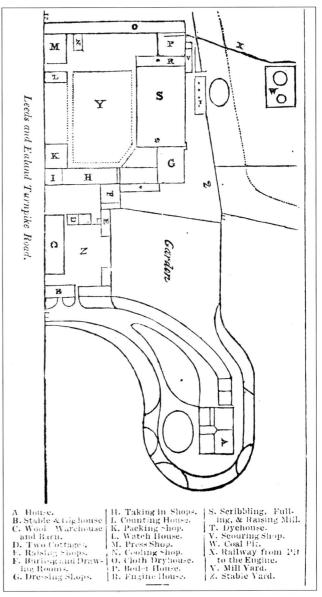

A. House.
B. Stable & Gighouse.
C. Wood Warehouse and Barn.
D. Two Cottages.
E. Raising Shops.
F. Burling and Drawing Rooms.
G. Dressing Shops.
H. Taking in Shops.
I. Counting House.
K. Packing Shop.
L. Watch House.
M. Press Shop.
N. Cooling Shop.
O. Cloth Dryhouse.
P. Boiler House.
R. Engine House.
S. Scribbling, Fulling, & Raising Mill.
T. Dyehouse.
V. Scouring Shop.
W. Coal Pit.
X. Railway from Pit to the Engine.
Y. Mill Yard.
Z. Stable Yard.

Figure 89: Plan of Butts Mill and Marsh House, from a sale advertisement of 1832 (Leeds Mercury 21 July 1832)

prospect' and surrounded by 'thriving plantations' was also put up for auction. This seemed a sorry end to the business and home which Hirst had established over the previous thirty years, and the whole estate was put on sale in August 1832 (Fig. 89).[37]

Evidently no purchaser could be found – many similar properties were on sale as numerous other manufacturers were in difficulties. William Hirst and his son continued to occupy the mill and house as tenants of the bank and carried on their business as before. They were both on the voters' list in 1840, Hirst senior at Marsh House and his son shown as joint tenant of the mill. Beckett, Blayds and Co. technically owned the property when the 1840 township valuation was drawn up, and the description of the mill shows the range of the Hirsts' business. They prepared wool by scribbling and carding, but were mainly engaged in finishing cloth – including dyeing, fulling and dressing (or cropping). Spinning and weaving were still done outside the mill. This is typical of the way in which factory-based merchant/manufacturers organised their activities at that time.

William Hirst senior was about seventy when the 1841 census was taken, still living at Marsh House and evidently wealthy enough to keep two resident servants. His son, by then aged about thirty-five, had married Sarah Sigston and by the mid century the younger Hirsts lived in Croft House, which Sarah had inherited from her family.

The elder William Hirst died in the early 1840s. Family fortunes were improving, assisted by Sarah's large inheritance, and in 1846 the younger William was able to buy back the mill, house and land from Beckett's. He settled his debt by paying £6,500 to the bank, and took a mortgage of £5,000 from one James Hargrave to cover the rest. By the time Hirst died in August 1850 he had repaid half the sum owing to Hargrave. His daughters sold the whole property in May 1851 to William Crowther of Little Gomersal, a manufacturing chemist. Crowther did not occupy the mill but let it to a firm of woollen manufacturers and merchants called Barker, Son and Brook.[38]

The factory was turned over to a variety of uses; tenants after 1850 included Mason and Wood, soap manufacturers; Houghton Bros., machine makers; James Howard & Co, sizers; and H.F. Cockill & Sons Ltd., curriers. By 1870, the lease of the mill had been bought by Shackleton Smith of Gomersal, a worsted spinner, who used the premises for preparing and spinning worsted yarn.[39]

In January 1877 Butts Mill was totally destroyed by fire. It is in reports of this fire that the best description of the old mill is found: it was a three storey building of eleven bays, with an attic. Much of it had been sublet by Smith; the top storey was occupied by John Holdsworth, blanket and flannel manufacturer, and the middle by Messrs Walker and Bridgewater. Other tenants were Oliver and Thomas Preston and John Illingworth. Fire had started in the middle room over the staircase, and the mill was said to have been 'unsavable'.[40]

Marsh House survived rather longer, changing its name eventually to Barrington House.[41] Its inhabitants included Shackleton Smith, and later John Wesley Hillard, founder of the grocery chain.[42]

The Company Mill

Union Mill was started as a co-partnership in 1837 to meet local demands for factory-produced yarn. Some of the partners joined the scheme because they needed a ready supply of wool for weaving; others saw it only as a financial investment and hoped to make a profit from the venture.

It is significant that the Union Mill project was floated after Castle Hill Mill had ceased wool processing, but before Thomas Burnley acquired his own factory (at this time he was still running a large business from Pollard Hall). Burnley was one of the instigators of Union Mill, and became a trustee. His name appeared at the head of the company along with that of Edwin Firth, a Heckmondwike blanket manufacturer. It is likely that these two were important customers of Union Mill in its early days.

The mill company was launched in 1837 with eighty shares, each of £50. By no means all the shareholders were from Gomersal, nor were they all directly involved in the woollen trade. Besides Burnley and Firth, the trustees were David Fox, a Cleckheaton cardmaker; Josiah Burrows of Castle House, who was a farmer and maltster; Samuel Porritt, who lived in Upper Lane but was evidently not a woollen manufacturer; Benjamin Fearnley, a Gomersal woolstapler; and two woollen manufacturers from Little Gomersal, William Hammond and William Walker. At least four other small manufacturers from Gomersal held shares, but so did a shopkeeper, two cardmakers and several others whose occupations cannot be traced but who were certainly not Gomersal clothiers.[43]

William Carr of Gomersal House recorded that his father had bought the site of the factory in the Beaumont sale of 1833.[44] All the evidence points to Union Mill having been built in 1837, and the company first appears in a directory of 1838 as Burnley, Firth & Co., scribbling millers.[45] The property was described in the 1840 township valuation as a scribbling and worsted mill, engine house, boiler house, wash house, counting house over Briggs' reservoir, and mill yard. At £200, its rateable value placed it among the larger factories of the village. (Cloth Hall Mill was valued at £320, Butts Mill at £300). The Ordnance Survey map of c.1850 confirms this, showing a concentration of buildings adjoining the Holme Lane End and Heckmondwike turnpike road, with three mill dams to the south and east. The mill had hardly altered forty years later at the time of the next Ordnance Survey revision.

Burnley maintained his interest in Union Mill even after taking over Gomersal Mills in 1850 – in 1853 the company was still called Burnley Firth & Co. The name had changed to Firth Burrows & Co. by 1876; Burnley, with all the carding and spinning facilities he could require available by then at Gomersal Mills, had evidently withdrawn from the partnership. Union Mill started to manufacture cloth as well as yarn after 1850.[46]

The Merchant Family

Even as the age of domestic textile manufacture was drawing to a close, merchants remained important figures in the woollen industry. Until full mechanization came, a large part of cloth manufacture was carried out in the home and organized by merchants. These men stood to make – and lose – fortunes.

One such merchant business in Gomersal was that of the Knowles family. Relative latecomers to the village – no trace of them has been found before 1765 – they were already wealthy when they arrived.[47] They built an extensive business in Great Gomersal, employing large numbers of domestic out-workers to make the army cloths in which they specialized. They had workshops and warehouses, eventually owned a factory, and are associated with several large and important houses in the village. The family was a prolific one, and records left by this dynasty reveal dramatic changes of fortune in the first half of the nineteenth century, along with fascinating details of their personal affairs.[48]

The first Lionel Knowles (b.1696) probably arrived in Gomersal from Rastrick. His wife was Jane Laverack, who may have been from the Spen family of maltsters. He was said to have lived at Hill Top House (which from 1769 was owned by one of his younger sons, Charles) until his death in 1779. Lionel was succeeded as head of the family by his eldest son Lionel [II] (1735-1802) who also lived at Hill Top House. Lionel [II] was a cloth merchant in partnership with his brother, John (1743-1801). Lionel had ten children – the fifth child and eldest son, Lionel [III], was taken into partnership with his father and uncle in 1794.

John lived at Low House, in Lower Lane (later Knowles Lane), Great Gomersal. He also had ten children, only one of whom was a son – John (1780-1853). The younger John became partner of his cousin Lionel [III] after the death in 1801 of John senior. However, this partnership did not last; John was certified a lunatic in 1807 and his affairs afterwards managed by a brother-in-law.[49]

The will of Lionel [II], made in 1801, the year before his death, gives some indication of his wealth.[50] He left his share of the business and 'all that new erected dryhouse in Upper Croft' to Lionel [III]. To the only other surviving son, James, he willed his dwellinghouse, barn, stable, garden and grounds of four acres – this was Hill Top House. Five daughters also survived him, and had been separately provided for. One, Sarah, had brought her family into relationship with another merchant dynasty through her marriage to William Burnley of Pollard Hall.

By the deaths of his father, uncle and only brother, and the insanity of his cousin, which all occurred between 1801 and 1807, Lionel [III] was left in sole charge of the business. With Britain at war with France for most of the period 1793-1815, this was a booming time for the army cloth trade, and Lionel [III] did more than any other member of his family to build their wealth and stature as cloth merchants. But there were also troubles in the woollen industry during this time, mainly stemming from the introduction of machinery into cloth finishing. In 1804 Knowles was forced to increase the wages of his twenty shearmen (croppers) when they threatened to strike, even though his rate of payment was the same as that of the other Gomersal merchants. He employed institution men, who had served recognised apprenticeships and paid heavy union dues. These unionised croppers, facing a threat to

their livelihood from mechanized cropping frames, tried desperately to hold on to their traditional high pay and privileges. Knowles' problems were described to a parliamentary select committee by his neighbour, Joshua Taylor of Red House, a merchant who would not employ institution men, preferring to train his own croppers. Taylor said that Lionel Knowles was the only Gomersal merchant threatened with a strike, and thus forced to raise wages.[51] Aside from these labour problems, though, the period was a highly successful one for Knowles.

Lionel [III] lived in an old house, now demolished, at Tenlands in Lower (Knowles) Lane; the family business was based there, and their warehouse and counting

Figure 90: *Tenlands (KCS RH4/53)*

house stood behind the dwelling (Fig. 90). He built West House, possibly in anticipation of the marriage of his elder son, Lionel [IV] (1792-1845). The style and size of this building testify to the success of the Knowles family at the time. Set back from the road in extensive grounds, West House is a mansion of the Regency period. It was built of ashlar and is now painted, has a slate roof and is of two storeys. The façade is symmetrical, of five bays with sash windows. The three central bays break forward slightly and are surmounted by a parapet topped by three urns. Over the front door is a semi-circular fanlight painted with a coat of arms, presumably that of the Knowles family. The door has a pediment and slender columns. Set back on either side of the main house are wings of one bay which appear to be of more recent construction (Fig. 91).

Lionel [IV] was living at West House by 1815.[52] In 1818 he married Lucy Dickinson, daughter of a Leeds merchant. (Two years later, his brother Stephen Hartley Knowles married Lucy's sister Ann). By the end of 1818 Lionel [IV] and Lucy, settled at West House, had a son, Lionel William (Lionel [V]). But the following year brought failure and tragedy. At a time when the family had perhaps overstretched its resources by building the mansion, post-war recession hit the country. Late in

Figure 91: *West House*

March 1819 Lionel [IV] was on a business trip to London when the Knowles partnership – himself, his father and brother – was bankrupted. Lionel wrote to his wife immediately to tell her this, but when Lucy went to see her father-in-law in his counting house she discovered that he had already heard the news. Lucy wrote back to her husband; far from being cast down by the situation, she pointed out to Lionel that many were worse off than themselves. 'Moreover we are far from destitute in pecuniary matters – far otherwise. What is settled upon me is a hansome thing. You are young and have good buseness as well as credit, whilst some young men at your age are but just entering upon it'.[53] Other letters written by Lucy at the time show deep affection for Lionel, and confidence in his abilities. She was expecting another baby, and the gloomy year 1819 ended with the birth and death of that son.

Lucy's optimism was ultimately rewarded. The 'hansome thing' was a legacy of £5,000 from her father, £4,000 of which was used to rescue the Knowles property in Gomersal from their creditors. Lionel [IV] was able to stay at West House and continue in business. Ann Dickinson brought a marriage portion of £5,000 to Stephen Hartley Knowles in 1820. Although the partnership was again in financial trouble in 1826, with West House and Tenlands and other property offered for sale, the business of Lionel Knowles and Sons, merchants and manufacturers, seems to have carried on much as before.[54] The old man died in 1837, and the business continued under the names of the two brothers.

In the early 1840s Lionel [IV] bought Clough Mill, at the Birkenshaw end of Lower Lane, and it was used by the brothers for wool scribbling. The previous owners had been clothiers called Crowther, and there is some indication that Joseph Crowther worked there in partnership with the Knowles family in the 1850s.[55]

Various branches of the family still lived around the warehouse and business premises in Lower Lane. Stephen Hartley Knowles had built a new house at

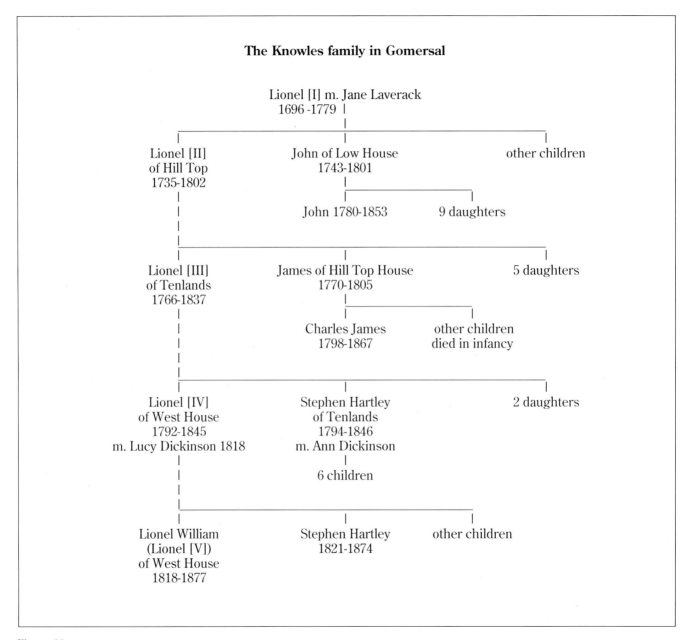

The Knowles family in Gomersal

Lionel [I] m. Jane Laverack
1696 -1779

Lionel [II]
of Hill Top
1735-1802

John of Low House
1743-1801

other children

John 1780-1853

9 daughters

Lionel [III]
of Tenlands
1766-1837

James of Hill Top House
1770-1805

5 daughters

Charles James
1798-1867

other children
died in infancy

Lionel [IV]
of West House
1792-1845
m. Lucy Dickinson 1818

Stephen Hartley
of Tenlands
1794-1846
m. Ann Dickinson

2 daughters

6 children

Lionel William
(Lionel [V])
of West House
1818-1877

Stephen Hartley
1821-1874

other children

Figure 92

Tenlands where he was living at the time of the 1841 census with Ann and their six children. By this time, Priscilla Knowles was the only one of John Knowles's ten children still at Low House, living there with a servant. Low House had been owned by a Joseph Dobson of Leeds and sold by his heir in 1813 to the Sigston brothers.[56] The Knowles family had ceased to be tenants there by 1851. Eventually part of The Wheatleys estate owned by one Ackroyd, it was sold at auction in 1900 and at that time was two dwellinghouses.[57]

Lionel [IV] and Lucy had thirteen children, eleven of whom outlived their parents. Shortly before his fifty-third birthday, Lionel, apparently at the peak of his business life, fell ill. He made a will in April 1845, in which the house and recent improvements to his garden were the first thing to concern him: 'I direct that the alterations now making by me in the pleasure grounds attached to my dwelling house called West House if incomplete at the time of my decease shall be completed by my executors ...'.[58] He was also in the process of building a wool warehouse next to Clough Mill, and instructed his trustees to complete the work. The will refers as well to Lionel's share in a dyeing business at Birstall which was carried on with his brother and one Edward Longbottom. His business premises were divided between various sons, with cash bequests to other children. Lionel [V] was to have West House, providing that Lucy and the unmarried children could have a home there. The six children who were not of age were to be 'brought up and educated in a liberal and becoming manner'. For one, John Dickinson Knowles, then seventeen, it was stipulated that he was to be sent to the University of Oxford or Cambridge. (The boy went to Cambridge, later becoming Vicar of Glossop.) Lionel did not live long after making the will. Lucy's death in September 1845 must have been a severe blow, and he followed her only a month later.

The census of 1851 shows that Lionel [V], then thirty-two, and described as a cloth merchant, was living at West House with his brothers Stephen Hartley Knowles (described as a dyer, though it appears he was never

well enough to work) and James, a cloth merchant, along with two unmarried sisters. Three resident servants made up the establishment. The widow of their uncle Stephen Hartley Knowles, Ann, lived still at Tenlands with some of her children, and three servants.

Ten years later, in 1861, Lionel [V] lived at West House with his wife Julia, a woman with aristocratic connections. His cousin Frederick had taken over at Tenlands and was also in business as a cloth merchant. The neighbouring Follingworth House had been built during the 1850s for Lionel [V]'s youngest brother, Arthur, perhaps at the time of his marriage in 1857, though on the site of an older house called Follingworth. Arthur was a dyer with a business employing forty men and eight boys. Another old house on the lane, Stringer House, now called Elmer Dene, had passed from the Knowles family to one John Woodhead.

Although this generation maintained links with the cloth trade, the connection was fast diminishing. Merchant-manufacturers had become redundant, and the woollen industry was now almost entirely factory-based. A member of the Knowles family, John Bruce Knowles, was still running Clough Mill in Cadman's time, around 1930, but it remained a small concern when compared with the businesses which descended from other Gomersal merchants. The failure of the Knowles family to build on their success as merchants was explained by William Carr, a Gomersal doctor, in his diary for 1867. Carr noted that a distant cousin of the Gomersal family, Charles James Knowles, Q.C., had bequeathed £2,600 to each child of the families of Lionel [IV] and his brother Hartley Knowles.[59] This, says Carr, would be 'very acceptable' as there had just occurred the stoppage of W. Greene & Co., in which the Knowles firm had been a partner. Carr continued: 'About this time various members of this family who had appeared so prosperous for the last 30 years broke up their Establishments and left the Neighbourhood – with a view to retrenchment. The sons of the late Lionel Knowles [IV] were none of them men of much capacity and of indolent habits and unfitted for business – and none of them have maintained their father's position'. Both Tenlands (still with its warehouse, counting house and dryhouse) and Follingworth were let, and sold at auction in 1872.[60]

Most of the children of Lionel [IV] retired to a spa town or to the seaside, and most died childless.

NOTES

1. *Parliamentary Papers* (House of Commons) 1839-40 (43).
2. The date of Taylor's Hunsworth Mill is usually said to be 1785, but a lease and letter of 1788 refer to his 'intended fulling mill at Hunsworth' (*YAS* MD 292/59).
3. The literal meaning of manufactory is a place where things were made by hand; usually, though, the term denotes a workshop where machinery was in use.
4. Cadman 1930, 54.
5. *WYAS K* DD/CA/7.
6. Grady 1987, 100-101; though plans to build a larger hall in Leeds were already under consideration in 1774 – see Grady, 111.
7. *WYAS L* DT 305/5/20.
8. *WYAS L* DT 305/5/18.
9. *Leeds Mercury* 28 Mar 1775.
10. *WYAS L* DB/M670/6; also reproduced as endpiece in Cadman 1930.
11. Barfoot and Wilkes 1793, 325.
12. *WYAS C* HAS/B:13/51.
13. *Guildhall Library* RE 7253/32a 183784.
14. *Leeds Intelligencer* 24 Oct 1803. For further information on the Crowther family in Gomersal and Churwell see Herbert Heaton 'Yorkshire Cloth Traders in the United States' *Thoresby Society* Misc. Vol XXXVII, 225-287.
15. *Leeds Intelligencer* 7 Apr 1806; 18 Jan 1808.
16. *Guildhall Library* Sun CR 11937/197 115361 and 115362.
17. *Parliamentary Papers* (House of Commons) 1834 (167) XX, C1, 154-5.
18. *WYAS C* FW:179/12; *WYAS K* DD/CA/4; see chapter 5.
19. Cudworth 1876, 527-8.
20. Anon 1952.
21. Census 1851 and 1861.
22. *Leeds Intelligencer.*
23. *Leeds Intelligencer* 20 July 1795 etc.
24. *Bretton* BEA/C3/B16/1.
25. *Bretton* BEA/C3/B16/6.
26. *Guildhall Library* RE 7253/32a 182275.
27. *Bretton* BEA/C3/B16/2.
28. *Leeds Intelligencer* 28 Dec 1818.
29. *Bretton* BEA/C3/B16/9.
30. *Bretton* BEA/C3/B16/5.
31. White 1838, 425.
32. Cadman 1930, 126.
33. White 1853, 325.
34. *WYAS HQ* QE Returns of cotton mills, and see Cloth Hall above.
35. *WYAS C* FW:179/1.
36. *WYAS C* FW:179/1.
37. *WYAS K* DD/HS/G/3/20; Cadman 1930, 78-9; *Leeds Mercury* 21 July 1832.
38. *WYAS K* DD/HS/G/3/22 and /23.
39. Cadman 1930, 78-9; *WYAS K* Spiking March 1870.
40. *WYAS K* DD/C4 Scrap Book 1.
41. The house is mentioned in Cradock's History of the Parish of Birstall, but there is no evidence to support Cradock's belief that a much older house, in existence in the 1650s, had been on this site. (Cradock 1933, 253).
42. Cadman 1930, 78-9.
43. *WYAS L* Acc 976 HS72; White 1838, 425.
44. *WYAS K* DD/CA/6.
45. White 1838, 425.
46. White 1853, 326; *WYAS K* Spiking Feb 1876.
47. Cudworth 1876, 521-2.
48. *WYAS HQ* C23. Most of the information about the Knowles family is derived from this archive, though some errors have been found in the accompanying family tree (C23/116).
49. *WYAS HQ* C23/3 and /4.
50. *WYAS HQ* C23/1.
51. *Parliamentary Papers* (House of Commons) 1806 (268) III, 378-381.
52. *WYAS HQ* C23/88.
53. *WYAS HQ* C23/88.
54. *WYAS HQ* C23/6; *Leeds Intelligencer* 27 April 1826.
55. Cudworth 1876, 521-2.
56. *WYAS K* DD/HS/C9.
57. *WYAS B* 1D78/68; see also chapter 5.
58. *WYAS HQ* C23/34.
59. *WYAS K* DD/CA/7; Charles James Knowles (1798-1867) was the only survivor of the family of James, son of Lionel II, and died unmarried; see figure 92.
60. *WYAS K* DD/CA/7.

Chapter 8

INNS AND PUBLIC HOUSES

Public houses provided a focus for all kinds of activities in Gomersal. Before the middle of the last century there were few public buildings in West Riding towns and villages, and business was often transacted at inns. Public houses accommodated and refreshed travellers and their horses, and acted as local centres of coach transport. They also provided rooms for public meetings, auctions, magistrates' sessions, coroners' courts, election and union meetings, and for employers to pay out wages. Some Leeds inns served as headquarters for Gomersal merchants and woollen manufacturers on their weekly visits to town.

Gomersal pubs varied in size between the large ones on main roads, which catered for travellers and could hold public meetings, and smaller taverns for very local needs. Most brewed their own beer. The smaller establishments did not provide a living for the publican and his or her family, and some doubled as blacksmith's or butcher's shops. Even the Black Bull, well established as the venue of major local events such as court sessions, auctions and railway company meetings, was partly run as a farm. What all these pubs did have in common was their importance in the lives of those living nearby. They offered warmth and comfort, and perhaps happy oblivion, to people whose everyday lives were hard and cheerless.

Common attitudes to beer and nutrition in the West Riding were described by a Pudsey man, Joseph Lawson, remembering life in his home town in 1830.[1] Lawson wrote about the time of the Corn Laws, when flour was dear, white bread scarce, and when the poor were lucky to eat meat once a week. Oat cake, brown bread, porridge pudding, skimmed milk, potatoes and home-brewed beer formed the staple diet, with tea, coffee, sugar, butter and treacle as occasional luxuries. Most households could and did brew their own beer,

but the ale-house still held great attractions. 'Nearly all the male population went there, more or less. People went there because they had nowhere else to go for society. Whatever took place then came off at the alehouse, and there were not the many other attractions there are today outside the public house,' said Lawson, writing in 1887 when Mechanics' Institutes, circulating libraries, and religious and temperance activities offered a wider range of pastimes to the working class.

Earlier in the century, customers of West Riding pubs could play at dominoes, shoving the penny, quoits and skittles, or join in communal singing, or just gossip. There were few books or papers about, and in any case the majority could scarcely read. Where most people worked at home, as they did in Gomersal, a visit to the pub was a good opportunity to find out what was going on in the wider world. The other attraction of the alehouse was of course the beer. There was a firm belief that alcohol was essential to health. Said Lawson: 'Even the poor looked upon intoxication as real strength and nourishment'. Beer was 3d. a pint or less and was exceptionally strong, and if you chose your pub carefully it was possible to become insensibly drunk for sixpence.

Gomersal had one or two alehouses, a category of unlicensed pub allowed to sell only beer. These often operated in the front room of an ordinary house and were known by the owner's name. They died out when licensing regulations became stricter. The pubs which have survived to the present day were those which were fully licensed, offering spirits and perhaps a more select tap of ale in the bar, as well as a common brew in the taproom. Better-paid working men, such as slubbers, could afford to patronise the bar, and looked down on the poorer handloom weavers who drank in the taproom.[2]

Most of the pubs of modern Gomersal have existed for over a century, and some go back much further.

The Black Bull

Strictly speaking the Black Bull is in Birstall, at the centre of the hamlet surrounding Birstall Church. The inn had a much wider importance in the district, though, as the parish was large and people came from as far as Wyke, Hightown and Tong to worship or marry at the mother church. Travelling mainly on foot, they needed rest and refreshment. The inn grew up in Kirkgate to cater for people visiting the church, and for travellers on the main roads. Because it was accessible, it developed other functions, notably as a venue for magistrates' courts and local election polls. By the end of the eighteenth century, auctions of Gomersal and Birstall property were frequently held at the Black Bull.

The building has seventeenth century features, which means that in part at least it pre-dates the Leeds – Elland turnpike road which ran along Kirkgate from 1740. But the Black Bull is on two much older long-distance routes, one an ancient road which passed Oakwell and Birstall Church before proceeding up Garfitt Hill to Popeley and Castle Hill, and the second a road which existed before turnpiking, described in 1655 as 'the stone causey leading between Halifax and Leeds at the way out of Gomersal ...'.[3] This causeway is shown as a section of the main York to Chester road in a national atlas of 1675; Birstall bridge, below the church, is marked, along with the Oakwell road 'to Bradforth'.[4] So the Black Bull occupied a position, even before 1740, where two main routes passed its door. This remained the case until Kirkgate was by-passed by a new section of road at the bottom of Church Lane in the present century.

There have been claims that the Black Bull Inn dates back over 800 years and was connected with the monks of Nostell Priory. We have not found any evidence to confirm this. The earliest external features are those of the seventeenth century at the rear of the inn, including two-light double chamfered windows from which the mullions have been removed, and a projecting porch. The front of the inn was rebuilt in about 1800 and consists mostly of eighteenth century and later features (Fig. 93). Further major alterations were made in 1960, including the demolition of the old brewhouse.

Inside, the first floor function room retains some of its original panelling, and a magistrate's box and prisoner's dock with painted panels and canopies. This is where the court, and presumably other events such as auctions and public meetings, were held. It is possible that the present structure hides a much older core, or that another building stood on the site before 1600, but this is speculation.

The story of the Black Bull is complicated by references to two inns of the same name in the Kirkgate area of Birstall, and also to an inn called the Chained Bull. One of the inns, often called the Old Black Bull or the Lower Black Bull, and now demolished, was a brick building at the bottom of Garfitt Hill. The pub which faces the church was sometimes called the Chained Bull by locals, but directories and newspapers consistently referred to it as the Black Bull Inn. From these and other sources it has been possible to discover the names of some landlords and landladies from 1775 when a Mr Thompson had it. Mrs Thompson, presumably his widow, was there in 1801, William Schofield in 1822, Martha Schofield in 1826 and Samuel Wood in 1838.[5] In 1839 or 1840 Joshua Kenyon took over; he died in about 1852 while still in his early forties and was succeeded by his widow Elizabeth (Betty). She kept on until after 1875, when a directory described her as 'farmer and victualler'. John Greenwood, 'maltster, wine and spirit merchant, families supplied', was at the Black Bull in 1881, followed by Jacob Maud (1887) and William Radforth (1893 and 1904).

The Garfitt Hill pub seems to have been smaller than the Kirkgate Black Bull. In the township valuation of 1840 the latter (called the Chained Bull Inn) was rated at £21 15s. 0d. The other (Old) Black Bull, with a brewhouse,

Figure 93: *The Black Bull at Birstall Church c.1900*

stable and garden, had a rateable value of £15 7s. 6d. The Old Black Bull was delicensed in the early years of this century, and was converted first to a laundry, then a dance hall and later into cottages.[6] It appears to have had a number of different landlords in the last century. Joshua Mann, sometimes described as a gardener as well as victualler, was probably there in 1822, and certainly occupied the pub from 1826 to 1841. He was followed by George Walker in 1847 and 1848 (at the 'Little Bull'), Thomas Crowther in 1851 and 1853, Thomas Elliott in 1857, James Booth in 1861 and Edward Vickers in 1881. The pub was rarely mentioned in directories after 1861, and the buildings had ceased to be marked as an inn on the Ordnance Survey map of 1888-92.

The White Horse

This bleak, box-like building with pan-tiled roof set in an expanse of tarmac hardly evokes the image of an eighteenth century coaching inn. But that is exactly what the White Horse once was, a hostelry catering for traffic using the two main roads which crossed at Gomersal Hill Top. It stands almost on the crossroads of the Leeds – Elland turnpike road and an old hilltop route which became part of the Holme Lane End and Heckmondwike turnpike after 1824/5. The present White Horse is a building of the nineteenth century, though much altered, and all its outbuildings have gone to make way for a car park (Fig. 94).

There were buildings on this site in 1714 when a plan of Ibbetson's newly acquired Gomersal estate was drawn up (Fig. 1). A house with a rear outshut faced the hilltop road. Nearer to the crossroads was a long two storey building at right angles to the road; it appears to have had chimneys and was probably a house. A third structure, possibly a barn, was sited a little nearer the crossroads and fronting on to the road. The three buildings were at the head of a field called Near Brier Close; this and neighbouring land was occupied by a Joseph Goodier. There is no indication as to whether these buildings were in use as an inn.

Figure 94: *The White Horse, Hill Top, c.1954*

The Ibbetson family owned the White Horse until 1843, but were never more than absentee landlords. The family whose name is bound up with the early history of the pub was called Lang. An innkeeper named Benjamin Lang, of Great Gomersal, was mentioned in a document of 1768 which did not state which inn he ran.[7] The name of Benjamin Lang occurred again in land tax returns of about 1800, when Lang was a tenant of Ibbetson and probably already at the White Horse. The Lang family kept the White Horse until about 1870, and also feature in the histories of the Bull's Head and the Old Saw.

The Langs were in business as farmers and butchers besides being innkeepers and brewers. Outbuildings surrounding the White Horse included a butcher's shop and farm buildings, besides the brewhouse and stables usually found at an inn. Joseph Lang, victualler at the White Horse in 1822, appeared in a directory of 1826 as 'victualler and butcher'. Lang made his will in 1834, describing himself as an innkeeper, and left the business to his two elder daughters, Nancy and Mary, mentioning particularly 'all the wines, spirituous and other liquors and all the brewing utensils and also the horses, cows, hay and corn of which I shall die possessed'. He had a young family – his only son, Joseph, was not yet of age. He asked that Nancy and Mary give a home to Joseph and three younger daughters until the children were of an age to marry. The White Horse he referred to as 'all that messuage or dwellinghouse with the cottages, barn, stable, and other outbuildings, closes [etc] at Gomersal which I hold under lease from Sir Charles Ibbetson of Denton'. The lease had run from 1823 and cost the Langs £50 a year.[8]

Lang must have died soon after making the will, for in 1838 Nancy and Mary Lang were listed in directories as victuallers at the White Horse. The 1840 township valuation mentioned a butcher's shop there besides the inn and brewhouse. It seems that their brother Joseph carried on the butchery business for many years before taking over as publican at the Old Saw in about 1868.

The elder Joseph Lang had bought the Bull's Head in Little Gomersal at Beaumont's auction in 1833, and his daughters were the owners in 1840, though it was managed by tenants. The sisters sold that property by 1849. They may have bought the White Horse in the 1840s. The pub then had two front rooms, a bar, kitchen, pantry and cellar, and outside a barn, stable, brewhouse and butcher's shop along with fifteen acres of farmland.

Mary Lang died in 1850.[9] Nancy had married John Sykes, and trade directories from this time gave Sykes's name as licensee of the White Horse. The last reference to him is found in an 1870 directory; he was followed as licensee in the 1870s by Samuel Hodgson, in the 1880s by a Joseph Gibson, and in 1893 by William Allatt.

The Bull's Head

The Bull's Head has existed as a pub since before 1800. For most of its history the inn occupied only part of the range at the junction of Lower Lane and Listing Lane, and the rest of the building was used as a blacksmith's shop and house (Fig. 95).

The present inn conforms to the same plan as a structure which stood on the site when Sir Thomas Wentworth's lands were surveyed in 1721, though in style it appears to date from later in that century. Whether the Bull's Head was used as an inn in the early 1700s is not known. It stands on land owned by the Popeley family which first passed by marriage to the Wentworths in 1650, and then by inheritance to the Beaumonts who sold their Gomersal estate in 1833. Lot 1 in that auction included 'a well-accustomed Inn, called the Bull's Head, with suitable conveniences, Stable, Barn, Mistal and Garden; also a cottage and Blacksmith's Shop adjoining', and more than five acres of land. It was bought for £745 by Joseph Lang, of the White Horse.[10]

Benjamin Ross was publican at the Bull's Head before 1800. In 1799 he was mentioned in the accounts of Castle Hill Mill, supplying both blacksmith's work for

Figure 95: *The Bull's Head, Little Gomersal, c.1900*

the mill, and beer to the millwrights.[11] It seems that three bays of the present Bull's Head formed the public house, with a smith's workshop in the middle section and a small dwelling house on the corner of Lower Lane. A blocked-off taking-in door can still be seen at first floor level on the gable wall of this cottage. Ross was still at the Bull's Head in 1822, when a directory described him as blacksmith and innkeeper.

After Joseph Lang bought the property, the inn was managed by William Dove. There are references to Dove's tenancy in 1837/8 and 1840, when he occupied 'The Bull's Head Inn, kitchen, barn, stable and garden and two fields nearby'.[12] However the Ross family still rented part of the premises. Benjamin Ross had died and the smithy was worked by his son, Joshua, who in 1841 was living in the adjoining cottage with his widowed mother, sister and an apprentice. Joshua Ross was still in business in part of the Bull's Head in 1853, though another blacksmith, John Todd, had taken over by 1861. Cadman says that the smithy became a rag warehouse in the twentieth century, and that the building was destroyed by fire in the 1920s and rebuilt – surely an exaggeration.[13]

By 1849 the Bull's Head was in the ownership of Benjamin Thornton, and there followed a rapid turnover of tenants. Census returns and directories have produced the following names, though exact dates of arrival and departure are difficult to determine: William Knowles (1841); Joseph Newsome (1847, 1848, 1851); John Peace (1853); Mary Clayton (1857); Joseph Hirst (1861); John Roberts jun. (1866); Mrs Emma Sykes (1870); Joseph Shaw (1875); Ben Thackrah (1881, 1887); John Sherwood (1893); John Smith (1904).

The Old Saw

In appearance, the Old Saw would seem to be one of the most ancient public houses in the district. The main building is certainly very old – perhaps 300 years – but its history as a pub does not go back so far. This oldest section is a double-fronted farmhouse which had stone mullioned windows. On to this was built, perhaps early in the last century, a single-bay cottage with bay-window projecting towards Spen Lane. There was also a small extension forward from the older house. All these buildings are retained, though details have been obliterated by rendering and by a modern entrance porch.

There is nothing to indicate that Spen had an inn of any importance in the early part of the last century. The hamlet was only a short distance from the White Horse at Gomersal Hill Top and the Nag's Head (now The George) in Cleckheaton, both of which were sited at the crossroads of long-distance routes. The Old Saw seems to have started out as a beer shop, presumably to cater for very local needs. The Gomersal township valuation of 1840 showed the Old Saw (though not named as such) as being in the ownership of one Hannah Ogden and tenanted by Thomas Iredale. The premises were described as a retail beer shop, brewhouse, laundry, mistal, shed and garden, with three cottages on the site, separately tenanted. There were no other licensed premises in Spen. This is strange, for the Ordnance Survey of 1847-51 had 'The Old Saw P.H.' in Lower Spen, below Spen Hall, in a pair of cottages which still

Figure 96: *The Old Saw, Spen, c.1890*

stand on the main road side. This could be dismissed as an error by the Ordnance Survey, but an inhabitant of one of these cottages has told us that deeds refer to his home's previous use as a pub. So it is not clear whether the name of the Old Saw was moved to a different establishment at some time between 1850 and 1870.

The Old Saw was certainly in its present location by 1871, when a sale plan for adjoining property showed the owner of the pub as Edward Atkinson Esq. (of Spen House and St Peg Mills).[14] The Atkinson family still owned the Old Saw in 1902.

Directories started to record the Old Saw in 1853, when Thomas Hardill was landlord. His name continued to appear until 1870, though this evidence is contradicted by spirit accounts which give the following list of licensees: Thomas Hardhill 1856-66; Thomas Kershaw 1866-7; Mary Kershaw 1867-8; Joseph Lang 1868-95; Priscilla Lang 1895-99; David H. Scott 1899-1910 (though a photograph of the signboard at this time shows the name as Stott).[15]

Joseph Lang was the younger brother of Nancy and Mary Lang of the White Horse. Before taking the Old

Saw, Lang had been a butcher at Hill Top. He was thirty-six years old and his wife Priscilla thirty-five when the 1851 census was taken, which means that they were eighty and eighty-three respectively when they left the Old Saw in the 1890s – presumably upon their deaths. During his time as landlord Lang was famed for his 'glee parties'. These were held whenever he killed a pig, and customers were invited to partake of pigs-fry.[16] It is just possible that Lang is the old man who appears on a photograph of the Old Saw taken at the end of the last century (Fig. 96).

The Wheatsheaf

The Wheatsheaf was a farmhouse long before it became an inn. The building is plainly and substantially built in stone in a vernacular style. It has been subjected to some rebuilding during its lifetime; there is a clear line to the right of the front door, marking the addition of an extension (Fig. 97). One would also expect to see quoins on a building of such age; their absence suggests that the eastern end of the pub may also have been altered. The chimneys and stonework indicate a possible date of around 1700, and the style of the stone surrounds of the upstairs windows suggests that some reconstruction could have taken place about a century later, possibly

Figure 97: *The Wheatsheaf, Little Gomersal*

replacing older mullioned window sets with the present surrounds. The western gable appears to be the oldest surviving part of the building. A small window with a chamfered surround and a formerly steep roof line, are evocative of seventeenth century architecture.

Before about 1858, there were two or three alehouses in the village of Little Gomersal, but no pub other than the Bull's Head. The Wheatsheaf Inn was opened by William Greenwood, who held the licence for about twenty years.[17] He was followed by Thomas Greenwood, who was there in 1881, John Gambles (1887) and Squire Roberts (1893). The early licensees continued to farm the land as well as run the pub. Cadman claimed that at one time the only lavatory in the whole of Little Gomersal was in the Wheatsheaf yard.[18]

The Shoulder of Mutton

Situated at the heart of Great Gomersal, the Shoulder of Mutton lies on the old main road through the village. The section of Oxford Road leading to Birkenshaw was built as recently as 1824-5. Previously travellers following the road from Hill Top continued either along Lower Lane (now Knowles Lane) or turned right down Moor Lane. The Shoulder of Mutton was not at a main crossroads, and was never a major coaching inn, but it was the only pub at the centre of this busy village.

It also stands above the Gomersal tunnel of the Heaton Lodge and Wortley railway line, and a man is said to have been killed 100 yards beneath the pub during the construction of the tunnel in 1896-1900.[19] Perhaps because of its situation over the line, the pub was owned by the LMS Railway Company in the early years of this century.

The present buildings of the Shoulder of Mutton have been much altered and modernized, though there is clearly an eighteenth century core to them (Fig. 98). The inn was sold at auction in 1827, when it included a barn, stable, butcher's shop and fold or yard.[20] Apparently the pub never had its own brewhouse, though like the White Horse it housed a butcher. Thomas Thornton, the tenant at the time of the auction, appeared in directories from 1822 as licensee, and was both a victualler and butcher. He may have bought the premises in 1827, as he appeared on the 1840 township valuation as owner.

By 1841 Joseph Fearnley Wigglesworth, another victualler-cum-butcher, was the innkeeper, and was still there in 1848. The publicans who followed him were not described as butchers, so it is possible that the butcher's shop closed in the middle of the nineteenth century.

Figure 98: *The Shoulder of Mutton, Great Gomersal*

NOTES

1. Lawson 1887, 79-84.
2. For a fuller account of changes in licensing laws during the nineteenth century, see Jennings 1985.
3. *WYAS K* DD/HS/G/1/19.
4. Ogilby 1675, number 89.
5. Cadman 1930, 52; *Halifax Journal* 1 August 1801; for the names of licensees of the inns referred to in this chapter, the following directories have been consulted: Baines 1822, 461, 509; Parson 1826, 219, 227; Parson and White 1830, 467; White 1837-8, 423, 425; White 1847, 368, 370; Slater 1848, 1040; White 1853, 323, 326; White 1857, 620, 623; White 1861, 736, 738; White 1866, 436, 442; White 1870, 503, 508; White 1875, 1123-4, 1126; Kelly 1881, 84, 353; Slater 1887, 33-5; Kelly 1893, 90, 369-70; Kelly 1904, 118, 285-6. See also census returns of 1841, 1851 and 1861 and Gomersal Township Valuation 1840. For further information on the Black Bull, see DoE list of buildings in the former Batley Borough; also notes on the history of the Black Bull, available from the landlord.
6. Cadman 1930, 112-4.
7. Cadman 1930, 159.
8. *WYAS K* DD/HS/J/16.
9. *WYAS K* DD/HS/J/18.
10. *Bretton* BEA/C2/B47/1; B60/1; and see the section on the White Horse, above.
11. *Bretton* BEA/C3/B16/6.
12. Gomersal Township Valuation.
13. Cadman 1930, 125-6.
14. *WYAS B* 1D78/82.
15. *WYAS K* KC210.
16. Cadman 1930, 87.
17. Cadman 1930, 134.
18. Cadman 1930, 117.
19. Cadman 1930, 41.
20. *Leeds Intelligencer* 10 May 1827.

APPENDIX 1

Maps relating to Gomersal

1619 Plan of part of the estate of John Gomersall deceased, by R.Saxton (*YAS* DD 70/9/17).

1675 Map of the road between York and Chester (John Ogilby 1675 *Britannia* Plate 89).

1714 A Map of Popeley, Stubley [etc.] ... in the Parish of Birstall ... Surveyed for Mr James Ibbitson of Leeds, merchant. By J. Dickinson Anno 1714 (in private ownership; see Fig. 1).

1721 Wentworth's estate (*Bretton* BEA/C2/MPD6/1).

1732 A Plan of the Estate at Gomersall and Burstall Surveyed by John Topham ye 23rd Octobr. 1732 (*YAS* MD132/B4; see Fig. 44).

1770 A Survey of the Glebe Lands ... belonging to the Rectory of Birstall ... Possessions of the master and Fellows of Trinity College, Cambridge 1770 (In private ownership; see Fig. 2).

1775 Thomas Jefferys' map of Yorkshire.

1798 A Plan of the Estate of Sir Henry Ibbetson Bart. situate in Gomersall ... Copied from a Plan Made in 1798 (*WYAS Leeds* DB/M 670/4).

1808 A Plan of an Estate situate at Gomersall ... by J. Green 1808 (*WYAS Leeds* DB/M 382).

1809 A Plan of an Estate situate at Gomersall the property of Messrs Sigstons Made March 1809 by Jonathan Taylor (*WYAS Kirklees* KC52 Sigston Box 2 Bundle 2; see Fig. 49).

1812 Plan of Popeley Estate (*WYAS Leeds* DB/M 670/2).

1815 Plans of Popeley Colliery (*WYAS Leeds* DB/M 670/1-4).

1822 Thorp's map of the district ten miles around Leeds.

1833 Beaumont Sale Catalogue with plans 1833 (*Bretton* BEA/C2/B21/1).

1839 Plan accompanying Gomersal Township Valuation 1840 (*WYAS Leeds* DB/M 506; copy at Cleckheaton Library).

1841 Plan of the estate of Sir Charles Henry Ibbetson Bart. (*WYAS Leeds* DB/M179).

1843 Plan of the estates in Gomersal and Heckmondwike; Ibbetson sale map (*WYAS Leeds* DB/M 607/4 and /8).

1849 Gomersal Tithe Map (*WYAS Kirklees*).

1847-51 Ordnance Survey 6" Sheet 232 Surveyed 1847-51 Published 1854.

1888-92 Ordnance Survey 25" Sheets 232.5, 232.6, 232.10; Resurveyed 1888-1892. Published 1893 and 1894.

1900 Sale plan re Ackroyd Deceased 9 August 1900 (*WYAS Bradford* 1D78/68).

APPENDIX 2

Notes on Sources

There is a plentiful supply of secondary material, though most is not specifically about Gomersal. H.A. Cadman's *Gomersal Past and Present* is the only book dealing with the whole of Gomersal in a general way. Cadman's style and lack of organization make this a difficult work to use with any confidence, though some of it has proved more accurate than expected. Where Cadman quotes from legal documents (presumably encountered in the course of his work as a Gomersal solicitor, though he does not cite references) his information has proved dependable when checked against other sources. Less reliable is the material in Cadman which relies on oral evidence; in many cases it has been impossible to verify what little detail is given, and sometimes the information is simply inaccurate.

Cradock's *History of the Ancient Parish of Birstall* is a stark contrast, meticulously researched and an excellent history of the wider parish, though limited to matters ecclesiastical. There are also some reputable studies of individual buildings (see Ferrett, Scraton and Scraton, Woledge, for example). More specialist, unpublished, reports have been prepared on certain buildings and sites by the West Yorkshire Archaeology Service, and these may be consulted in the Sites and Monuments Record in Wakefield.

Primary material concerning Gomersal is to be found in a number of record offices. The local branch of West Yorkshire Archive Service at Huddersfield (*WYAS K*) holds a number of significant documents, particularly township and estate maps; it also houses some of the archive of Hellewell and Sutton solicitors, and the diary of Dr William Carr of Little Gomersal, both of which contain much on local property transactions. Copies of some of the maps and lists of local items in the Kirklees archive are kept at Cleckheaton Library.

The West Yorkshire Archive Service office in Leeds (*WYAS L*) has other material belonging to Hellewell and Sutton, though not all of this is catalogued. This office also has a number of the more interesting Gomersal maps, some of which relate to the Ibbetson estate. Further Ibbetson documents are deposited at the North Yorkshire County Record Office, Northallerton (*NYCRO*).

Also in Leeds, the Yorkshire Archaeological Society (*YAS*) has a collection of some of the finest early documentation about Gomersal, including seventeenth century church pew lists and the 1641 tax list. They hold part of Lord Allendale's collection of family papers dating back to Wentworth's predecessors in Little Gomersal, the Popeleys and Gomersalls. A further large holding of Wentworth, Beaumont and earlier material is kept at the old family seat, now Bretton Hall College of Higher Education.

The headquarters of West Yorkshire Archive Service in Wakefield (*WYAS HQ*) has the Registry of Deeds and other general material such as land tax returns, which form a rich source for any study of buildings or landscape in West Yorkshire. This office also holds some specifically Gomersal material, notably the papers of the Knowles family, which are mainly deeds and letters. In Bradford (*WYAS B*) are a number of miscellaneous items, among which the Preston Papers rank high in importance, containing as they do transcriptions of medieval documents and various genealogies. The Calderdale archives (*WYAS C*) also have miscellaneous Gomersal references, some of it in solicitors' collections.

The Batt papers are held by the Thoresby Society in Leeds; the early seventeenth century rentals in this archive are particularly important. Finally, wills and probate papers can be consulted in York at the Borthwick Institute.

BIBLIOGRAPHY

Anon 1742 *The Poll for a Representative in Parliament for the County of York ... 1742* (York).

Anon 1899 'Duchy of Lancaster Depositions' *Thoresby Society* Vol IX for 1897-9, 5-22.

Anon 1902 'Index of Wills in the York Registry 1620-27' *YASRS* Vol XXXII for 1902.

Anon 1952 *Two Centuries of Thomas Burnley & Sons Limited* (Gomersal).

George J. Armytage 1881 'Extracts from Dodsworth's Manuscripts relating to Brighouse, Clifton, Kirklees and Hartshead' *YAJ* Vol VI for 1881, 73-79.

George A. Auden 1909 'Two Early Sculptured Stones in Birstall Church' *YAJ* Vol XX for 1909, 20-23.

W.P. Baildon and S. Margerison (eds.) 1904 'The Calverley Charters' *Thoresby Society* Vol VI for 1904.

A. Ronald Bielby 1978 *Churches and Chapels of Kirklees* (Huddersfield).

W. Brown (ed.) 1898 'Yorkshire Inquisitions Vol II' *YASRS* Vol XXIII for 1897.

William Brown (ed.) 1907 'The Register of William Wickwane' *Publications of the Surtees Society* Vol CXIV for 1907.

W. Brown (ed.) 1909 'Yorkshire Deeds' *YASRS* XXXIX for 1907.

W. Brown (ed.) 1914 'Yorkshire Deeds Vol II' *YASRS* Vol L for 1913.

H. Ashwell Cadman 1930 *Gomersal Past and Present* (Leeds).

James J. Cartwright 1873 'A Subsidy Roll for the Wapentake of Agbrigg and Morley' *YAJ* Vol II for 1871-2, 43-60.

C.T. Clay (ed.) 1932 'Yorkshire Deeds Vol VII' *YASRS* Vol LXXXIII for 1932.

C.T. Clay (ed.) 1940 'Yorkshire Deeds Vol VIII' *YASRS* Vol CII for 1940.

J.W. Clay (ed.) 1904 'Yorkshire Church Notes 1619-1631 by Roger Dodsworth' *YASRS* Vol XXXIV for 1904, 55-56.

J.W. Clay (ed.) 1907 *Dugdale's Visitation of Yorkshire* Vol II (Exeter).

W.G. Collingwood 1915 'Anglian and Anglo-Danish Sculpture in the West Riding' *YAJ* Vol XXIII for 1915, 129-299.

F. Collins (ed.) 1889 'Index of Wills in the York Registry 1389-1514' *YASRS* Vol VI for 1888.

F. Collins (ed.) 1891 'Index of Wills in the York Registry 1514-1553' *YASRS* Vol XI for 1891, Appendix 1.

Robert Beilby Cook 1915 'Wills of Leeds and District' *Thoresby Society* Vol XXII for 1912-14, 235-264.

Gillian Cookson 1988 *Spen Valley in Old Picture Postcards* (Zaltbommel).

Gillian Cookson 1992 'Brookhouses' *Journal of the Spen Valley Historical Society* 1992, 14-17.

H.C. Cradock 1933 *A History of the Ancient Parish of Birstall*.

William Cudworth 1876 *Round About Bradford* (Bradford).

F.W. Dendy (ed.) 1921 'Visitations of the North' *Publications of the Surtees Society* Vol CXXXIII for 1920.

Department of the Environment 1984 *List of Buildings of Special Architectural or Historic Interest: Borough of Kirklees*.

A.S. Ellis 1895 'Yorkshire Receipts and Bonds' *YAJ* Vol XIII for 1895, 77-83.

Ifor M. Evans and Heather Lawrence 1979 *Christopher Saxton: Elizabethan Map Maker* (Wakefield).

M.L. Faull and S.A. Moorhouse (eds) 1981 *West Yorkshire: an Archaeological Survey to AD 1500* (Wakefield).

Mabel Ferrett 1987 *The Taylors of the Red House* (Huddersfield).

Amy G. Foster 1954 'Oakwell Hall, Birstall: Inventory of Goods 1611' *Thoresby Society* Vol XLI for 1946-53, 114-7.

Colum Giles 1986 *Rural Houses of West Yorkshire 1400-1830*.

Sir Stephen Glynne 1918 'Notes on Yorkshire Churches' *YAJ* Vol XXIV for 1917, 187.

Armitage Goodall 1953 *Spenlandia* (Dewsbury).

Kevin Grady 1989 'The Georgian Public Buildings of Leeds and the West Riding' *Thoresby Society* Vol LXII No 133 for 1987.

T.W. Hanson 1922-3 'The Story of Spen Valley' series in *Cleckheaton and Spenborough Guardian* 1922-3.

Henry Harrison 1910 'Old Cleckheaton' *Cleckheaton Guardian* 14 Oct 1910.

Joseph Hunter 1831 *South Yorkshire* Vol II.

Paul Jennings 1985 *Inns and Pubs of Old Bradford* (Bradford).

W.T. Lancaster 1924 'Birstall, Gomersal and Heckmondwike: A genealogical paper' *Thoresby Society* Vol XXVI for 1924, 15-40.

Joseph Lawson 1887 *Progress in Pudsey* (Stanningley).

Derek Linstrum 1978 *West Yorkshire Architects and Architecture*.

John Lister (ed.) 1915 'West Riding Sessions Records 1611-1642' *YASRS* Vol LIV for 1915.

G.R. Lloyd 1955 *Two Hundred Years of Christian Witness: at Gomersal, Mirfield and at Wyke*.

J.W. Morkill 'Manor and Park of Roundhay' *Thoresby Society* Vol II for 1891, 215-248.

John Nussey (ed.) 1983 *The Parish Register of Birstall Vol I 1558-1635* (YAS Parish Register Section).

John Nussey (ed.) 1987 *The Parish Register of Birstall Vol II 1636-1687* (YAS Parish Register Section).

S.L. Ollard and P.C. Walker (eds.) 1928 'Archbishop Herring's Visitation Returns 1743 Vol I' *YASRS* Vol LXXI for 1927, 60-62.

Frank Peel 1891 *Nonconformity in Spen Valley* (Heckmondwike).

Frank Peel 1893 *Spen Valley Past and Present* (Heckmondwike).

Nikolaus Pevsner 1967 *The Buildings of England: Yorkshire: The West Riding* (Harmondsworth).

Plantagenet-Harrison 1879 *The History of Yorkshire.*

James Raine 1872 'The Register, or Rolls, of Walter Gray, Lord Archbishop of York' *Publications of the Surtees Society* Vol LVI for 1870, 27-8.

James Rusby 1891 'Miscellaneous Genealogical Notes' *Thoresby Society* Vol II for 1891, 36-50.

Pamela Scraton and R.E.Scraton 1974 *A Brief History of Spen Hall* (Bradford).

F.H. Slingsby (ed.) 1956 'Feet of Fines for the County of York from 1272 to 1300' *YASRS* Vol CXXI for 1955.

William Smith 1886 *Morley: Ancient and Modern.*

Thomas William Thompson 1925 *The Spen Valley* (Heckmondwike).

R.C.N. Thornes 1981 *West Yorkshire: A Noble Scene of Industry* (Wakefield).

J.W. Walker (ed.) 1924 'Abstracts of the Chartularies of the Priory of Monkbretton' *YASRS* Vol LXVI for 1924.

R.G. Wilson 1988 'Merchants and Land – the Ibbetsons of Leeds and Denton 1650-1850' *Northern History* Vol 24 1988, 75-100.

Geoffrey Woledge 1978 *Oakwell Hall* (Huddersfield).

Note on Trade Directories

Directories consulted include Barfoot and Wilkes 1793; Baines 1822; Parson 1826; Parson and White 1830; White 1837/8, 1847, 1853, 1857, 1861, 1866, 1870, 1875; Slater 1848, 1887; Kelly 1881, 1893, 1904. These are all available at Leeds City Reference Library, and most of them are also at other local libraries.

INDEX